ALBANIAN
VOCABULARY

ENGLISH-
ALBANIAN

The most useful words
To expand your lexicon and sharpen
your language skills

9000 words

Albanian vocabulary for English speakers - 9000 words

By Andrey Taranov

T&P Books vocabularies are intended for helping you learn, memorize and review foreign words. The dictionary is divided into themes, covering all major spheres of everyday activities, business, science, culture, etc.

The process of learning words using T&P Books' theme-based dictionaries gives you the following advantages:

- Correctly grouped source information predetermines success at subsequent stages of word memorization
- Availability of words derived from the same root allowing memorization of word units (rather than separate words)
- Small units of words facilitate the process of establishing associative links needed for consolidation of vocabulary
- Level of language knowledge can be estimated by the number of learned words

T&P Books Publishing
www.tpbooks.com

ISBN: 978-1-78716-995-1

This book is also available in E-book formats.
Please visit www.tpbooks.com or the major online bookstores.

ALBANIAN VOCABULARY
for English speakers

T&P Books vocabularies are intended to help you learn, memorize, and review foreign words. The vocabulary contains over 9000 commonly used words arranged thematically.

- Vocabulary contains the most commonly used words
- Recommended as an addition to any language course
- Meets the needs of beginners and advanced learners of foreign languages
- Convenient for daily use, revision sessions, and self-testing activities
- Allows you to assess your vocabulary

Special features of the vocabulary

- Words are organized according to their meaning, not alphabetically
- Words are presented in three columns to facilitate the reviewing and self-testing processes
- Words in groups are divided into small blocks to facilitate the learning process
- The vocabulary offers a convenient and simple transcription of each foreign word

The vocabulary has 256 topics including:

Basic Concepts, Numbers, Colors, Months, Seasons, Units of Measurement, Clothing & Accessories, Food & Nutrition, Restaurant, Family Members, Relatives, Character, Feelings, Emotions, Diseases, City, Town, Sightseeing, Shopping, Money, House, Home, Office, Working in the Office, Import & Export, Marketing, Job Search, Sports, Education, Computer, Internet, Tools, Nature, Countries, Nationalities and more ...

T&P BOOKS' THEME-BASED DICTIONARIES

The Correct System for Memorizing Foreign Words

Acquiring vocabulary is one of the most important elements of learning a foreign language, because words allow us to express our thoughts, ask questions, and provide answers. An inadequate vocabulary can impede communication with a foreigner and make it difficult to understand a book or movie well.

The pace of activity in all spheres of modern life, including the learning of modern languages, has increased. Today, we need to memorize large amounts of information (grammar rules, foreign words, etc.) within a short period. However, this does not need to be difficult. All you need to do is to choose the right training materials, learn a few special techniques, and develop your individual training system.

Having a system is critical to the process of language learning. Many people fail to succeed in this regard; they cannot master a foreign language because they fail to follow a system comprised of selecting materials, organizing lessons, arranging new words to be learned, and so on. The lack of a system causes confusion and eventually, lowers self-confidence.

T&P Books' theme-based dictionaries can be included in the list of elements needed for creating an effective system for learning foreign words. These dictionaries were specially developed for learning purposes and are meant to help students effectively memorize words and expand their vocabulary.

Generally speaking, the process of learning words consists of three main elements:

- Reception (creation or acquisition) of a training material, such as a word list
- Work aimed at memorizing new words
- Work aimed at reviewing the learned words, such as self-testing

All three elements are equally important since they determine the quality of work and the final result. All three processes require certain skills and a well-thought-out approach.

New words are often encountered quite randomly when learning a foreign language and it may be difficult to include them all in a unified list. As a result, these words remain written on scraps of paper, in book margins, textbooks, and so on. In order to systematize such words, we have to create and continually update a "book of new words." A paper notebook, a netbook, or a tablet PC can be used for these purposes.

This "book of new words" will be your personal, unique list of words. However, it will only contain the words that you came across during the learning process. For example, you might have written down the words "Sunday," "Tuesday," and "Friday." However, there are additional words for days of the week, for example, "Saturday," that are missing, and your list of words would be incomplete. Using a theme dictionary, in addition to the "book of new words," is a reasonable solution to this problem.

The theme-based dictionary may serve as the basis for expanding your vocabulary.

It will be your big "book of new words" containing the most frequently used words of a foreign language already included. There are quite a few theme-based dictionaries available, and you should ensure that you make the right choice in order to get the maximum benefit from your purchase.

Therefore, we suggest using theme-based dictionaries from T&P Books Publishing as an aid to learning foreign words. Our books are specially developed for effective use in the sphere of vocabulary systematization, expansion and review.

Theme-based dictionaries are not a magical solution to learning new words. However, they can serve as your main database to aid foreign-language acquisition. Apart from theme dictionaries, you can have copybooks for writing down new words, flash cards, glossaries for various texts, as well as other resources; however, a good theme dictionary will always remain your primary collection of words.

T&P Books' theme-based dictionaries are specialty books that contain the most frequently used words in a language.

The main characteristic of such dictionaries is the division of words into themes. For example, the *City* theme contains the words "street," "crossroads," "square," "fountain," and so on. The *Talking* theme might contain words like "to talk," "to ask," "question," and "answer".

All the words in a theme are divided into smaller units, each comprising 3–5 words. Such an arrangement improves the perception of words and makes the learning process less tiresome. Each unit contains a selection of words with similar meanings or identical roots. This allows you to learn words in small groups and establish other associative links that have a positive effect on memorization.

The words on each page are placed in three columns: a word in your native language, its translation, and its transcription. Such positioning allows for the use of techniques for effective memorization. After closing the translation column, you can flip through and review foreign words, and vice versa. "This is an easy and convenient method of review – one that we recommend you do often."

Our theme-based dictionaries contain transcriptions for all the foreign words. Unfortunately, none of the existing transcriptions are able to convey the exact nuances of foreign pronunciation. That is why we recommend using the transcriptions only as a supplementary learning aid. Correct pronunciation can only be acquired with the help of sound. Therefore our collection includes audio theme-based dictionaries.

The process of learning words using T&P Books' theme-based dictionaries gives you the following advantages:

- You have correctly grouped source information, which predetermines your success at subsequent stages of word memorization
- Availability of words derived from the same root (lazy, lazily, lazybones), allowing you to memorize word units instead of separate words
- Small units of words facilitate the process of establishing associative links needed for consolidation of vocabulary
- You can estimate the number of learned words and hence your level of language knowledge
- The dictionary allows for the creation of an effective and high-quality revision process
- You can revise certain themes several times, modifying the revision methods and techniques
- Audio versions of the dictionaries help you to work out the pronunciation of words and develop your skills of auditory word perception

The T&P Books' theme-based dictionaries are offered in several variants differing in the number of words: 1.500, 3.000, 5.000, 7.000, and 9.000 words. There are also dictionaries containing 15,000 words for some language combinations. Your choice of dictionary will depend on your knowledge level and goals.

We sincerely believe that our dictionaries will become your trusty assistant in learning foreign languages and will allow you to easily acquire the necessary vocabulary.

TABLE OF CONTENTS

Education 140

Arts 147

Rest. Entertainment. Travel 153

TECHNICAL EQUIPMENT. TRANSPORTATION 162
Technical equipment 162

MISCELLANEOUS   250

MAIN 500 VERBS   257

PRONUNCIATION GUIDE

T&P phonetic alphabet	Albanian example	English example
[a]	flas [flas]	shorter than in ask
[e], [ɛ]	melodi [mɛlodí]	absent, pet
[ə]	kërkoj [kərkój]	driver, teacher
[i]	pikë [píkə]	shorter than in feet
[o]	motor [motór]	pod, John
[u]	fuqi [fucí]	book
[y]	myshk [myʃk]	fuel, tuna
[b]	brakë [brákə]	baby, book
[c]	oqean [ocɛán]	Irish - ceist
[d]	adoptoj [adoptój]	day, doctor
[dz]	lexoj [lɛdzój]	beads, kids
[dʒ]	xham [dʒam]	joke, general
[ð]	dhomë [ðómə]	weather, together
[f]	i fortë [i fórtə]	face, food
[g]	bullgari [buɫgarí]	game, gold
[h]	jaht [jáht]	home, have
[j]	hyrje [hýrjɛ]	yes, New York
[ɟ]	zgjedh [zɟɛð]	geese
[k]	korik [korík]	clock, kiss
[l]	lëviz [ləvíz]	lace, people
[ɫ]	shkallë [ʃkáɫə]	feel
[m]	medalje [mɛdáljɛ]	magic, milk
[n]	klan [klan]	name, normal
[ɲ]	spanjoll [spaɲóɫ]	canyon, new
[ŋ]	trung [truŋ]	ring
[p]	polici [politsí]	pencil, private
[r]	i erët [i érət]	rice, radio
[ɾ]	groshë [gróʃə]	Spanish - pero
[s]	spital [spitál]	city, boss
[ʃ]	shes [ʃɛs]	machine, shark
[t]	tapet [tapét]	tourist, trip
[ts]	batica [batítsa]	cats, tsetse fly
[tʃ]	kaçube [katʃúbɛ]	church, French
[v]	javor [javór]	very, river
[z]	horizont [horizónt]	zebra, please
[ʒ]	kuzhinë [kuʒínə]	forge, pleasure
[θ]	përkthej [pərkθéj]	month, tooth

ABBREVIATIONS
used in the vocabulary

English abbreviations

ab.	-	about
adj	-	adjective
adv	-	adverb
anim.	-	animate
as adj	-	attributive noun used as adjective
e.g.	-	for example
etc.	-	et cetera
fam.	-	familiar
fem.	-	feminine
form.	-	formal
inanim.	-	inanimate
masc.	-	masculine
math	-	mathematics
mil.	-	military
n	-	noun
pl	-	plural
pron.	-	pronoun
sb	-	somebody
sing.	-	singular
sth	-	something
v aux	-	auxiliary verb
vi	-	intransitive verb
vi, vt	-	intransitive, transitive verb
vt	-	transitive verb

Albanian abbreviations

f	-	feminine noun
m	-	masculine noun
pl	-	plural

BASIC CONCEPTS

Basic concepts. Part 1

1. Pronouns

I, me	Unë, mua	[unə], [múa]
you	ti, ty	[ti], [ty]
he	ai	[aí]
she	ajo	[ajó]
it	ai	[aí]
we	ne	[nɛ]
you (to a group)	ju	[ju]
they (masc.)	ata	[atá]
they (fem.)	ato	[ató]

2. Greetings. Salutations. Farewells

Hello! (fam.)	Përshëndetje!	[pərʃəndétjɛ!]
Hello! (form.)	Përshëndetje!	[pərʃəndétjɛ!]
Good morning!	Mirëmëngjes!	[mirəmənɟés!]
Good afternoon!	Mirëdita!	[mirədíta!]
Good evening!	Mirëmbrëma!	[mirəmbréma!]
to say hello	përshëndes	[pərʃəndés]
Hi! (hello)	Ç'kemi!	[tʃʼkémi!]
greeting (n)	përshëndetje (f)	[pərʃəndétjɛ]
to greet (vt)	përshëndes	[pərʃəndés]
How are you? (form.)	Si jeni?	[si jéni?]
How are you? (fam.)	Si je?	[si jɛ?]
What's new?	Çfarë ka të re?	[tʃfárə ká tə ré?]
Goodbye!	Mirupafshim!	[mirupáfʃim!]
Bye!	U pafshim!	[u páfʃim!]
See you soon!	Shihemi së shpejti!	[ʃíhɛmi sə ʃpéjti!]
Farewell!	Lamtumirë!	[lamtumírə!]
to say goodbye	përshëndetem	[pərʃəndétɛm]
So long!	Tungjatjeta!	[tunɟatjéta!]

Thank you!	Faleminderit!	[falɛmindéɾit!]
Thank you very much!	Faleminderit shumë!	[falɛmindéɾit ʃúmə!]
You're welcome	Të lutem	[tə lútɛm]
Don't mention it!	Asgjë!	[asɟə́!]
It was nothing	Asgjë	[asɟə́]

Excuse me! (fam.)	Më fal!	[mə fal!]
Excuse me! (form.)	Më falni!	[mə fálni!]
to excuse (forgive)	fal	[fal]

to apologize (vi)	kërkoj falje	[kərkój fáljɛ]
My apologies	Kërkoj ndjesë	[kərkój ndjésə]
I'm sorry!	Më vjen keq!	[mə vjɛn kɛc!]
to forgive (vt)	fal	[fal]
It's okay! (that's all right)	S'ka gjë!	[s'ka ɟə!]
please (adv)	të lutem	[tə lútɛm]

Don't forget!	Mos harro!	[mos haró!]
Certainly!	Sigurisht!	[siguɾíʃt!]
Of course not!	Sigurisht që jo!	[siguɾíʃt cə jo!]
Okay! (I agree)	Në rregull!	[nə réguɫ!]
That's enough!	Mjafton!	[mjaftón!]

3. How to address

Excuse me, ...	Më falni, ...	[mə fálni, ...]
mister, sir	zotëri	[zotəɾí]
ma'am	zonjë	[zóɲə]
miss	zonjushë	[zoɲúʃə]

young man	djalë i ri	[djálə i ɾí]
young man (little boy, kid)	djalosh	[djalóʃ]
miss (little girl)	vajzë	[vájzə]

4. Cardinal numbers. Part 1

0 zero	zero	[zéɾo]
1 one	një	[ɲə]
2 two	dy	[dy]
3 three	tre	[tɾɛ]
4 four	katër	[kátəɾ]

5 five	pesë	[pésə]
6 six	gjashtë	[ɟáʃtə]
7 seven	shtatë	[ʃtátə]
8 eight	tetë	[tétə]
9 nine	nëntë	[nəntə]

10 ten	dhjetë	[ðjétə]
11 eleven	njëmbëdhjetë	[ɲəmbəðjétə]
12 twelve	dymbëdhjetë	[dymbəðjétə]
13 thirteen	trembëdhjetë	[trɛmbəðjétə]
14 fourteen	katërmbëdhjetë	[katərmbəðjétə]

15 fifteen	pesëmbëdhjetë	[pɛsəmbəðjétə]
16 sixteen	gjashtëmbëdhjetë	[ɟaʃtəmbəðjétə]
17 seventeen	shtatëmbëdhjetë	[ʃtatəmbəðjétə]
18 eighteen	tetëmbëdhjetë	[tɛtəmbəðjétə]
19 nineteen	nëntëmbëdhjetë	[nəntəmbəðjétə]

20 twenty	njëzet	[ɲəzét]
21 twenty-one	njëzet e një	[ɲəzét ɛ ɲə]
22 twenty-two	njëzet e dy	[ɲəzét ɛ dy]
23 twenty-three	njëzet e tre	[ɲəzét ɛ trɛ]

30 thirty	tridhjetë	[triðjétə]
31 thirty-one	tridhjetë e një	[triðjétə ɛ ɲə]
32 thirty-two	tridhjetë e dy	[triðjétə ɛ dy]
33 thirty-three	tridhjetë e tre	[triðjétə ɛ trɛ]

40 forty	dyzet	[dyzét]
41 forty-one	dyzet e një	[dyzét ɛ ɲə]
42 forty-two	dyzet e dy	[dyzét ɛ dy]
43 forty-three	dyzet e tre	[dyzét ɛ trɛ]

50 fifty	pesëdhjetë	[pɛsəðjétə]
51 fifty-one	pesëdhjetë e një	[pɛsəðjétə ɛ ɲə]
52 fifty-two	pesëdhjetë e dy	[pɛsəðjétə ɛ dy]
53 fifty-three	pesëdhjetë e tre	[pɛsəðjétə ɛ trɛ]

60 sixty	gjashtëdhjetë	[ɟaʃtəðjétə]
61 sixty-one	gjashtëdhjetë e një	[ɟaʃtəðjétə ɛ ɲə]
62 sixty-two	gjashtëdhjetë e dy	[ɟaʃtəðjétə ɛ dý]
63 sixty-three	gjashtëdhjetë e tre	[ɟaʃtəðjétə ɛ tré]

70 seventy	shtatëdhjetë	[ʃtatəðjétə]
71 seventy-one	shtatëdhjetë e një	[ʃtatəðjétə ɛ ɲə]
72 seventy-two	shtatëdhjetë e dy	[ʃtatəðjétə ɛ dy]
73 seventy-three	shtatëdhjetë e tre	[ʃtatəðjétə ɛ trɛ]

80 eighty	tetëdhjetë	[tɛtəðjétə]
81 eighty-one	tetëdhjetë e një	[tɛtəðjétə ɛ ɲə]
82 eighty-two	tetëdhjetë e dy	[tɛtəðjétə ɛ dy]
83 eighty-three	tetëdhjetë e tre	[tɛtəðjétə ɛ trɛ]

90 ninety	nëntëdhjetë	[nəntəðjétə]
91 ninety-one	nëntëdhjetë e një	[nəntəðjétə ɛ ɲə]
92 ninety-two	nëntëdhjetë e dy	[nəntəðjétə ɛ dy]
93 ninety-three	nëntëdhjetë e tre	[nəntəðjétə ɛ trɛ]

5. Cardinal numbers. Part 2

100 one hundred	njëqind	[ɲəcínd]
200 two hundred	dyqind	[dycínd]
300 three hundred	treqind	[trɛcínd]
400 four hundred	katërqind	[katərcínd]
500 five hundred	pesëqind	[pɛsəcínd]
600 six hundred	gjashtëqind	[ɟaʃtəcínd]
700 seven hundred	shtatëqind	[ʃtatəcínd]
800 eight hundred	tetëqind	[tɛtəcínd]
900 nine hundred	nëntëqind	[nəntəcínd]
1000 one thousand	një mijë	[ɲə míjə]
2000 two thousand	dy mijë	[dy míjə]
3000 three thousand	tre mijë	[trɛ míjə]
10000 ten thousand	dhjetë mijë	[ðjétə míjə]
one hundred thousand	njëqind mijë	[ɲəcínd míjə]
million	milion (m)	[milión]
billion	miliardë (f)	[miliárdə]

6. Ordinal numbers

first (adj)	i pari	[i pári]
second (adj)	i dyti	[i dýti]
third (adj)	i treti	[i tréti]
fourth (adj)	i katërti	[i kátərti]
fifth (adj)	i pesti	[i pésti]
sixth (adj)	i gjashti	[i ɟáʃti]
seventh (adj)	i shtati	[i ʃtáti]
eighth (adj)	i teti	[i téti]
ninth (adj)	i nënti	[i nénti]
tenth (adj)	i dhjeti	[i ðjéti]

7. Numbers. Fractions

fraction	thyesë (f)	[θýɛsə]
one half	gjysma	[ɟýsma]
one third	një e treta	[ɲə ɛ tréta]
one quarter	një e katërta	[ɲə ɛ kátərta]
one eighth	një e teta	[ɲə ɛ téta]
one tenth	një e dhjeta	[ɲə ɛ ðjéta]
two thirds	dy të tretat	[dy tə trétat]
three quarters	tre të katërtat	[trɛ tə kátərtat]

8. Numbers. Basic operations

subtraction	zbritje (f)	[zbrítjɛ]
to subtract (vi, vt)	zbres	[zbrɛs]
division	pjesëtim (m)	[pjɛsətím]
to divide (vt)	pjesëtoj	[pjɛsətój]

addition	mbledhje (f)	[mbléðjɛ]
to add up (vt)	shtoj	[ʃtoj]
to add (vi, vt)	mbledh	[mbléð]
multiplication	shumëzim (m)	[ʃuməzím]
to multiply (vt)	shumëzoj	[ʃuməzój]

9. Numbers. Miscellaneous

digit, figure	shifër (f)	[ʃífər]
number	numër (m)	[númər]
numeral	numerik (m)	[numɛrík]
minus sign	minus (m)	[minús]
plus sign	plus (m)	[plus]
formula	formulë (f)	[formúlə]
calculation	llogaritje (f)	[ɬogarítjɛ]
to count (vi, vt)	numëroj	[numərój]
to count up	llogaris	[ɬogarís]
to compare (vt)	krahasoj	[krahasój]

How much?	Sa?	[sa?]
sum, total	shuma (f)	[ʃúma]
result	rezultat (m)	[rɛzultát]
remainder	mbetje (f)	[mbétjɛ]
a few (e.g., ~ years ago)	disa	[disá]
little (I had ~ time)	pak	[pak]
few (I have ~ friends)	disa	[disá]
a little (~ water)	pak	[pak]
the rest	mbetje (f)	[mbétjɛ]
one and a half	një e gjysmë (f)	[ɲə ɛ ɟýsmə]
dozen	dyzinë (f)	[dyzínə]

in half (adv)	përgjysmë	[pərɟýsmə]
equally (evenly)	gjysmë për gjysmë	[ɟýsmə pər ɟýsmə]
half	gjysmë (f)	[ɟýsmə]
time (three ~s)	herë (f)	[hérə]

10. The most important verbs. Part 1

to advise (vt)	këshilloj	[kəʃiɫój]
to agree (say yes)	bie dakord	[bíɛ dakórd]

to answer (vi, vt)	përgjigjem	[pərɟíɟɛm]
to apologize (vi)	kërkoj falje	[kərkój fáljɛ]
to arrive (vi)	arrij	[aríj]

to ask (~ oneself)	pyes	[pýɛs]
to ask (~ sb to do sth)	pyes	[pýɛs]
to be (vi)	jam	[jam]

to be afraid	kam frikë	[kam fríkə]
to be hungry	kam uri	[kam urí]
to be interested in ...	interesohem ...	[intɛrɛsóhɛm ...]
to be needed	nevojitet	[nɛvojítɛt]
to be surprised	çuditem	[tʃudítɛm]

to be thirsty	kam etje	[kam étjɛ]
to begin (vt)	filloj	[fiłój]
to belong to ...	përkas ...	[pərkás ...]
to boast (vi)	mburrem	[mbúrɛm]
to break (split into pieces)	ndahem	[ndáhɛm]

to call (~ for help)	thërras	[θərás]
can (v aux)	mund	[mund]
to catch (vt)	kap	[kap]
to change (vt)	ndryshoj	[ndryʃój]
to choose (select)	zgjedh	[zɟɛð]

to come down (the stairs)	zbres	[zbrɛs]
to compare (vt)	krahasoj	[krahasój]
to complain (vi, vt)	ankohem	[ankóhɛm]
to confuse (mix up)	ngatërroj	[ŋatərój]
to continue (vt)	vazhdoj	[vaʒdój]
to control (vt)	kontrolloj	[kontrołój]

to cook (dinner)	gatuaj	[gatúaj]
to cost (vt)	kushton	[kuʃtón]
to count (add up)	numëroj	[numərój]
to count on ...	mbështetem ...	[mbəʃtétɛm ...]
to create (vt)	krijoj	[krijój]
to cry (weep)	qaj	[caj]

11. The most important verbs. Part 2

to deceive (vi, vt)	mashtroj	[maʃtrój]
to decorate (tree, street)	zbukuroj	[zbukurój]
to defend (a country, etc.)	mbroj	[mbrój]
to demand (request firmly)	kërkoj	[kərkój]
to dig (vt)	gërmoj	[gərmój]

| to discuss (vt) | diskutoj | [diskutój] |
| to do (vt) | bëj | [bəj] |

to doubt (have doubts)	dyshoj	[dyʃój]
to drop (let fall)	lëshoj	[ləʃój]
to enter (room, house, etc.)	hyj	[hyj]

to excuse (forgive)	fal	[fal]
to exist (vi)	ekzistoj	[ɛkzistój]
to expect (foresee)	parashikoj	[paraʃikój]
to explain (vt)	shpjegoj	[ʃpjɛgój]
to fall (vi)	bie	[bíɛ]

to find (vt)	gjej	[ɟéj]
to finish (vt)	përfundoj	[pərfundój]
to fly (vi)	fluturoj	[fluturój]
to follow ... (come after)	ndjek ...	[ndjék ...]
to forget (vi, vt)	harroj	[harój]

to forgive (vt)	fal	[fal]
to give (vt)	jap	[jap]
to give a hint	aludoj	[aludój]
to go (on foot)	ec në këmbë	[ɛts nə kémbə]

to go for a swim	notoj	[notój]
to go out (for dinner, etc.)	dal	[dal]
to guess (the answer)	hamendësoj	[hamɛndəsój]

to have (vt)	kam	[kam]
to have breakfast	ha mëngjes	[ha mənɟés]
to have dinner	ha darkë	[ha dárkə]
to have lunch	ha drekë	[ha drékə]
to hear (vt)	dëgjoj	[dəɟój]

to help (vt)	ndihmoj	[ndihmój]
to hide (vt)	fsheh	[fʃéh]
to hope (vi, vt)	shpresoj	[ʃprɛsój]
to hunt (vi, vt)	dal për gjah	[dál pər ɟáh]
to hurry (vi)	nxitoj	[ndzitój]

12. The most important verbs. Part 3

to inform (vt)	informoj	[informój]
to insist (vi, vt)	këmbëngul	[kəmbəŋúl]
to insult (vt)	fyej	[fýɛj]
to invite (vt)	ftoj	[ftoj]
to joke (vi)	bëj shaka	[bəj ʃaká]

to keep (vt)	mbaj	[mbáj]
to keep silent, to hush	hesht	[hɛʃt]
to kill (vt)	vras	[vras]
to know (sb)	njoh	[ɲóh]

to know (sth)	di	[di]
to laugh (vi)	qesh	[cɛʃ]

to liberate (city, etc.)	çliroj	[tʃlirój]
to like (I like …)	pëlqej	[pəlcéj]
to look for … (search)	kërkoj …	[kərkój …]
to love (sb)	dashuroj	[daʃurój]
to make a mistake	gaboj	[gabój]

to manage, to run	drejtoj	[drɛjtój]
to mean (signify)	nënkuptoj	[nənkuptój]
to mention (talk about)	përmend	[pərménd]
to miss (school, etc.)	humbas	[humbás]
to notice (see)	vërej	[vəréj]

to object (vi, vt)	kundërshtoj	[kundərʃtój]
to observe (see)	vëzhgoj	[vəʒgój]
to open (vt)	hap	[hap]
to order (meal, etc.)	porosis	[porosís]
to order (mil.)	urdhëroj	[urðərój]
to own (possess)	zotëroj	[zotərój]

to participate (vi)	marr pjesë	[mar pjésə]
to pay (vi, vt)	paguaj	[pagúaj]
to permit (vt)	lejoj	[lɛjój]
to plan (vt)	planifikoj	[planifikój]
to play (children)	luaj	[lúaj]

to pray (vi, vt)	lutem	[lútɛm]
to prefer (vt)	preferoj	[prɛfɛrój]
to promise (vt)	premtoj	[prɛmtój]
to pronounce (vt)	shqiptoj	[ʃciptój]
to propose (vt)	propozoj	[propozój]
to punish (vt)	ndëshkoj	[ndəʃkój]

13. The most important verbs. Part 4

to read (vi, vt)	lexoj	[lɛdzój]
to recommend (vt)	rekomandoj	[rɛkomandój]
to refuse (vi, vt)	refuzoj	[rɛfuzój]
to regret (be sorry)	pendohem	[pɛndóhɛm]
to rent (sth from sb)	marr me qira	[mar mɛ cirá]

to repeat (say again)	përsëris	[pərsərís]
to reserve, to book	rezervoj	[rɛzɛrvój]
to run (vi)	vrapoj	[vrapój]
to save (rescue)	shpëtoj	[ʃpətój]
to say (~ thank you)	them	[θɛm]
to scold (vt)	qortoj	[cortój]
to see (vt)	shikoj	[ʃikój]

to sell (vt)	shes	[ʃɛs]
to send (vt)	dërgoj	[dərgój]
to shoot (vi)	qëlloj	[cətój]

to shout (vi)	bërtas	[bərtás]
to show (vt)	tregoj	[trɛgój]
to sign (document)	nënshkruaj	[nənʃkrúaj]
to sit down (vi)	ulem	[úlɛm]

to smile (vi)	buzëqesh	[buzəcéʃ]
to speak (vi, vt)	flas	[flas]
to steal (money, etc.)	vjedh	[vjɛð]
to stop (for pause, etc.)	ndaloj	[ndalój]
to stop (please ~ calling me)	ndaloj	[ndalój]

to study (vt)	studioj	[studiój]
to swim (vi)	notoj	[notój]
to take (vt)	marr	[mar]
to think (vi, vt)	mendoj	[mɛndój]
to threaten (vt)	kërcënoj	[kərtsənój]

to touch (with hands)	prek	[prɛk]
to translate (vt)	përkthej	[pərkθéj]
to trust (vt)	besoj	[bɛsój]
to try (attempt)	përpiqem	[pərpícɛm]
to turn (e.g., ~ left)	kthej	[kθɛj]

to underestimate (vt)	nënvlerësoj	[nənvlɛrəsój]
to understand (vt)	kuptoj	[kuptój]
to unite (vt)	bashkoj	[baʃkój]
to wait (vt)	pres	[prɛs]

to want (wish, desire)	dëshiroj	[dəʃirój]
to warn (vt)	paralajmëroj	[paralajmərój]
to work (vi)	punoj	[punój]
to write (vt)	shkruaj	[ʃkrúaj]
to write down	mbaj shënim	[mbáj ʃəním]

14. Colors

color	ngjyrë (f)	[ɲýrə]
shade (tint)	nuancë (f)	[nuántsə]
hue	tonalitet (m)	[tonalitét]
rainbow	ylber (m)	[ylbér]

white (adj)	e bardhë	[ɛ bárðə]
black (adj)	e zezë	[ɛ zézə]
gray (adj)	gri	[gri]
green (adj)	jeshile	[jɛʃílɛ]

yellow (adj)	e verdhë	[ɛ vérðə]
red (adj)	e kuqe	[ɛ kúcɛ]
blue (adj)	blu	[blu]
light blue (adj)	bojëqielli	[bojəciéɬi]
pink (adj)	rozë	[rózə]
orange (adj)	portokalli	[portokáɬi]
violet (adj)	bojëvjollcë	[bojəvjóɬtsə]
brown (adj)	kafe	[káfɛ]
golden (adj)	e artë	[ɛ ártə]
silvery (adj)	e argjendtë	[ɛ arɲéndtə]
beige (adj)	bezhë	[béʒə]
cream (adj)	krem	[krɛm]
turquoise (adj)	e bruztë	[ɛ brúztə]
cherry red (adj)	qershi	[cɛrʃí]
lilac (adj)	jargavan	[jargaván]
crimson (adj)	e kuqe e thellë	[ɛ kúcɛ ɛ θéɬə]
light (adj)	e hapur	[ɛ hápuɾ]
dark (adj)	e errët	[ɛ érət]
bright, vivid (adj)	e ndritshme	[ɛ ndrítʃmɛ]
colored (pencils)	e ngjyrosur	[ɛ ɲɟyrósuɾ]
color (e.g., ~ film)	ngjyrë	[ɲɟýrə]
black-and-white (adj)	bardhë e zi	[bárðə ɛ zi]
plain (one-colored)	njëngjyrëshe	[nənɟýrəʃɛ]
multicolored (adj)	shumëngjyrëshe	[ʃumənɟýrəʃɛ]

15. Questions

Who?	Kush?	[kuʃ?]
What?	Çka?	[tʃká?]
Where? (at, in)	Ku?	[ku?]
Where (to)?	Për ku?	[pər ku?]
From where?	Nga ku?	[ŋa ku?]
When?	Kur?	[kur?]
Why? (What for?)	Pse?	[psɛ?]
Why? (~ are you crying?)	Pse?	[psɛ?]
What for?	Për çfarë arsye?	[pər tʃfárə arsýɛ?]
How? (in what way)	Si?	[si?]
What? (What kind of ...?)	Çfarë?	[tʃfárə?]
Which?	Cili?	[tsíli?]
To whom?	Kujt?	[kújt?]
About whom?	Për kë?	[pər kə?]
About what?	Për çfarë?	[pər tʃfárə?]
With whom?	Me kë?	[mɛ kə?]

| How many? How much? | **Sa?** | [sa?] |
| Whose? | **Të kujt?** | [tə kujt?] |

16. Prepositions

with (accompanied by)	**me**	[mɛ]
without	**pa**	[pa]
to (indicating direction)	**për në**	[pər nə]
about (talking ~ ...)	**për**	[pər]
before (in time)	**përpara**	[pərpára]
in front of ...	**para ...**	[pára ...]

under (beneath, below)	**nën**	[nən]
above (over)	**mbi**	[mbí]
on (atop)	**mbi**	[mbí]
from (off, out of)	**nga**	[ŋa]
of (made from)	**nga**	[ŋa]

| in (e.g., ~ ten minutes) | **për** | [pər] |
| over (across the top of) | **sipër** | [sípər] |

17. Function words. Adverbs. Part 1

Where? (at, in)	**Ku?**	[ku?]
here (adv)	**këtu**	[kətú]
there (adv)	**atje**	[atjé]

| somewhere (to be) | **diku** | [dikú] |
| nowhere (not in any place) | **askund** | [askúnd] |

| by (near, beside) | **afër** | [áfər] |
| by the window | **tek dritarja** | [tɛk dritárja] |

Where (to)?	**Për ku?**	[pər ku?]
here (e.g., come ~!)	**këtu**	[kətú]
there (e.g., to go ~)	**atje**	[atjé]
from here (adv)	**nga këtu**	[ŋa kətú]
from there (adv)	**nga atje**	[ŋa atjɛ]

| close (adv) | **pranë** | [pránə] |
| far (adv) | **larg** | [larg] |

near (e.g., ~ Paris)	**afër**	[áfər]
nearby (adv)	**pranë**	[pránə]
not far (adv)	**jo larg**	[jo lárg]

| left (adj) | **majtë** | [májtə] |
| on the left | **majtas** | [májtas] |

to the left	në të majtë	[nə tə májtə]
right (adj)	djathtë	[djáθtə]
on the right	djathtas	[djáθtas]
to the right	në të djathtë	[nə tə djáθtə]

in front (adv)	përballë	[pərbáɫə]
front (as adj)	i përparmë	[i pərpármə]
ahead (the kids ran ~)	përpara	[pərpára]

behind (adv)	prapa	[prápa]
from behind	nga prapa	[ŋa prápa]
back (towards the rear)	pas	[pas]

middle	mes (m)	[mɛs]
in the middle	në mes	[nə mɛs]

at the side	në anë	[nə anə]
everywhere (adv)	kudo	[kúdo]
around (in all directions)	përreth	[pəréθ]

from inside	nga brenda	[ŋa brénda]
somewhere (to go)	diku	[dikú]
straight (directly)	drejt	[dréjt]
back (e.g., come ~)	pas	[pas]

from anywhere	nga kudo	[ŋa kúdo]
from somewhere	nga diku	[ŋa dikú]

firstly (adv)	së pari	[sə pári]
secondly (adv)	së dyti	[sə dýti]
thirdly (adv)	së treti	[sə tréti]

suddenly (adv)	befas	[béfas]
at first (in the beginning)	në fillim	[nə fiɫím]
for the first time	për herë të parë	[pər hérə tə párə]
long before ...	shumë përpara ...	[ʃúmə pərpára ...]
anew (over again)	sërish	[səríʃ]
for good (adv)	një herë e mirë	[ɲə hérə ɛ mírə]

never (adv)	kurrë	[kúrə]
again (adv)	përsëri	[pərsərí]
now (at present)	tani	[táni]
often (adv)	shpesh	[ʃpɛʃ]
then (adv)	atëherë	[atəhérə]
urgently (quickly)	urgjent	[urɟént]
usually (adv)	zakonisht	[zakoníʃt]

by the way, ...	meqë ra fjala, ...	[mécə ra fjála, ...]
possibly	ndoshta	[ndóʃta]
probably (adv)	mundësisht	[mundəsíʃt]
maybe (adv)	mbase	[mbásɛ]
besides ...	përveç	[pərvétʃ]

that's why ...	ja përse ...	[ja pərsé ...]
in spite of ...	pavarësisht se ...	[pavarəsíʃt sɛ ...]
thanks to ...	falë ...	[fálə ...]

what (pron.)	çfarë	[tʃfárə]
that (conj.)	që	[cə]
something	diçka	[ditʃká]
anything (something)	ndonji gjë	[ndoɲí ɟə]
nothing	asgjë	[asɟə́]

who (pron.)	kush	[kuʃ]
someone	dikush	[dikúʃ]
somebody	dikush	[dikúʃ]

nobody	askush	[askúʃ]
nowhere (a voyage to ~)	askund	[askúnd]
nobody's	i askujt	[i askújt]
somebody's	i dikujt	[i dikújt]

so (I'm ~ glad)	aq	[ác]
also (as well)	gjithashtu	[ɟiθaʃtú]
too (as well)	gjithashtu	[ɟiθaʃtú]

18. Function words. Adverbs. Part 2

Why?	Pse?	[psɛ?]
for some reason	për një arsye	[pər ɲə arsýɛ]
because ...	sepse ...	[sɛpsé ...]
for some purpose	për ndonjë shkak	[pər ndóɲə ʃkak]

and	dhe	[ðɛ]
or	ose	[ósɛ]
but	por	[por]
for (e.g., ~ me)	për	[pər]

too (~ many people)	tepër	[tépər]
only (exclusively)	vetëm	[vétəm]
exactly (adv)	pikërisht	[pikəríʃt]
about (more or less)	rreth	[rɛθ]

approximately (adv)	përafërsisht	[pərafərsíʃt]
approximate (adj)	përafërt	[pəráfərt]
almost (adv)	pothuajse	[poθúajsɛ]
the rest	mbetje (f)	[mbétjɛ]

the other (second)	tjetri	[tjétri]
other (different)	tjetër	[tjétər]
each (adj)	çdo	[tʃdo]
any (no matter which)	çfarëdo	[tʃfarədó]
many (adj)	disa	[disá]

much (adv)	shumë	[ʃúmə]
many people	shumë njerëz	[ʃúmə ɲérəz]
all (everyone)	të gjithë	[tə ɟíθə]

in return for …	në vend të …	[nə vénd tə …]
in exchange (adv)	në shkëmbim të …	[nə ʃkəmbím tə …]
by hand (made)	me dorë	[mɛ dórə]
hardly (negative opinion)	vështirë se …	[vəʃtírə sɛ …]

probably (adv)	mundësisht	[mundəsíʃt]
on purpose (intentionally)	me qëllim	[mɛ cəɫím]
by accident (adv)	aksidentalisht	[aksidɛntalíʃt]

very (adv)	shumë	[ʃúmə]
for example (adv)	për shembull	[pər ʃémbuɫ]
between	midis	[midís]
among	rreth	[rɛθ]
so much (such a lot)	kaq shumë	[kác ʃúmə]
especially (adv)	veçanërisht	[vɛtʃanəríʃt]

Basic concepts. Part 2

19. Weekdays

Monday	E hënë (f)	[ɛ hénə]
Tuesday	E martë (f)	[ɛ mártə]
Wednesday	E mërkurë (f)	[ɛ mərkúrə]
Thursday	E enjte (f)	[ɛ éɲtɛ]
Friday	E premte (f)	[ɛ prémtɛ]
Saturday	E shtunë (f)	[ɛ ʃtúnə]
Sunday	E dielë (f)	[ɛ díɛlə]
today (adv)	sot	[sot]
tomorrow (adv)	nesër	[nésər]
the day after tomorrow	pasnesër	[pasnésər]
yesterday (adv)	dje	[djé]
the day before yesterday	pardje	[pardjé]
day	ditë (f)	[dítə]
working day	ditë pune (f)	[dítə púnɛ]
public holiday	festë kombëtare (f)	[féstə kombətárɛ]
day off	ditë pushim (m)	[dítə puʃím]
weekend	fundjavë (f)	[fundjávə]
all day long	gjithë ditën	[ɟíθə dítən]
the next day (adv)	ditën pasardhëse	[dítən pasárðəsɛ]
two days ago	dy ditë më parë	[dy dítə mə párə]
the day before	një ditë më parë	[ɲə dítə mə párə]
daily (adj)	ditor	[ditór]
every day (adv)	çdo ditë	[tʃdo dítə]
week	javë (f)	[jávə]
last week (adv)	javën e kaluar	[jávən ɛ kalúar]
next week (adv)	javën e ardhshme	[jávən ɛ árðʃmɛ]
weekly (adj)	javor	[javór]
every week (adv)	çdo javë	[tʃdo jávə]
twice a week	dy herë në javë	[dy hérə nə jávə]
every Tuesday	çdo të martë	[tʃdo tə mártə]

20. Hours. Day and night

morning	mëngjes (m)	[mənɟés]
in the morning	në mëngjes	[nə mənɟés]
noon, midday	mesditë (f)	[mɛsdítə]

in the afternoon	pasdite	[pasdítɛ]
evening	mbrëmje (f)	[mbrə́mjɛ]
in the evening	në mbrëmje	[nə mbrə́mjɛ]
night	natë (f)	[nátə]
at night	natën	[nátən]
midnight	mesnatë (f)	[mɛsnátə]

second	sekondë (f)	[sɛkóndə]
minute	minutë (f)	[minútə]
hour	orë (f)	[órə]
half an hour	gjysmë ore (f)	[ɟýsmə órɛ]
a quarter-hour	çerek ore (m)	[tʃɛrék órɛ]
fifteen minutes	pesëmbëdhjetë minuta	[pɛsəmbəðjétə minútə]
24 hours	24 orë	[ɲəzét ɛ kátər órə]

sunrise	agim (m)	[agím]
dawn	agim (m)	[agím]
early morning	mëngjes herët (m)	[mənɟés hérət]
sunset	perëndim dielli (m)	[pɛrəndím diéɬi]

early in the morning	herët në mëngjes	[hérət nə mənɟés]
this morning	sot në mëngjes	[sot nə mənɟés]
tomorrow morning	nesër në mëngjes	[nésər nə mənɟés]

this afternoon	sot pasdite	[sot pasdítɛ]
in the afternoon	pasdite	[pasdítɛ]
tomorrow afternoon	nesër pasdite	[nésər pasdítɛ]

| tonight (this evening) | sonte në mbrëmje | [sóntɛ nə mbrəmjɛ] |
| tomorrow night | nesër në mbrëmje | [nésər nə mbrə́mjɛ] |

at 3 o'clock sharp	në orën 3 fiks	[nə órən trɛ fiks]
about 4 o'clock	rreth orës 4	[rɛθ órəs kátər]
by 12 o'clock	deri në orën 12	[déri nə órən dymbəðjétə]

in 20 minutes	për 20 minuta	[pər ɲəzét minúta]
in an hour	për një orë	[pər ɲə órə]
on time (adv)	në orar	[nə orár]

a quarter to …	çerek …	[tʃɛrék …]
within an hour	brenda një ore	[brénda ɲə órɛ]
every 15 minutes	çdo 15 minuta	[tʃdo pɛsəmbəðjétə minúta]
round the clock	gjithë ditën	[ɟíθə dítən]

21. Months. Seasons

January	Janar (m)	[janár]
February	Shkurt (m)	[ʃkurt]
March	Mars (m)	[mars]
April	Prill (m)	[priɬ]

| May | **Maj** (m) | [maj] |
| June | **Qershor** (m) | [cɛrʃór] |

July	**Korrik** (m)	[korík]
August	**Gusht** (m)	[guʃt]
September	**Shtator** (m)	[ʃtatór]
October	**Tetor** (m)	[tɛtór]
November	**Nëntor** (m)	[nəntór]
December	**Dhjetor** (m)	[ðjɛtór]

spring	**pranverë** (f)	[pranvérə]
in spring	**në pranverë**	[nə pranvérə]
spring (as adj)	**pranveror**	[pranvɛrór]

summer	**verë** (f)	[vérə]
in summer	**në verë**	[nə vérə]
summer (as adj)	**veror**	[vɛrór]

fall	**vjeshtë** (f)	[vjéʃtə]
in fall	**në vjeshtë**	[nə vjéʃtə]
fall (as adj)	**vjeshtor**	[vjéʃtor]

winter	**dimër** (m)	[dímər]
in winter	**në dimër**	[nə dímər]
winter (as adj)	**dimëror**	[dimərór]

month	**muaj** (m)	[múaj]
this month	**këtë muaj**	[kətə múaj]
next month	**muajin tjetër**	[múajin tjétər]
last month	**muajin e kaluar**	[múajin ɛ kalúar]

a month ago	**para një muaji**	[pára ɲə múaji]
in a month (a month later)	**pas një muaji**	[pas ɲə múaji]
in 2 months (2 months later)	**pas dy muajsh**	[pas dy múajʃ]
the whole month	**gjithë muajin**	[ɟíθə múajin]
all month long	**gjatë gjithë muajit**	[ɟátə ɟíθə múajit]

monthly (~ magazine)	**mujor**	[mujór]
monthly (adv)	**mujor**	[mujór]
every month	**çdo muaj**	[tʃdo múaj]
twice a month	**dy herë në muaj**	[dy hérə nə múaj]

year	**vit** (m)	[vit]
this year	**këtë vit**	[kətə vít]
next year	**vitin tjetër**	[vítin tjétər]
last year	**vitin e kaluar**	[vítin ɛ kalúar]

a year ago	**para një viti**	[pára ɲə víti]
in a year	**për një vit**	[pər ɲə vit]
in two years	**për dy vite**	[pər dy vítɛ]
the whole year	**gjithë vitin**	[ɟíθə vítin]

all year long	gjatë gjithë vitit	[ɟátə ɟíθə vítit]
every year	çdo vit	[tʃdo vít]
annual (adj)	vjetor	[vjɛtór]
annually (adv)	çdo vit	[tʃdo vít]
4 times a year	4 herë në vit	[kátər hérə nə vit]

date (e.g., today's ~)	datë (f)	[dátə]
date (e.g., ~ of birth)	data (f)	[dáta]
calendar	kalendar (m)	[kalɛndár]

half a year	gjysmë viti	[ɟýsmə víti]
six months	gjashtë muaj	[ɟáʃtə múaj]
season (summer, etc.)	stinë (f)	[stínə]
century	shekull (m)	[ʃékuɫ]

22. Time. Miscellaneous

time	kohë (f)	[kóhə]
moment	çast, moment (m)	[tʃást], [momént]
instant (n)	çast (m)	[tʃást]
instant (adj)	i çastit	[i tʃástit]
lapse (of time)	interval (m)	[intɛrvál]
life	jetë (f)	[jétə]
eternity	përjetësi (f)	[pərjɛtəsí]

epoch	epokë (f)	[ɛpókə]
era	erë (f)	[érə]
cycle	cikël (m)	[tsíkəl]
period	periudhë (f)	[pɛriúðə]
term (short-~)	afat (m)	[afát]

the future	ardhmëria (f)	[arðməría]
future (as adj)	e ardhme	[ɛ árðmɛ]
next time	herën tjetër	[hérən tjétər]
the past	e shkuara (f)	[ɛ ʃkúara]
past (recent)	kaluar	[kalúar]
last time	herën e fundit	[hérən ɛ fúndit]

later (adv)	më vonë	[mə vónə]
after (prep.)	pas	[pas]
nowadays (adv)	në këto kohë	[nə kəto kóhə]
now (at this moment)	tani	[táni]
immediately (adv)	menjëherë	[mɛɲəhérə]
soon (adv)	së shpejti	[sə ʃpéjti]
in advance (beforehand)	paraprakisht	[paraprakíʃt]

a long time ago	para shumë kohësh	[pára ʃúmə kóhəʃ]
recently (adv)	së fundmi	[sə fúndmi]
destiny	fat (m)	[fat]
memories (childhood ~)	kujtime (pl)	[kujtímɛ]

archives	arkiva (f)	[arkíva]
during …	gjatë …	[ɟátə …]
long, a long time (adv)	gjatë, kohë e gjatë	[ɟátə], [kóhə ɛ ɟátə]
not long (adv)	jo gjatë	[jo ɟátə]
early (in the morning)	herët	[hérət]
late (not early)	vonë	[vónə]

forever (for good)	përjetë	[pərjétə]
to start (begin)	filloj	[fiɫój]
to postpone (vt)	shtyj	[ʃtyj]

at the same time	njëkohësisht	[ɲəkohəsíʃt]
permanently (adv)	përhershëm	[pərhérʃəm]
constant (noise, pain)	vazhdueshme	[vaʒdúɛʃmɛ]
temporary (adj)	i përkohshëm	[i pərkóhʃəm]

sometimes (adv)	ndonjëherë	[ndoɲəhérə]
rarely (adv)	rrallë	[ráɫə]
often (adv)	shpesh	[ʃpɛʃ]

23. Opposites

| rich (adj) | i pasur | [i pásur] |
| poor (adj) | i varfër | [i várfər] |

| ill, sick (adj) | i sëmurë | [i səmúrə] |
| well (not sick) | mirë | [mírə] |

| big (adj) | i madh | [i máð] |
| small (adj) | i vogël | [i vógəl] |

| quickly (adv) | shpejt | [ʃpɛjt] |
| slowly (adv) | ngadalë | [ŋadálə] |

| fast (adj) | i shpejtë | [i ʃpéjtə] |
| slow (adj) | i ngadaltë | [i ŋadáltə] |

| glad (adj) | i kënaqur | [i kənácur] |
| sad (adj) | i mërzitur | [i mərzítur] |

| together (adv) | së bashku | [sə báʃku] |
| separately (adv) | veç e veç | [vɛtʃ ɛ vɛtʃ] |

| aloud (to read) | me zë | [mɛ zə] |
| silently (to oneself) | pa zë | [pa zə] |

tall (adj)	i lartë	[i lártə]
low (adj)	i ulët	[i úlət]
deep (adj)	i thellë	[i θéɫə]
shallow (adj)	i cekët	[i tsékət]

yes	po	[po]
no	jo	[jo]
distant (in space)	i largët	[i lárgət]
nearby (adj)	afër	[áfər]
far (adv)	larg	[larg]
nearby (adv)	pranë	[pránə]
long (adj)	i gjatë	[i ɟátə]
short (adj)	i shkurtër	[i ʃkúrtər]
good (kindhearted)	i mirë	[i mírə]
evil (adj)	djallëzor	[djaɫəzór]
married (adj)	i martuar	[i martúar]
single (adj)	beqar	[bɛcár]
to forbid (vt)	ndaloj	[ndalój]
to permit (vt)	lejoj	[lɛjój]
end	fund (m)	[fund]
beginning	fillim (m)	[fiɫím]
left (adj)	majtë	[májtə]
right (adj)	djathtë	[djáθtə]
first (adj)	i pari	[i pári]
last (adj)	i fundit	[i fúndit]
crime	krim (m)	[krim]
punishment	ndëshkim (m)	[ndəʃkím]
to order (vt)	urdhëroj	[urðərój]
to obey (vi, vt)	bindem	[bíndɛm]
straight (adj)	i drejtë	[i dréjtə]
curved (adj)	i harkuar	[i harkúar]
paradise	parajsë (f)	[parájsə]
hell	ferr (m)	[fɛr]
to be born	lind	[lind]
to die (vi)	vdes	[vdɛs]
strong (adj)	i fortë	[i fórtə]
weak (adj)	i dobët	[i dóbət]
old (adj)	plak	[plak]
young (adj)	i ri	[i rí]
old (adj)	i vjetër	[i vjétər]
new (adj)	i ri	[i rí]

| hard (adj) | i fortë | [i fórtə] |
| soft (adj) | i butë | [i bútə] |

| warm (tepid) | ngrohtë | [ŋróhtə] |
| cold (adj) | i ftohtë | [i ftóhtə] |

| fat (adj) | i shëndoshë | [i ʃəndóʃə] |
| thin (adj) | i dobët | [i dóbət] |

| narrow (adj) | i ngushtë | [i ŋúʃtə] |
| wide (adj) | i gjerë | [i ɟérə] |

| good (adj) | i mirë | [i mírə] |
| bad (adj) | i keq | [i kéc] |

| brave (adj) | guximtar | [gudzimtáɾ] |
| cowardly (adj) | frikacak | [frikatsák] |

24. Lines and shapes

square	katror (m)	[katrór]
square (as adj)	katrore	[katrórɛ]
circle	rreth (m)	[rɛθ]
round (adj)	i rrumbullakët	[i rumbuɫákət]
triangle	trekëndësh (m)	[trékəndəʃ]
triangular (adj)	trekëndor	[trɛkəndór]

oval	oval (f)	[ovál]
oval (as adj)	ovale	[oválɛ]
rectangle	drejtkëndësh (m)	[drɛjtkéndəʃ]
rectangular (adj)	drejtkëndor	[drɛjtkəndór]

pyramid	piramidë (f)	[piramídə]
rhombus	romb (m)	[romb]
trapezoid	trapezoid (m)	[trapɛzoíd]
cube	kub (m)	[kub]
prism	prizëm (m)	[prízəm]

circumference	perimetër (m)	[pɛrimétər]
sphere	sferë (f)	[sférə]
ball (solid sphere)	top (m)	[top]
diameter	diametër (m)	[diamétər]
radius	sipërfaqe (f)	[sipərfácɛ]
perimeter (circle's ~)	perimetër (m)	[pɛrimétər]
center	qendër (f)	[céndər]

horizontal (adj)	horizontal	[horizontál]
vertical (adj)	vertikal	[vɛrtikál]
parallel (n)	paralele (f)	[paralélɛ]
parallel (as adj)	paralel	[paralél]

line	vijë (f)	[víjə]
stroke	vizë (f)	[vízə]
straight line	vijë e drejtë (f)	[víjə ɛ dréjtə]
curve (curved line)	kurbë (f)	[kúrbə]
thin (line, etc.)	e hollë	[ɛ hółə]
contour (outline)	kontur (f)	[kontúr]

intersection	kryqëzim (m)	[krycəzím]
right angle	kënd i drejtë (m)	[kənd i dréjtə]
segment	segment (m)	[sɛgmént]
sector (circular ~)	sektor (m)	[sɛktór]
side (of triangle)	anë (f)	[ánə]
angle	kënd (m)	[kə́nd]

25. Units of measurement

weight	peshë (f)	[péʃə]
length	gjatësi (f)	[ɟatəsí]
width	gjerësi (f)	[ɟɛrəsí]
height	lartësi (f)	[lartəsí]
depth	thellësi (f)	[θɛɫəsí]
volume	vëllim (m)	[vətím]
area	sipërfaqe (f)	[sipərfácɛ]

gram	gram (m)	[gram]
milligram	miligram (m)	[miligrám]
kilogram	kilogram (m)	[kilográm]
ton	ton (m)	[ton]
pound	paund (m)	[páund]
ounce	ons (m)	[ons]

meter	metër (m)	[métər]
millimeter	milimetër (m)	[milimétər]
centimeter	centimetër (m)	[tsɛntimétər]
kilometer	kilometër (m)	[kilométər]
mile	milje (f)	[míljɛ]

inch	inç (m)	[intʃ]
foot	këmbë (f)	[kə́mbə]
yard	jard (m)	[járd]

square meter	metër katror (m)	[métər katrór]
hectare	hektar (m)	[hɛktár]

liter	litër (m)	[lítər]
degree	gradë (f)	[grádə]
volt	volt (m)	[volt]
ampere	amper (m)	[ampér]
horsepower	kuaj-fuqi (f)	[kúaj-fucí]
quantity	sasi (f)	[sasí]

a little bit of ...	pak ...	[pak ...]
half	gjysmë (f)	[ɟýsmə]
dozen	dyzinë (f)	[dyzínə]
piece (item)	copë (f)	[tsópə]

| size | madhësi (f) | [maðəsí] |
| scale (map ~) | shkallë (f) | [ʃkáɫə] |

minimal (adj)	minimale	[minimálɛ]
the smallest (adj)	më i vogli	[mə i vógli]
medium (adj)	i mesëm	[i mésəm]
maximal (adj)	maksimale	[maksimálɛ]
the largest (adj)	më i madhi	[mə i máði]

26. Containers

canning jar (glass ~)	kavanoz (m)	[kavanóz]
can	kanoçe (f)	[kanótʃɛ]
bucket	kovë (f)	[kóvə]
barrel	fuçi (f)	[futʃí]

wash basin (e.g., plastic ~)	legen (m)	[lɛgén]
tank (100L water ~)	tank (m)	[tank]
hip flask	faqore (f)	[facórɛ]
jerrycan	bidon (m)	[bidón]
tank (e.g., tank car)	cisternë (f)	[tsistérnə]

mug	tas (m)	[tas]
cup (of coffee, etc.)	filxhan (m)	[fildʒán]
saucer	pjatë filxhani (f)	[pjátə fildʒáni]
glass (tumbler)	gotë (f)	[gótə]
wine glass	gotë vere (f)	[gótə vérɛ]
stock pot (soup pot)	tenxhere (f)	[tɛndʒérɛ]

| bottle (~ of wine) | shishe (f) | [ʃíʃɛ] |
| neck (of the bottle, etc.) | grykë | [grýkə] |

carafe (decanter)	brokë (f)	[brókə]
pitcher	shtambë (f)	[ʃtámbə]
vessel (container)	enë (f)	[énə]
pot (crock, stoneware ~)	enë (f)	[énə]
vase	vazo (f)	[vázo]

flacon, bottle (perfume ~)	shishe (f)	[ʃíʃɛ]
vial, small bottle	shishkë (f)	[ʃíʃkə]
tube (of toothpaste)	tubet (f)	[tubét]

sack (bag)	thes (m)	[θɛs]
bag (paper ~, plastic ~)	qese (f)	[césɛ]
pack (of cigarettes, etc.)	paketë (f)	[pakétə]

box (e.g., shoebox)	kuti (f)	[kutí]
crate	arkë (f)	[árkə]
basket	shportë (f)	[ʃpórtə]

27. Materials

material	material (m)	[matɛriál]
wood (n)	dru (m)	[dru]
wood-, wooden (adj)	prej druri	[prɛj drúri]

| glass (n) | qelq (m) | [cɛlc] |
| glass (as adj) | prej qelqi | [prɛj célci] |

| stone (n) | gur (m) | [guɾ] |
| stone (as adj) | guror | [guɾóɾ] |

| plastic (n) | plastikë (f) | [plastíkə] |
| plastic (as adj) | plastike | [plastíkɛ] |

| rubber (n) | gomë (f) | [gómə] |
| rubber (as adj) | prej gome | [prɛj gómɛ] |

| cloth, fabric (n) | pëlhurë (f) | [pəlhúrə] |
| fabric (as adj) | nga pëlhura | [ŋa pəlhúra] |

| paper (n) | letër (f) | [létəɾ] |
| paper (as adj) | prej letre | [prɛj létrɛ] |

| cardboard (n) | karton (m) | [kartón] |
| cardboard (as adj) | prej kartoni | [prɛj kartóni] |

polyethylene	polietilen (m)	[poliétilɛn]
cellophane	celofan (m)	[tsɛlofán]
linoleum	linoleum (m)	[linolɛúm]
plywood	kompensatë (f)	[kompɛnsátə]

porcelain (n)	porcelan (m)	[portsɛlán]
porcelain (as adj)	prej porcelani	[prɛj portsɛláni]
clay (n)	argjilë (f)	[aɲílə]
clay (as adj)	prej argjile	[prɛj aɲílɛ]
ceramic (n)	qeramikë (f)	[cɛramíkə]
ceramic (as adj)	prej qeramike	[prɛj cɛramíkɛ]

28. Metals

metal (n)	metal (m)	[mɛtál]
metal (as adj)	prej metali	[prɛj mɛtáli]
alloy (n)	aliazh (m)	[aliáʒ]

gold (n)	ar (m)	[ár]
gold, golden (adj)	prej ari	[prɛj ári]
silver (n)	argjend (m)	[arɟénd]
silver (as adj)	prej argjendi	[prɛj arɟéndi]

iron (n)	hekur (m)	[hékur]
iron-, made of iron (adj)	prej hekuri	[prɛj hékuri]
steel (n)	çelik (m)	[tʃɛlík]
steel (as adj)	prej çeliku	[prɛj tʃɛlíku]
copper (n)	bakër (m)	[bákər]
copper (as adj)	prej bakri	[prɛj bákri]

aluminum (n)	alumin (m)	[alumín]
aluminum (as adj)	prej alumini	[prɛj alumíni]
bronze (n)	bronz (m)	[bronz]
bronze (as adj)	prej bronzi	[prɛj brónzi]

brass	tunxh (m)	[tundʒ]
nickel	nikel (m)	[nikél]
platinum	platin (m)	[platín]
mercury	merkur (m)	[mɛrkúr]
tin	kallaj (m)	[kałáj]
lead	plumb (m)	[plúmb]
zinc	zink (m)	[zink]

HUMAN BEING

Human being. The body

29. Humans. Basic concepts

human being	qenie njerëzore (f)	[cɛníɛ ɲɛrəzóɾɛ]
man (adult male)	burrë (m)	[búrə]
woman	grua (f)	[grúa]
child	fëmijë (f)	[fəmíjə]
girl	vajzë (f)	[vájzə]
boy	djalë (f)	[djálə]
teenager	adoleshent (m)	[adolɛʃént]
old man	plak (m)	[plak]
old woman	plakë (f)	[plákə]

30. Human anatomy

organism (body)	organizëm (m)	[organízəm]
heart	zemër (f)	[zémər]
blood	gjak (m)	[ɟak]
artery	arterie (f)	[artériɛ]
vein	venë (f)	[vénə]
brain	tru (m)	[tru]
nerve	nerv (m)	[nɛrv]
nerves	nerva (f)	[nérva]
vertebra	vertebër (f)	[vɛrtébər]
spine (backbone)	shtyllë kurrizore (f)	[ʃtýłə kurizóɾɛ]
stomach (organ)	stomak (m)	[stomák]
intestines, bowels	zorrët (f)	[zórət]
intestine (e.g., large ~)	zorrë (f)	[zórə]
liver	mëlçi (f)	[məltʃí]
kidney	veshkë (f)	[véʃkə]
bone	kockë (f)	[kótskə]
skeleton	skelet (m)	[skɛlét]
rib	brinjë (f)	[bríɲə]
skull	kafkë (f)	[káfkə]
muscle	muskul (m)	[múskul]
biceps	biceps (m)	[bitséps]

triceps	triceps (m)	[tritséps]
tendon	tendon (f)	[tɛndón]
joint	nyje (f)	[nýjɛ]
lungs	mushkëri (m)	[muʃkərí]
genitals	organe gjenitale (f)	[orgánɛ ɉɛnitálɛ]
skin	lëkurë (f)	[ləkúrə]

31. Head

head	kokë (f)	[kókə]
face	fytyrë (f)	[fytýrə]
nose	hundë (f)	[húndə]
mouth	gojë (f)	[gójə]

eye	sy (m)	[sy]
eyes	sytë	[sýtə]
pupil	bebëz (f)	[bébəz]
eyebrow	vetull (f)	[vétuɫ]
eyelash	qerpik (m)	[cɛrpík]
eyelid	qepallë (f)	[cɛpáɫə]

tongue	gjuhë (f)	[ɉúhə]
tooth	dhëmb (m)	[ðəmb]
lips	buzë (f)	[búzə]
cheekbones	mollëza (f)	[móɫəza]
gum	mishrat e dhëmbëve	[míʃrat ɛ ðəmbəvɛ]
palate	qiellzë (f)	[ciéɫzə]

nostrils	vrimat e hundës (pl)	[vrímat ɛ húndəs]
chin	mjekër (f)	[mjékər]
jaw	nofull (f)	[nófuɫ]
cheek	faqe (f)	[fácɛ]

forehead	ball (m)	[báɫ]
temple	tëmth (m)	[təmθ]
ear	vesh (m)	[vɛʃ]
back of the head	zverk (m)	[zvɛrk]
neck	qafë (f)	[cáfə]
throat	fyt (m)	[fyt]

hair	flokë (pl)	[flókə]
hairstyle	model flokësh (m)	[modél flókəʃ]
haircut	prerje flokësh (f)	[prérɉɛ flókəʃ]
wig	paruke (f)	[parúkɛ]

mustache	mustaqe (f)	[mustácɛ]
beard	mjekër (f)	[mjékər]
to have (a beard, etc.)	lë mjekër	[lə mjékər]
braid	gërshet (m)	[gərʃét]
sideburns	baseta (f)	[baséta]

red-haired (adj)	flokëkuqe	[flokəkúcɛ]
gray (hair)	thinja	[θíɲa]
bald (adj)	qeros	[cɛrós]
bald patch	tullë (f)	[túɫə]

| ponytail | bishtalec (m) | [biʃtaléts] |
| bangs | balluke (f) | [baɫúkɛ] |

32. Human body

hand	dorë (f)	[dórə]
arm	krah (m)	[krah]
finger	gisht i dorës (m)	[gíʃt i dórəs]
toe	gisht i këmbës (m)	[gíʃt i kə́mbəs]
thumb	gishti i madh (m)	[gíʃti i máð]
little finger	gishti i vogël (m)	[gíʃti i vógəl]
nail	thua (f)	[θúa]

fist	grusht (m)	[grúʃt]
palm	pëllëmbë dore (f)	[pəɫə́mbə dórɛ]
wrist	kyç (m)	[kytʃ]
forearm	parakrah (m)	[parakráh]
elbow	bërryl (m)	[bərýl]
shoulder	shpatull (f)	[ʃpátuɫ]

leg	këmbë (f)	[kə́mbə]
foot	shputë (f)	[ʃpútə]
knee	gju (m)	[ɟú]
calf (part of leg)	pulpë (f)	[púlpə]
hip	ijë (f)	[íjə]
heel	thembër (f)	[θémbər]

body	trup (m)	[trup]
stomach	stomak (m)	[stomák]
chest	kraharor (m)	[kraharór]
breast	gjoks (m)	[ɟóks]
flank	krah (m)	[krah]
back	kurriz (m)	[kuríz]
lower back	fundshpina (f)	[fundʃpína]
waist	beli (m)	[béli]

navel (belly button)	kërthizë (f)	[kərθízə]
buttocks	vithe (f)	[víθɛ]
bottom	prapanica (f)	[prapanítsa]

beauty mark	nishan (m)	[niʃán]
birthmark (café au lait spot)	shenjë lindjeje (f)	[ʃéɲə líndjɛjɛ]
tattoo	tatuazh (m)	[tatuáʒ]
scar	shenjë (f)	[ʃéɲə]

Clothing & Accessories

33. Outerwear. Coats

clothes	rroba (f)	[róba]
outerwear	veshje e sipërme (f)	[véʃjɛ ɛ sípərmɛ]
winter clothing	veshje dimri (f)	[véʃjɛ dímri]
coat (overcoat)	pallto (f)	[páɫto]
fur coat	gëzof (m)	[gəzóf]
fur jacket	xhaketë lëkure (f)	[dʒakétə ləkúrɛ]
down coat	xhup (m)	[dʒup]
jacket (e.g., leather ~)	xhaketë (f)	[dʒakétə]
raincoat (trenchcoat, etc.)	pardesy (f)	[pardɛsý]
waterproof (adj)	kundër shiut	[kúndər ʃíut]

34. Men's & women's clothing

shirt (button shirt)	këmishë (f)	[kəmíʃə]
pants	pantallona (f)	[pantaɫóna]
jeans	xhinse (f)	[dʒínsɛ]
suit jacket	xhaketë kostumi (f)	[dʒakétə kostúmi]
suit	kostum (m)	[kostúm]
dress (frock)	fustan (m)	[fustán]
skirt	fund (m)	[fund]
blouse	bluzë (f)	[blúzə]
knitted jacket (cardigan, etc.)	xhaketë me thurje (f)	[dʒakétə mɛ θúrjɛ]
jacket (of woman's suit)	xhaketë femrash (f)	[dʒakétə fémraʃ]
T-shirt	bluzë (f)	[blúzə]
shorts (short trousers)	pantallona të shkurtra (f)	[pantaɫóna tə ʃkúrtra]
tracksuit	tuta sportive (f)	[túta sportívɛ]
bathrobe	peshqir trupi (m)	[pɛʃcír trúpi]
pajamas	pizhame (f)	[piʒámɛ]
sweater	triko (f)	[tríko]
pullover	pulovër (m)	[pulóvər]
vest	jelek (m)	[jɛlék]
tailcoat	frak (m)	[frak]
tuxedo	smoking (m)	[smokíŋ]

uniform	uniformë (f)	[unifórmə]
workwear	rroba pune (f)	[róba púnɛ]
overalls	kominoshe (f)	[kominóʃɛ]
coat (e.g., doctor's smock)	uniformë (f)	[unifórmə]

35. Clothing. Underwear

underwear	të brendshme (f)	[tə bréndʃmɛ]
boxers, briefs	boksera (f)	[bokséra]
panties	brekë (f)	[brékə]
undershirt (A-shirt)	fanellë (f)	[fanétə]
socks	çorape (pl)	[tʃorápɛ]

nightdress	këmishë nate (f)	[kəmíʃə nátɛ]
bra	sytjena (f)	[sytjéna]
knee highs (knee-high socks)	çorape déri tek gjuri (pl)	[tʃorápɛ déri ték ɟúri]
pantyhose	geta (f)	[géta]
stockings (thigh highs)	çorape të holla (pl)	[tʃorápɛ tə hóta]
bathing suit	rrobë banje (f)	[róbə báɲɛ]

36. Headwear

hat	kapelë (f)	[kapélə]
fedora	kapelë republike (f)	[kapélə rɛpublíkɛ]
baseball cap	kapelë bejsbolli (f)	[kapélə bɛjsbóti]
flatcap	kapelë e sheshtë (f)	[kapélə ɛ ʃéʃtə]

beret	beretë (f)	[bɛrétə]
hood	kapuç (m)	[kapútʃ]
panama hat	kapelë panama (f)	[kapélə panamá]
knit cap (knitted hat)	kapuç leshi (m)	[kapútʃ léʃi]

headscarf	shami (f)	[ʃamí]
women's hat	kapelë femrash (f)	[kapélə fémraʃ]
hard hat	helmetë (f)	[hɛlmétə]
garrison cap	kapelë ushtrie (f)	[kapélə uʃtríɛ]
helmet	helmetë (f)	[hɛlmétə]

| derby | kapelë derby (f) | [kapélə dérby] |
| top hat | kapelë cilindër (f) | [kapélə tsilíndər] |

37. Footwear

| footwear | këpucë (pl) | [kəpútsə] |
| shoes (men's shoes) | këpucë burrash (pl) | [kəpútsə búraʃ] |

shoes (women's shoes)	**këpucë grash** (pl)	[kəpútsə gráʃ]
boots (e.g., cowboy ~)	**çizme** (pl)	[tʃízmɛ]
slippers	**pantofla** (pl)	[pantófla]

tennis shoes (e.g., Nike ~)	**atlete tenisi** (pl)	[atlétɛ tɛnísi]
sneakers	**atlete** (pl)	[atlétɛ]
(e.g., Converse ~)		
sandals	**sandale** (pl)	[sandálɛ]

cobbler (shoe repairer)	**këpucëtar** (m)	[kəputsətár]
heel	**takë** (f)	[tákə]
pair (of shoes)	**palë** (f)	[pálə]

shoestring	**lidhëse këpucësh** (f)	[liðəsɛ kəpútsəʃ]
to lace (vt)	**lidh këpucët**	[lið kəpútsət]
shoehorn	**lugë këpucësh** (f)	[lúgə kəpútsəʃ]
shoe polish	**bojë këpucësh** (f)	[bójə kəpútsəʃ]

38. Textile. Fabrics

cotton (n)	**pambuk** (m)	[pambúk]
cotton (as adj)	**i pambuktë**	[i pambúktə]
flax (n)	**li** (m)	[li]
flax (as adj)	**prej liri**	[prɛj líri]

silk (n)	**mëndafsh** (m)	[məndáfʃ]
silk (as adj)	**i mëndafshtë**	[i məndáfʃtə]
wool (n)	**lesh** (m)	[lɛʃ]
wool (as adj)	**i leshtë**	[i léʃtə]

velvet	**kadife** (f)	[kadífɛ]
suede	**kamosh** (m)	[kamóʃ]
corduroy	**kadife me riga** (f)	[kadífɛ mɛ ríga]

nylon (n)	**najlon** (m)	[najlón]
nylon (as adj)	**prej najloni**	[prɛj najlóni]
polyester (n)	**poliestër** (m)	[poliéstər]
polyester (as adj)	**prej poliestri**	[prɛj poliéstri]

leather (n)	**lëkurë** (f)	[ləkúrə]
leather (as adj)	**prej lëkure**	[prɛj ləkúrɛ]
fur (n)	**gëzof** (m)	[gəzóf]
fur (e.g., ~ coat)	**prej gëzofi**	[prɛj gəzófi]

39. Personal accessories

gloves	**dorëza** (pl)	[dórəza]
mittens	**doreza** (f)	[doréza]

scarf (muffler)	shall (m)	[ʃał]
glasses (eyeglasses)	syze (f)	[sýzɛ]
frame (eyeglass ~)	skelet syzesh (m)	[skɛlét sýzɛʃ]
umbrella	çadër (f)	[tʃádər]
walking stick	bastun (m)	[bastún]
hairbrush	furçë flokësh (f)	[fúrtʃə flókəʃ]
fan	erashkë (f)	[ɛráʃkə]

tie (necktie)	kravatë (f)	[kravátə]
bow tie	papion (m)	[papión]
suspenders	aski (pl)	[askí]
handkerchief	shami (f)	[ʃamí]

comb	krehër (m)	[kréhər]
barrette	kapëse flokësh (f)	[kápəsɛ flókəʃ]
hairpin	karficë (f)	[karfítsə]
buckle	tokëz (f)	[tókəz]

| belt | rrip (m) | [rip] |
| shoulder strap | rrip supi (m) | [rip súpi] |

bag (handbag)	çantë dore (f)	[tʃántə dórɛ]
purse	çantë (f)	[tʃántə]
backpack	çantë shpine (f)	[tʃántə ʃpínɛ]

40. Clothing. Miscellaneous

fashion	modë (f)	[módə]
in vogue (adj)	në modë	[nə módə]
fashion designer	stilist (m)	[stilíst]

collar	jakë (f)	[jákə]
pocket	xhep (m)	[dʒɛp]
pocket (as adj)	i xhepit	[i dʒépit]
sleeve	mëngë (f)	[mə́ŋə]
hanging loop	hallkë për varje (f)	[háłkə pər várjɛ]
fly (on trousers)	zinxhir (m)	[zindʒír]

zipper (fastener)	zinxhir (m)	[zindʒír]
fastener	kapëse (f)	[kápəsɛ]
button	kopsë (f)	[kópsə]
buttonhole	vrimë kopse (f)	[vrímə kópsɛ]
to come off (ab. button)	këputet	[kəpútɛt]

to sew (vi, vt)	qep	[cɛp]
to embroider (vi, vt)	qëndis	[cəndís]
embroidery	qëndisje (f)	[cəndísjɛ]
sewing needle	gjilpërë për qepje (f)	[ɟilpə́rə pər cépjɛ]
thread	pe (m)	[pɛ]
seam	tegel (m)	[tɛgél]

to get dirty (vi)	**bëhem pis**	[béhɛm pis]
stain (mark, spot)	**njollë** (f)	[ɲółə]
to crease, crumple (vt)	**zhubros**	[ʒubrós]
to tear, to rip (vt)	**gris**	[gris]
clothes moth	**molë rrobash** (f)	[móla róbaʃ]

41. Personal care. Cosmetics

toothpaste	**pastë dhëmbësh** (f)	[pástə ðémbəʃ]
toothbrush	**furçë dhëmbësh** (f)	[fúrtʃə ðémbəʃ]
to brush one's teeth	**laj dhëmbët**	[laj ðémbət]
razor	**brisk** (m)	[brísk]
shaving cream	**pastë rroje** (f)	[pástə rójɛ]
to shave (vi)	**rruhem**	[rúhɛm]
soap	**sapun** (m)	[sapún]
shampoo	**shampo** (f)	[ʃampó]
scissors	**gërshërë** (f)	[gərʃérə]
nail file	**limë thonjsh** (f)	[límə θóɲʃ]
nail clippers	**prerëse thonjsh** (f)	[prérəsɛ θóɲʃ]
tweezers	**piskatore vetullash** (f)	[piskatórɛ vétułaʃ]
cosmetics	**kozmetikë** (f)	[kozmɛtíkə]
face mask	**maskë fytyre** (f)	[máskə fytýrɛ]
manicure	**manikyr** (m)	[manikýr]
to have a manicure	**bëj manikyr**	[bəj manikýr]
pedicure	**pedikyr** (m)	[pɛdikýr]
make-up bag	**çantë kozmetike** (f)	[tʃántə kozmɛtíkɛ]
face powder	**pudër fytyre** (f)	[púdər fytýrɛ]
powder compact	**pudër kompakte** (f)	[púdər kompáktɛ]
blusher	**ruzh** (m)	[ruʒ]
perfume (bottled)	**parfum** (m)	[parfúm]
toilet water (lotion)	**parfum** (m)	[parfúm]
lotion	**krem** (m)	[krɛm]
cologne	**kolonjë** (f)	[kolóɲə]
eyeshadow	**rimel** (m)	[rimél]
eyeliner	**laps për sy** (m)	[láps pər sy]
mascara	**rimel** (m)	[rimél]
lipstick	**buzëkuq** (m)	[buzəkúc]
nail polish, enamel	**llak për thonj** (m)	[łak pər θóɲ]
hair spray	**llak flokësh** (m)	[łak flókəʃ]
deodorant	**deodorant** (m)	[dɛodoránt]
cream	**krem** (m)	[krɛm]
face cream	**krem për fytyrë** (m)	[krɛm pər fytýrə]

hand cream	krem për duar (m)	[krɛm pər dúar]
anti-wrinkle cream	krem kundër rrudhave (m)	[krɛm kúndər rúðavɛ]
day cream	krem dite (m)	[krɛm dítɛ]
night cream	krem nate (m)	[krɛm nátɛ]
day (as adj)	dite	[dítɛ]
night (as adj)	nate	[nátɛ]

tampon	tampon (m)	[tampón]
toilet paper (toilet roll)	letër higjienike (f)	[létər hiʝiɛníkɛ]
hair dryer	tharëse flokësh (f)	[θárəsɛ flókəʃ]

42. Jewelry

jewelry, jewels	bizhuteri (f)	[biʒutɛrí]
precious (e.g., ~ stone)	i çmuar	[i tʃmúar]
hallmark stamp	vulë dalluese (f)	[vúlə dałúɛsɛ]

ring	unazë (f)	[unázə]
wedding ring	unazë martese (f)	[unázə martésɛ]
bracelet	byzylyk (m)	[byzylýk]

earrings	vathë (pl)	[váθə]
necklace (~ of pearls)	gjerdan (m)	[ʝɛrdán]
crown	kurorë (f)	[kurórə]
bead necklace	qafore me rruaza (f)	[cafórɛ mɛ ruáza]

diamond	diamant (m)	[diamánt]
emerald	smerald (m)	[smɛráld]
ruby	rubin (m)	[rubín]
sapphire	safir (m)	[safír]
pearl	perlë (f)	[pérlə]
amber	qelibar (m)	[cɛlibár]

43. Watches. Clocks

watch (wristwatch)	orë dore (f)	[órə dórɛ]
dial	faqe e orës (f)	[fácɛ ɛ órəs]
hand (of clock, watch)	akrep (m)	[akrép]
metal watch band	rrip metalik ore (m)	[rip mɛtalík órɛ]
watch strap	rrip ore (m)	[rip órɛ]

battery	bateri (f)	[batɛrí]
to be dead (battery)	e shkarkuar	[ɛ ʃkarkúar]
to change a battery	ndërroj baterinë	[ndərój batɛrínə]
to run fast	kalon shpejt	[kalón ʃpéjt]
to run slow	ngel prapa	[ŋɛl prápa]
wall clock	orë muri (f)	[órə múri]
hourglass	orë rëre (f)	[órə rərɛ]

sundial	orë diellore (f)	[órə diɛłórɛ]
alarm clock	orë me zile (f)	[órə mɛ zílɛ]
watchmaker	orëndreqës (m)	[orəndrécəs]
to repair (vt)	ndreq	[ndréc]

Food. Nutricion

44. Food

meat	mish (m)	[miʃ]
chicken	pulë (f)	[púlə]
Rock Cornish hen (poussin)	mish pule (m)	[miʃ púlɛ]
duck	rosë (f)	[rósə]
goose	patë (f)	[pátə]
game	gjah (m)	[ɟáh]
turkey	mish gjel deti (m)	[miʃ ɟɛl déti]
pork	mish derri (m)	[miʃ déri]
veal	mish viçi (m)	[miʃ vítʃi]
lamb	mish qengji (m)	[miʃ cénɟi]
beef	mish lope (m)	[miʃ lópɛ]
rabbit	mish lepuri (m)	[miʃ lépuri]
sausage (bologna, etc.)	salsiçe (f)	[salsítʃɛ]
vienna sausage (frankfurter)	salsiçe vjeneze (f)	[salsítʃɛ vjɛnézɛ]
bacon	proshutë (f)	[proʃútə]
ham	sallam (m)	[saɬám]
gammon	kofshë derri (f)	[kófʃə déri]
pâté	pate (f)	[paté]
liver	mëlçi (f)	[məltʃí]
hamburger (ground beef)	hamburger (m)	[hamburgér]
tongue	gjuhë (f)	[ɟúhə]
egg	ve (f)	[vɛ]
eggs	vezë (pl)	[vézə]
egg white	e bardhë veze (f)	[ɛ bárðə vézɛ]
egg yolk	e verdhë veze (f)	[ɛ vérðə vézɛ]
fish	peshk (m)	[pɛʃk]
seafood	fruta deti (pl)	[frúta déti]
crustaceans	krustace (pl)	[krustátsɛ]
caviar	havjar (m)	[havjár]
crab	gaforre (f)	[gafórɛ]
shrimp	karkalec (m)	[karkaléts]
oyster	midhje (f)	[míðjɛ]
spiny lobster	karavidhe (f)	[karavíðɛ]
octopus	oktapod (m)	[oktapód]

squid	kallamarë (f)	[kałamárə]
sturgeon	bli (m)	[blí]
salmon	salmon (m)	[salmón]
halibut	shojzë e Atlantikut Verior (f)	[ʃójzə ɛ atlantíkut vɛɾiór]
cod	merluc (m)	[mɛrlúts]
mackerel	skumbri (m)	[skúmbri]
tuna	tunë (f)	[túnə]
eel	ngjalë (f)	[nɟálə]
trout	troftë (f)	[tróftə]
sardine	sardele (f)	[sardélɛ]
pike	mlysh (m)	[mlýʃ]
herring	harengë (f)	[haréŋə]
bread	bukë (f)	[búkə]
cheese	djath (m)	[djáθ]
sugar	sheqer (m)	[ʃɛcér]
salt	kripë (f)	[krípə]
rice	oriz (m)	[oríz]
pasta (macaroni)	makarona (f)	[makaróna]
noodles	makarona petë (f)	[makaróna pétə]
butter	gjalp (m)	[ɟalp]
vegetable oil	vaj vegjetal (m)	[vaj vɛɟɛtál]
sunflower oil	vaj luledielli (m)	[vaj lulɛdiéłi]
margarine	margarinë (f)	[margarínə]
olives	ullinj (pl)	[ułíɲ]
olive oil	vaj ulliri (m)	[vaj ułíri]
milk	qumësht (m)	[cúməʃt]
condensed milk	qumësht i kondensuar (m)	[cúməʃt i kondɛnsúar]
yogurt	kos (m)	[kos]
sour cream	salcë kosi (f)	[sáltsə kosi]
cream (of milk)	krem qumështi (m)	[krɛm cúməʃti]
mayonnaise	majonezë (f)	[majonézə]
buttercream	krem gjalpi (m)	[krɛm ɟálpi]
groats (barley ~, etc.)	drithëra (pl)	[dríθəra]
flour	miell (m)	[míɛł]
canned food	konserva (f)	[konsérva]
cornflakes	kornfleiks (m)	[kornfléiks]
honey	mjaltë (f)	[mjáltə]
jam	reçel (m)	[rɛtʃél]
chewing gum	çamçakëz (m)	[tʃamtʃakéz]

45. Drinks

water	ujë (m)	[újə]
drinking water	ujë i pijshëm (m)	[újə i píʃʃəm]
mineral water	ujë mineral (m)	[újə minɛrál]

still (adj)	ujë natyral	[újə natyrál]
carbonated (adj)	ujë i karbonuar	[újə i karbonúar]
sparkling (adj)	ujë i gazuar	[újə i gazúar]
ice	akull (m)	[ákuɫ]
with ice	me akull	[mɛ ákuɫ]

non-alcoholic (adj)	jo alkoolik	[jo alkoolík]
soft drink	pije e lehtë (f)	[píjɛ ɛ léhtə]
refreshing drink	pije freskuese (f)	[píjɛ frɛskúɛsɛ]
lemonade	limonadë (f)	[limonádə]

liquors	likere (pl)	[likérɛ]
wine	verë (f)	[vérə]
white wine	verë e bardhë (f)	[vérə ɛ bárðə]
red wine	verë e kuqe (f)	[vérə ɛ kúcɛ]

liqueur	liker (m)	[likér]
champagne	shampanjë (f)	[ʃampáɲə]
vermouth	vermut (m)	[vɛrmút]

whiskey	uiski (m)	[víski]
vodka	vodkë (f)	[vódkə]
gin	xhin (m)	[dʒin]
cognac	konjak (m)	[koɲák]
rum	rum (m)	[rum]

coffee	kafe (f)	[káfɛ]
black coffee	kafe e zezë (f)	[káfɛ ɛ zézə]
coffee with milk	kafe me qumësht (m)	[káfɛ mɛ cúməʃt]
cappuccino	kapuçino (m)	[kaputʃíno]
instant coffee	neskafe (f)	[nɛskáfɛ]

milk	qumësht (m)	[cúməʃt]
cocktail	koktej (m)	[koktéj]
milkshake	milkshake (f)	[milkʃákɛ]

juice	lëng frutash (m)	[ləŋ frútaʃ]
tomato juice	lëng domatesh (m)	[ləŋ domátɛʃ]
orange juice	lëng portokalli (m)	[ləŋ portokáɫi]
freshly squeezed juice	lëng frutash i freskët (m)	[ləŋ frútaʃ i fréskət]

beer	birrë (f)	[bírə]
light beer	birrë e lehtë (f)	[bíra ɛ léhtə]
dark beer	birrë e zezë (f)	[bíra ɛ zézə]
tea	çaj (m)	[tʃáj]

| black tea | çaj i zi (m) | [tʃáj i zí] |
| green tea | çaj jeshil (m) | [tʃáj jɛʃíl] |

46. Vegetables

| vegetables | perime (pl) | [pɛrímɛ] |
| greens | zarzavate (pl) | [zarzavátɛ] |

tomato	domate (f)	[domátɛ]
cucumber	kastravec (m)	[kastravéts]
carrot	karotë (f)	[karótə]
potato	patate (f)	[patátɛ]
onion	qepë (f)	[cépə]
garlic	hudhër (f)	[húðər]

cabbage	lakër (f)	[lákər]
cauliflower	lulelakër (f)	[lulɛlákər]
Brussels sprouts	lakër Brukseli (f)	[lákər brukséli]
broccoli	brokoli (m)	[brókoli]

beet	panxhar (m)	[pandʒár]
eggplant	patëllxhan (m)	[patətɫdʒán]
zucchini	kungulleshë (m)	[kuŋuɫéʃə]
pumpkin	kungull (m)	[kúŋuɫ]
turnip	rrepë (f)	[répə]

parsley	majdanoz (m)	[majdanóz]
dill	kopër (f)	[kópər]
lettuce	sallatë jeshile (f)	[saɫátə jɛʃílɛ]
celery	selino (f)	[sɛlíno]
asparagus	asparagus (m)	[asparágus]
spinach	spinaq (m)	[spinác]

pea	bizele (f)	[bizélɛ]
beans	fasule (f)	[fasúlɛ]
corn (maize)	misër (m)	[mísər]
kidney bean	groshë (f)	[gróʃə]

bell pepper	spec (m)	[spɛts]
radish	rrepkë (f)	[répkə]
artichoke	angjinare (f)	[aɲinárɛ]

47. Fruits. Nuts

fruit	frut (m)	[frut]
apple	mollë (f)	[móɫə]
pear	dardhë (f)	[dárðə]
lemon	limon (m)	[limón]

| orange | portokall (m) | [portokát] |
| strawberry (garden ~) | luleshtrydhe (f) | [luleʃtrýðɛ] |

mandarin	mandarinë (f)	[mandarínə]
plum	kumbull (f)	[kúmbuł]
peach	pjeshkë (f)	[pjéʃkə]
apricot	kajsi (f)	[kajsí]
raspberry	mjedër (f)	[mjédər]
pineapple	ananas (m)	[ananás]

banana	banane (f)	[banánɛ]
watermelon	shalqi (m)	[ʃalcí]
grape	rrush (m)	[ruʃ]
sour cherry	qershi vishnje (f)	[cɛrʃí víʃɲɛ]
sweet cherry	qershi (f)	[cɛrʃí]
melon	pjepër (m)	[pjépər]

grapefruit	grejpfrut (m)	[grɛjpfrút]
avocado	avokado (f)	[avokádo]
papaya	papaja (f)	[papája]
mango	mango (f)	[máŋo]
pomegranate	shegë (f)	[ʃégə]

redcurrant	kaliboba e kuqe (f)	[kalibóba ɛ kúcɛ]
blackcurrant	kaliboba e zezë (f)	[kalibóba ɛ zézə]
gooseberry	kulumbri (f)	[kulumbrí]
bilberry	boronicë (f)	[boronítsə]
blackberry	manaferra (f)	[manaféra]

raisin	rrush i thatë (m)	[ruʃ i θátə]
fig	fik (m)	[fik]
date	hurmë (f)	[húrmə]

peanut	kikirik (m)	[kikirík]
almond	bajame (f)	[bajámɛ]
walnut	arrë (f)	[árə]
hazelnut	lajthi (f)	[lajθí]
coconut	arrë kokosi (f)	[árə kokósi]
pistachios	fëstëk (m)	[fəsták]

48. Bread. Candy

bakers' confectionery (pastry)	ëmbëlsira (pl)	[əmbəlsíra]
bread	bukë (f)	[búkə]
cookies	biskota (pl)	[biskóta]

chocolate (n)	çokollatë (f)	[tʃokołátə]
chocolate (as adj)	prej çokollate	[prɛj tʃokołátɛ]
candy (wrapped)	karamele (f)	[karamélɛ]

cake (e.g., cupcake)	kek (m)	[kék]
cake (e.g., birthday ~)	tortë (f)	[tórtə]

pie (e.g., apple ~)	tortë (f)	[tórtə]
filling (for cake, pie)	mbushje (f)	[mbúʃɛ]

jam (whole fruit jam)	reçel (m)	[rɛtʃél]
marmalade	marmelatë (f)	[marmɛlátə]
wafers	vafera (pl)	[vaféra]
ice-cream	akullore (f)	[akuɫórɛ]
pudding	puding (m)	[pudíŋ]

49. Cooked dishes

course, dish	pjatë (f)	[pjátə]
cuisine	kuzhinë (f)	[kuʒínə]
recipe	recetë (f)	[rɛtsétə]
portion	racion (m)	[ratsión]

salad	sallatë (f)	[saɫátə]
soup	supë (f)	[súpə]

clear soup (broth)	lëng mishi (m)	[lən míʃi]
sandwich (bread)	sandviç (m)	[sandvítʃ]
fried eggs	vezë të skuqura (pl)	[vézə tə skúcura]

hamburger (beefburger)	hamburger	[hamburgér]
beefsteak	biftek (m)	[bifték]

side dish	garniturë (f)	[garnitúrə]
spaghetti	shpageti (pl)	[ʃpagéti]
mashed potatoes	pure patatesh (f)	[puré patátɛʃ]
pizza	pica (f)	[pítsa]
porridge (oatmeal, etc.)	qull (m)	[cuɫ]
omelet	omëletë (f)	[oməlétə]

boiled (e.g., ~ beef)	i zier	[i zíɛr]
smoked (adj)	i tymosur	[i tymósur]
fried (adj)	i skuqur	[i skúcur]
dried (adj)	i tharë	[i θárə]
frozen (adj)	i ngrirë	[i ŋrírə]
pickled (adj)	i marinuar	[i marinúar]

sweet (sugary)	i ëmbël	[i ə́mbəl]
salty (adj)	i kripur	[i krípur]
cold (adj)	i ftohtë	[i ftóhtə]
hot (adj)	i nxehtë	[i ndzéhtə]
bitter (adj)	i hidhur	[i híður]
tasty (adj)	i shijshëm	[i ʃíjʃəm]
to cook in boiling water	ziej	[zíɛj]

to cook (dinner)	**gatuaj**	[gatúaj]
to fry (vt)	**skuq**	[skuc]
to heat up (food)	**ngroh**	[ŋróh]

to salt (vt)	**hedh kripë**	[hɛð krípə]
to pepper (vt)	**hedh piper**	[hɛð pipér]
to grate (vt)	**rendoj**	[rɛndój]
peel (n)	**lëkurë** (f)	[ləkúrə]
to peel (vt)	**qëroj**	[cərój]

50. Spices

salt	**kripë** (f)	[krípə]
salty (adj)	**i kripur**	[i krípur]
to salt (vt)	**hedh kripë**	[hɛð krípə]

black pepper	**piper i zi** (m)	[pipér i zi]
red pepper (milled ~)	**piper i kuq** (m)	[pipér i kuc]

mustard	**mustardë** (f)	[mustárdə]
horseradish	**rrepë djegëse** (f)	[répə djégəsɛ]

condiment	**salcë** (f)	[sáltsə]
spice	**erëz** (f)	[érəz]
sauce	**salcë** (f)	[sáltsə]
vinegar	**uthull** (f)	[úθuɬ]

anise	**anisetë** (f)	[anisétə]
basil	**borzilok** (m)	[borzilók]
cloves	**karafil** (m)	[karafíl]

ginger	**xhenxhefil** (m)	[dʒɛndʒɛfíl]
coriander	**koriandër** (m)	[koriándər]
cinnamon	**kanellë** (f)	[kanéɬə]

sesame	**susam** (m)	[susám]
bay leaf	**gjeth dafine** (m)	[ɟɛθ dafínɛ]
paprika	**spec** (m)	[spɛts]
caraway	**kumin** (m)	[kumín]
saffron	**shafran** (m)	[ʃafrán]

51. Meals

food	**ushqim** (m)	[uʃcím]
to eat (vi, vt)	**ha**	[ha]

breakfast	**mëngjes** (m)	[mənɟés]
to have breakfast	**ha mëngjes**	[ha mənɟés]

| lunch | **drekë** (f) | [drékə] |
| to have lunch | **ha drekë** | [ha drékə] |

| dinner | **darkë** (f) | [dárkə] |
| to have dinner | **ha darkë** | [ha dárkə] |

| appetite | **oreks** (m) | [oréks] |
| Enjoy your meal! | **Të bëftë mirë!** | [tə bəftə mírə!] |

to open (~ a bottle)	**hap**	[hap]
to spill (liquid)	**derdh**	[dérð]
to spill out (vi)	**derdhje**	[dérðjɛ]

to boil (vi)	**ziej**	[zíɛj]
to boil (vt)	**ziej**	[zíɛj]
boiled (~ water)	**i zier**	[i zíɛr]
to chill, cool down (vt)	**ftoh**	[ftoh]
to chill (vi)	**ftohje**	[ftóhjɛ]

| taste, flavor | **shije** (f) | [ʃíjɛ] |
| aftertaste | **shije** (f) | [ʃíjɛ] |

to slim down (lose weight)	**dobësohem**	[dobəsóhɛm]
diet	**dietë** (f)	[diétə]
vitamin	**vitaminë** (f)	[vitamínə]
calorie	**kalori** (f)	[kalorí]
vegetarian (n)	**vegjetarian** (m)	[vɛɟɛtarián]
vegetarian (adj)	**vegjetarian**	[vɛɟɛtarián]

fats (nutrient)	**yndyrë** (f)	[yndýrə]
proteins	**proteinë** (f)	[protɛínə]
carbohydrates	**karbohidrat** (m)	[karbohidrát]

slice (of lemon, ham)	**fetë** (f)	[fétə]
piece (of cake, pie)	**copë** (f)	[tsópə]
crumb	**dromcë** (f)	[drómtsə]
(of bread, cake, etc.)		

52. Table setting

spoon	**lugë** (f)	[lúgə]
knife	**thikë** (f)	[θíkə]
fork	**pirun** (m)	[pirún]

| cup (e.g., coffee ~) | **filxhan** (m) | [fildʒán] |
| plate (dinner ~) | **pjatë** (f) | [pjátə] |

saucer	**pjatë filxhani** (f)	[pjátə fildʒáni]
napkin (on table)	**pecetë** (f)	[pɛsétə]
toothpick	**kruajtëse dhëmbësh** (f)	[krúajtəsɛ ðə́mbəʃ]

53. Restaurant

restaurant	**restorant** (m)	[rɛstoránt]
coffee house	**kafene** (f)	[kafɛné]
pub, bar	**pab** (m), **pijetore** (f)	[pab], [pijɛtórɛ]
tearoom	**çajtore** (f)	[tʃajtórɛ]
waiter	**kamerier** (m)	[kamɛriér]
waitress	**kameriere** (f)	[kamɛriérɛ]
bartender	**banakier** (m)	[banakiér]
menu	**menu** (f)	[mɛnú]
wine list	**menu verërash** (f)	[mɛnú vérəraʃ]
to book a table	**rezervoj një tavolinë**	[rɛzɛrvój ɲə tavolínə]
course, dish	**pjatë** (f)	[pjátə]
to order (meal)	**porosis**	[porosís]
to make an order	**bëj porosinë**	[bəj porosínə]
aperitif	**aperitiv** (m)	[apɛritív]
appetizer	**antipastë** (f)	[antipástə]
dessert	**ëmbëlsirë** (f)	[əmbəlsírə]
check	**faturë** (f)	[fatúrə]
to pay the check	**paguaj faturën**	[pagúaj fatúrən]
to give change	**jap kusur**	[jap kusúr]
tip	**bakshish** (m)	[bakʃíʃ]

Family, relatives and friends

54. Personal information. Forms

name (first name)	emër (m)	[émər]
surname (last name)	mbiemër (m)	[mbiémər]
date of birth	datëlindje (f)	[datəlíndjɛ]
place of birth	vendlindje (f)	[vɛndlíndjɛ]
nationality	kombësi (f)	[kombəsí]
place of residence	vendbanim (m)	[vɛndbaním]
country	shtet (m)	[ʃtɛt]
profession (occupation)	profesion (m)	[profɛsión]
gender, sex	gjinia (f)	[ɟinía]
height	gjatësia (f)	[ɟatəsía]
weight	peshë (f)	[péʃə]

55. Family members. Relatives

mother	nënë (f)	[nénə]
father	baba (f)	[babá]
son	bir (m)	[bir]
daughter	bijë (f)	[bíjə]
younger daughter	vajza e vogël (f)	[vájza ɛ vógəl]
younger son	djali i vogël (m)	[djáli i vógəl]
eldest daughter	vajza e madhe (f)	[vájza ɛ máðɛ]
eldest son	djali i vogël (m)	[djáli i vógəl]
brother	vëlla (m)	[vətá]
elder brother	vëllai i madh (m)	[vətái i mað]
younger brother	vëllai i vogël (m)	[vətái i vógəl]
sister	motër (f)	[mótər]
elder sister	motra e madhe (f)	[mótra ɛ máðɛ]
younger sister	motra e vogël (f)	[mótra ɛ vógəl]
cousin (masc.)	kushëri (m)	[kuʃərí]
cousin (fem.)	kushërirë (f)	[kuʃərírə]
mom, mommy	mami (f)	[mámi]
dad, daddy	babi (m)	[bábi]
parents	prindër (pl)	[príndər]
child	fëmijë (f)	[fəmíjə]

children	**fëmijë** (pl)	[fəmíjə]
grandmother	**gjyshe** (f)	[ɟýʃɛ]
grandfather	**gjysh** (m)	[ɟyʃ]
grandson	**nip** (m)	[nip]
granddaughter	**mbesë** (f)	[mbésə]
grandchildren	**nipër e mbesa** (pl)	[nípər ɛ mbésa]

uncle	**dajë** (f)	[dájə]
aunt	**teze** (f)	[tézɛ]
nephew	**nip** (m)	[nip]
niece	**mbesë** (f)	[mbésə]

mother-in-law (wife's mother)	**vjehrrë** (f)	[vjéhrə]
father-in-law (husband's father)	**vjehrri** (m)	[vjéhri]
son-in-law (daughter's husband)	**dhëndër** (m)	[ðə́ndər]

| stepmother | **njerkë** (f) | [ɲérkə] |
| stepfather | **njerk** (m) | [ɲérk] |

infant	**foshnjë** (f)	[fóʃɲə]
baby (infant)	**fëmijë** (f)	[fəmíjə]
little boy, kid	**djalosh** (m)	[djalóʃ]

| wife | **bashkëshorte** (f) | [baʃkəʃórtɛ] |
| husband | **bashkëshort** (m) | [baʃkəʃórt] |

| spouse (husband) | **bashkëshort** (m) | [baʃkəʃórt] |
| spouse (wife) | **bashkëshorte** (f) | [baʃkəʃórtɛ] |

married (masc.)	**i martuar**	[i martúar]
married (fem.)	**e martuar**	[ɛ martúar]
single (unmarried)	**beqar**	[bɛcár]
bachelor	**beqar** (m)	[bɛcár]
divorced (masc.)	**i divorcuar**	[i divortsúar]

| widow | **vejushë** (f) | [vɛjúʃə] |
| widower | **vejan** (m) | [vɛján] |

| relative | **kushëri** (m) | [kuʃərí] |
| close relative | **kushëri i afërt** (m) | [kuʃərí i áfərt] |

| distant relative | **kushëri i largët** (m) | [kuʃərí i lárgət] |
| relatives | **kushërinj** (pl) | [kuʃəríɲ] |

orphan (boy)	**jetim** (m)	[jɛtím]
orphan (girl)	**jetime** (f)	[jɛtímɛ]
guardian (of a minor)	**kujdestar** (m)	[kujdɛstár]
to adopt (a boy)	**adoptoj**	[adoptój]
to adopt (a girl)	**adoptoj**	[adoptój]

56. Friends. Coworkers

friend (masc.)	**mik** (m)	[mik]
friend (fem.)	**mike** (f)	[míkɛ]
friendship	**miqësi** (f)	[micəsí]
to be friends	**të miqësohem**	[tə micəsóhɛm]
buddy (masc.)	**shok** (m)	[ʃok]
buddy (fem.)	**shoqe** (f)	[ʃócɛ]
partner	**partner** (m)	[partnér]
chief (boss)	**shef** (m)	[ʃɛf]
superior (n)	**epror** (m)	[ɛprór]
owner, proprietor	**pronar** (m)	[pronár]
subordinate (n)	**vartës** (m)	[vártəs]
colleague	**koleg** (m)	[kolég]
acquaintance (person)	**i njohur** (m)	[i ɲóhur]
fellow traveler	**bashkudhëtar** (m)	[baʃkuðətár]
classmate	**shok klase** (m)	[ʃok klásɛ]
neighbor (masc.)	**komshi** (m)	[komʃí]
neighbor (fem.)	**komshike** (f)	[komʃíkɛ]
neighbors	**komshinj** (pl)	[komʃíɲ]

57. Man. Woman

woman	**grua** (f)	[grúa]
girl (young woman)	**vajzë** (f)	[vájzə]
bride	**nuse** (f)	[núsɛ]
beautiful (adj)	**i bukur**	[i búkur]
tall (adj)	**i gjatë**	[i ɟátə]
slender (adj)	**i hollë**	[i hółə]
short (adj)	**i shkurtër**	[i ʃkúrtər]
blonde (n)	**bionde** (f)	[bióndɛ]
brunette (n)	**zeshkane** (f)	[zɛʃkánɛ]
ladies' (adj)	**për femra**	[pər fémra]
virgin (girl)	**virgjëreshë** (f)	[virɟəréʃə]
pregnant (adj)	**shtatzënë**	[ʃtatzénə]
man (adult male)	**burrë** (m)	[búrə]
blond (n)	**biond** (m)	[biónd]
brunet (n)	**zeshkan** (m)	[zɛʃkán]
tall (adj)	**i gjatë**	[i ɟátə]
short (adj)	**i shkurtër**	[i ʃkúrtər]
rude (rough)	**i vrazhdë**	[i vráʒdə]

stocky (adj)	trupngjeshur	[trupnɟéʃur]
robust (adj)	i fuqishëm	[i fucíʃəm]
strong (adj)	i fortë	[i fórtə]
strength	forcë (f)	[fórtsə]

stout, fat (adj)	bullafiq	[buɫafíc]
swarthy (adj)	zeshkan	[zɛʃkán]
slender (well-built)	i hollë	[i hóɫə]
elegant (adj)	elegant	[ɛlɛgánt]

58. Age

age	moshë (f)	[móʃə]
youth (young age)	rini (f)	[riní]
young (adj)	i ri	[i rí]

| younger (adj) | më i ri | [mə i rí] |
| older (adj) | më i vjetër | [mə i vjétər] |

young man	djalë i ri (m)	[djálə i rí]
teenager	adoleshent (m)	[adolɛʃént]
guy, fellow	djalë (f)	[djálə]

| old man | plak (m) | [plak] |
| old woman | plakë (f) | [pɫákə] |

adult (adj)	i rritur	[i rítur]
middle-aged (adj)	mesoburrë	[mɛsobúrə]
elderly (adj)	i moshuar	[i moʃúar]
old (adj)	i vjetër	[i vjétər]

retirement	pension (m)	[pɛnsión]
to retire (from job)	dal në pension	[dál nə pɛnsión]
retiree	pensionist (m)	[pɛnsioníst]

59. Children

child	fëmijë (f)	[fəmíjə]
children	fëmijë (pl)	[fəmíjə]
twins	binjakë (pl)	[biɲákə]

cradle	djep (m)	[djép]
rattle	rraketake (f)	[rakɛtákɛ]
diaper	pelenë (f)	[pɛlénə]

pacifier	biberon (m)	[bibɛrón]
baby carriage	karrocë për bebe (f)	[karótsə pər bébɛ]
kindergarten	kopsht fëmijësh (m)	[kópʃt fəmíjəʃ]

babysitter	dado (f)	[dádo]
childhood	fëmijëri (f)	[fəmijərí]
doll	kukull (f)	[kúkuɫ]
toy	lodër (f)	[lódər]
construction set (toy)	lodër për ndërtim (m)	[lódər pər ndərtím]

well-bred (adj)	i edukuar	[i ɛdukúar]
ill-bred (adj)	i paedukuar	[i paɛdukúar]
spoiled (adj)	i llastuar	[i ɫastúar]

to be naughty	trazovaç	[trazovátʃ]
mischievous (adj)	mistrec	[mistréts]
mischievousness	shpirtligësi (f)	[ʃpirtligəsí]
mischievous child	fëmijë mistrec (m)	[fəmíjə mistréts]

| obedient (adj) | i bindur | [i bíndur] |
| disobedient (adj) | i pabindur | [i pabíndur] |

docile (adj)	i butë	[i bútə]
clever (smart)	i zgjuar	[i zɟúar]
child prodigy	fëmijë gjeni (m)	[fəmíjə ɟɛní]

60. Married couples. Family life

to kiss (vt)	puth	[puθ]
to kiss (vi)	puthem	[púθɛm]
family (n)	familje (f)	[famíljɛ]
family (as adj)	familjare	[familjárɛ]
couple	çift (m)	[tʃíft]
marriage (state)	martesë (f)	[martésə]
hearth (home)	vatra (f)	[vátra]
dynasty	dinasti (f)	[dinastí]

| date | takim (m) | [takím] |
| kiss | puthje (f) | [púθjɛ] |

love (for sb)	dashuri (f)	[daʃurí]
to love (sb)	dashuroj	[daʃurój]
beloved	i dashur	[i dáʃur]

tenderness	ndjeshmëri (f)	[ndjɛʃmərí]
tender (affectionate)	i ndjeshëm	[i ndjéʃəm]
faithfulness	besnikëri (f)	[bɛsnikərí]
faithful (adj)	besnik	[bɛsník]
care (attention)	kujdes (m)	[kujdés]
caring (~ father)	i dashur	[i dáʃur]
newlyweds	të porsamartuar (pl)	[tə porsamartúar]
honeymoon	muaj mjalti (m)	[múaj mjálti]
to get married (ab. woman)	martohem	[martóhɛm]

to get married (ab. man)	martohem	[martóhɛm]
wedding	dasmë (f)	[dásmə]
golden wedding	martesë e artë (f)	[martésə ɛ ártə]
anniversary	përvjetor (m)	[pərvjɛtór]

| lover (masc.) | dashnor (m) | [daʃnór] |
| mistress (lover) | dashnore (f) | [daʃnórɛ] |

adultery	tradhti bashkëshortore (f)	[traðtí baʃkəʃortórɛ]
to cheat on ... (commit adultery)	tradhtoj ...	[traðtój ...]
jealous (adj)	xheloz	[dʒɛlóz]
to be jealous	jam xheloz	[jam dʒɛlóz]
divorce	divorc (m)	[divórts]
to divorce (vi)	divorcoj	[divortsój]

to quarrel (vi)	grindem	[gríndɛm]
to be reconciled (after an argument)	pajtohem	[pajtóhɛm]
together (adv)	së bashku	[sə báʃku]
sex	seks (m)	[sɛks]

happiness	lumturi (f)	[lumturí]
happy (adj)	i lumtur	[i lúmtur]
misfortune (accident)	fatkeqësi (f)	[fatkɛcəsí]
unhappy (adj)	i trishtuar	[i triʃtúar]

Character. Feelings. Emotions

61. Feelings. Emotions

feeling (emotion)	ndjenjë (f)	[ndjéɲə]
feelings	ndjenja (pl)	[ndjéɲa]
to feel (vt)	ndjej	[ndjéj]
hunger	uri (f)	[urí]
to be hungry	kam uri	[kam urí]
thirst	etje (f)	[étjɛ]
to be thirsty	kam etje	[kam étjɛ]
sleepiness	përgjumësi (f)	[pəɾjuməsí]
to feel sleepy	përgjumje	[pəɾjúmjɛ]
tiredness	lodhje (f)	[lóðjɛ]
tired (adj)	i lodhur	[i lóðuɾ]
to get tired	lodhem	[lóðɛm]
mood (humor)	humor (m)	[humóɾ]
boredom	mërzitje (f)	[mərzítjɛ]
to be bored	mërzitem	[mərzítɛm]
seclusion	izolim (m)	[izolím]
to seclude oneself	izolohem	[izolóhɛm]
to worry (make anxious)	shqetësoj	[ʃcɛtəsój]
to be worried	shqetësohem	[ʃcɛtəsóhɛm]
worrying (n)	shqetësim (m)	[ʃcɛtəsím]
anxiety	ankth (m)	[ankθ]
preoccupied (adj)	i merakosur	[i mɛrakósuɾ]
to be nervous	nervozohem	[nɛrvozóhɛm]
to panic (vi)	më zë paniku	[mə zə paníku]
hope	shpresë (f)	[ʃprésə]
to hope (vi, vt)	shpresoj	[ʃprɛsój]
certainty	siguri (f)	[sigurí]
certain, sure (adj)	i sigurt	[i síguɾt]
uncertainty	pasiguri (f)	[pasigurí]
uncertain (adj)	i pasigurt	[i pasíguɾt]
drunk (adj)	i dehur	[i déhuɾ]
sober (adj)	i kthjellët	[i kθjéɫət]
weak (adj)	i dobët	[i dóbət]
happy (adj)	i lumtur	[i lúmtuɾ]
to scare (vt)	tremb	[trɛmb]

fury (madness)	tërbim (m)	[tərbím]
rage (fury)	inat (m)	[inát]

depression	depresion (m)	[dɛprɛsión]
discomfort (unease)	parehati (f)	[parɛhatí]
comfort	rehati (f)	[rɛhatí]
to regret (be sorry)	pendohem	[pɛndóhɛm]
regret	pendim (m)	[pɛndím]
bad luck	ters (m)	[tɛrs]
sadness	trishtim (m)	[triʃtím]

shame (remorse)	turp (m)	[turp]
gladness	gëzim (m)	[gəzím]
enthusiasm, zeal	entuziazëm (m)	[ɛntuziázəm]
enthusiast	entuziast (m)	[ɛntuziást]
to show enthusiasm	tregoj entuziazëm	[trɛgój ɛntuziázəm]

62. Character. Personality

character	karakter (m)	[karaktér]
character flaw	dobësi karakteri (f)	[dobəsí karaktéri]
mind	mendje (f)	[méndjɛ]
reason	arsye (f)	[arsýɛ]

conscience	ndërgjegje (f)	[ndərɟéɟɛ]
habit (custom)	zakon (m)	[zakón]
ability (talent)	aftësi (f)	[aftəsí]
can (e.g., ~ swim)	mund	[mund]

patient (adj)	i duruar	[i durúar]
impatient (adj)	i paduruar	[i padurúar]
curious (inquisitive)	kurioz	[kurióz]
curiosity	kuriozitet (m)	[kuriozitét]

modesty	modesti (f)	[modɛstí]
modest (adj)	modest	[modést]
immodest (adj)	i paturpshëm	[i patúrpʃəm]

laziness	dembeli (f)	[dɛmbɛlí]
lazy (adj)	dembel	[dɛmbél]
lazy person (masc.)	dembel (m)	[dɛmbél]

cunning (n)	dinakëri (f)	[dinakərí]
cunning (as adj)	dinak	[dinák]
distrust	mosbesim (m)	[mosbɛsím]
distrustful (adj)	mosbesues	[mosbɛsúɛs]

generosity	zemërgjerësi (f)	[zɛmərɟɛrəsí]
generous (adj)	zemërgjerë	[zɛmərɟérə]
talented (adj)	i talentuar	[i talɛntúar]

talent	talent (m)	[talént]
courageous (adj)	i guximshëm	[i gudzímʃəm]
courage	guxim (m)	[gudzím]
honest (adj)	i ndershëm	[i ndérʃəm]
honesty	ndershmëri (f)	[ndɛrʃmərí]

careful (cautious)	i kujdesshëm	[i kujdésʃəm]
brave (courageous)	trim, guximtar	[trim], [gudzimtár]
serious (adj)	serioz	[sɛrióz]
strict (severe, stern)	i rreptë	[i réptə]

decisive (adj)	i vendosur	[i vɛndósur]
indecisive (adj)	i pavendosur	[i pavɛndósur]
shy, timid (adj)	i turpshëm	[i túrpʃəm]
shyness, timidity	turp (m)	[turp]

confidence (trust)	besim në vetvete (m)	[bɛsím nə vɛtvétɛ]
to believe (trust)	besoj	[bɛsój]
trusting (credulous)	i besueshëm	[i bɛsúɛʃəm]

sincerely (adv)	sinqerisht	[síncɛriʃt]
sincere (adj)	i sinqertë	[i sincértə]
sincerity	sinqeritet (m)	[sincɛritét]
open (person)	i hapur	[i hápur]

calm (adj)	i qetë	[i cétə]
frank (sincere)	i dëlirë	[i dəlírə]
naïve (adj)	naiv	[naív]
absent-minded (adj)	i hutuar	[i hutúar]
funny (odd)	zbavitës	[zbavítəs]

greed, stinginess	lakmi (f)	[lakmí]
greedy, stingy (adj)	lakmues	[lakmúɛs]
stingy (adj)	koprrac	[kopráts]
evil (adj)	djallëzor	[djaɫəzór]
stubborn (adj)	kokëfortë	[kokəfórtə]
unpleasant (adj)	i pakëndshëm	[i pakéndʃəm]

selfish person (masc.)	egoist (m)	[ɛgoíst]
selfish (adj)	egoist	[ɛgoíst]
coward	frikacak (m)	[frikatsák]
cowardly (adj)	frikacak	[frikatsák]

63. Sleep. Dreams

to sleep (vi)	fle	[flɛ]
sleep, sleeping	gjumë (m)	[ɟúmə]
dream	ëndërr (m)	[éndər]
to dream (in sleep)	ëndërroj	[əndərój]
sleepy (adj)	përgjumshëm	[pərɟúmʃəm]

bed	shtrat (m)	[ʃtrat]
mattress	dyshek (m)	[dyʃék]
blanket (comforter)	mbulesë (f)	[mbulésə]
pillow	jastëk (m)	[jasték]
sheet	çarçaf (m)	[tʃartʃáf]

insomnia	pagjumësi (f)	[paɟuməsí]
sleepless (adj)	i pagjumë	[i paɟúmə]
sleeping pill	ilaç gjumi (m)	[ilátʃ ɟúmi]
to take a sleeping pill	marr ilaç gjumi	[mar ilátʃ ɟúmi]

to feel sleepy	përgjumje	[pərɟúmjɛ]
to yawn (vi)	më hapet goja	[mə hápɛt gója]
to go to bed	shkoj të fle	[ʃkoj tə flɛ]
to make up the bed	rregulloj shtratin	[rɛguɫój ʃtrátin]
to fall asleep	më zë gjumi	[mə zə ɟúmi]

nightmare	ankth (m)	[ankθ]
snore, snoring	gërhitje (f)	[gərhítjɛ]
to snore (vi)	gërhas	[gərhás]

alarm clock	orë me zile (f)	[órə mɛ zílɛ]
to wake (vt)	zgjoj	[zɟoj]
to wake up	zgjohem nga gjumi	[zɟóhɛm ŋa ɟúmi]
to get up (vi)	ngrihem	[ŋríhɛm]
to wash up (wash face)	laj	[laj]

64. Humour. Laughter. Gladness

humor (wit, fun)	humor (m)	[humór]
sense of humor	sens humori (m)	[sɛns humóri]
to enjoy oneself	kënaqem	[kənácɛm]
cheerful (merry)	gëzueshëm	[gəzúɛʃəm]
merriment (gaiety)	gëzim (m)	[gəzím]

smile	buzëqeshje (f)	[buzəcéʃjɛ]
to smile (vi)	buzëqesh	[buzəcéʃ]
to start laughing	filloj të qesh	[fiɫój tə céʃ]
to laugh (vi)	qesh	[cɛʃ]
laugh, laughter	qeshje (f)	[céʃjɛ]

anecdote	anekdotë (f)	[anɛkdótə]
funny (anecdote, etc.)	për të qeshur	[pər tə céʃur]
funny (odd)	zbavitës	[zbavítəs]

to joke (vi)	bëj shaka	[bəj ʃaká]
joke (verbal)	shaka (f)	[ʃaká]
joy (emotion)	gëzim (m)	[gəzím]
to rejoice (vi)	ngazëllohem	[ŋazəɫóhɛm]
joyful (adj)	gazmor	[gazmór]

65. Discussion, conversation. Part 1

communication	komunikim (m)	[komunikím]
to communicate	komunikoj	[komunikój]

conversation	bisedë (f)	[bisédə]
dialog	dialog (m)	[dialóg]
discussion (discourse)	diskutim (m)	[diskutím]
dispute (debate)	mosmarrëveshje (f)	[mosmarəvéʃɛ]
to dispute	kundërshtoj	[kundərʃtój]

interlocutor	bashkëbisedues (m)	[baʃkəbisɛdúɛs]
topic (theme)	temë (f)	[témə]
point of view	pikëpamje (f)	[pikəpámjɛ]
opinion (point of view)	opinion (m)	[opinión]
speech (talk)	fjalim (m)	[fjalím]

discussion (of report, etc.)	diskutim (m)	[diskutím]
to discuss (vt)	diskutoj	[diskutój]
talk (conversation)	bisedë (f)	[bisédə]
to talk (to chat)	bisedoj	[bisɛdój]
meeting (encounter)	takim (m)	[takím]
to meet (vi, vt)	takoj	[takój]

proverb	fjalë e urtë (f)	[fjálə ɛ úrtə]
saying	thënie (f)	[θéniɛ]
riddle (poser)	gjëegjëzë (f)	[ɟəéjəzə]
to pose a riddle	them gjëegjëzë	[θɛm ɟəéjəzə]
password	fjalëkalim (m)	[fjaləkalím]
secret	sekret (m)	[sɛkrét]

oath (vow)	betim (m)	[bɛtím]
to swear (an oath)	betohem	[bɛtóhɛm]
promise	premtim (m)	[prɛmtím]
to promise (vt)	premtoj	[prɛmtój]

advice (counsel)	këshillë (f)	[kəʃítə]
to advise (vt)	këshilloj	[kəʃitój]
to follow one's advice	ndjek këshillën	[ndjék kəʃítən]
to listen to ... (obey)	bindem ...	[bíndɛm ...]

news	lajme (f)	[lájmɛ]
sensation (news)	ndjesi (f)	[ndjɛsí]
information (report)	informacion (m)	[informatsión]
conclusion (decision)	përfundim (m)	[pərfundím]
voice	zë (f)	[zə]
compliment	kompliment (m)	[komplimént]
kind (nice)	i mirë	[i mírə]

word	fjalë (f)	[fjálə]
phrase	frazë (f)	[frázə]

answer	përgjigje (f)	[pəɾjíʝɛ]
truth	e vërtetë (f)	[ɛ vərtétə]
lie	gënjeshtër (f)	[gəɲéʃtər]

thought	mendim (m)	[mɛndím]
idea (inspiration)	ide (f)	[idé]
fantasy	fantazi (f)	[fantazí]

66. Discussion, conversation. Part 2

respected (adj)	i nderuar	[i ndɛɾúaɾ]
to respect (vt)	nderoj	[ndɛrój]
respect	nder (m)	[ndéɾ]
Dear ... (letter)	i dashur ...	[i dáʃuɾ ...]

| to introduce (sb to sb) | prezantoj | [prɛzantój] |
| to make acquaintance | njoftoj | [ɲoftój] |

intention	qëllim (m)	[cətím]
to intend (have in mind)	kam ndërmend	[kam ndərménd]
wish	dëshirë (f)	[dəʃírə]
to wish (~ good luck)	dëshiroj	[dəʃirój]

surprise (astonishment)	surprizë (f)	[surprízə]
to surprise (amaze)	befasoj	[bɛfasój]
to be surprised	çuditem	[tʃudítɛm]

to give (vt)	jap	[jap]
to take (get hold of)	marr	[maɾ]
to give back	kthej	[kθɛj]
to return (give back)	rikthej	[rikθéj]

to apologize (vi)	kërkoj falje	[kərkój fáljɛ]
apology	falje (f)	[fáljɛ]
to forgive (vt)	fal	[fal]

to talk (speak)	flas	[flas]
to listen (vi)	dëgjoj	[dəjój]
to hear out	tregoj vëmendje	[trɛgój vəméndjɛ]
to understand (vt)	kuptoj	[kuptój]

to show (to display)	tregoj	[trɛgój]
to look at ...	shikoj ...	[ʃikój ...]
to call (yell for sb)	thërras	[θərás]
to distract (disturb)	tërheq vëmendjen	[tərhéc vəméndjɛn]
to disturb (vt)	shqetësoj	[ʃcɛtəsój]
to pass (to hand sth)	jap	[jap]

| demand (request) | kërkesë (f) | [kərkésə] |
| to request (ask) | kërkoj | [kərkój] |

| demand (firm request) | kërkesë (f) | [kərkésə] |
| to demand (request firmly) | kërkoj | [kərkój] |

to tease (call names)	ngacmoj	[ŋatsmój]
to mock (make fun of)	tallem	[táɫɛm]
mockery, derision	tallje (f)	[táɫjɛ]
nickname	pseudonim (m)	[psɛudoním]

insinuation	nënkuptim (m)	[nənkuptím]
to insinuate (imply)	nënkuptoj	[nənkuptój]
to mean (vt)	dua të them	[dúa tə θém]

description	përshkrim (m)	[pərʃkrím]
to describe (vt)	përshkruaj	[pərʃkrúaj]
praise (compliments)	lëvdatë (f)	[ləvdátə]
to praise (vt)	lavdëroj	[lavdərój]

disappointment	zhgënjim (m)	[ʒgəɲím]
to disappoint (vt)	zhgënjej	[ʒgəɲéj]
to be disappointed	zhgënjehem	[ʒgəɲéhɛm]

supposition	supozim (m)	[supozím]
to suppose (assume)	supozoj	[supozój]
warning (caution)	paralajmërim (m)	[paralajmərim]
to warn (vt)	paralajmëroj	[paralajmərój]

67. Discussion, conversation. Part 3

| to talk into (convince) | bind | [bínd] |
| to calm down (vt) | qetësoj | [cɛtəsój] |

silence (~ is golden)	heshtje (f)	[héʃtjɛ]
to be silent (not speaking)	i heshtur	[i héʃtur]
to whisper (vi, vt)	pëshpëris	[pəʃpərís]
whisper	pëshpërimë (f)	[pəʃpərímə]

| frankly, sincerely (adv) | sinqerisht | [síncɛriʃt] |
| in my opinion ... | sipas mendimit tim ... | [sipás mɛndímit tim ...] |

detail (of the story)	detaj (m)	[dɛtáj]
detailed (adj)	i detajuar	[i dɛtajúar]
in detail (adv)	hollësisht	[hoɫəsíʃt]

| hint, clue | sugjerim (m) | [suɟɛrím] |
| to give a hint | aludoj | [aludój] |

look (glance)	shikim (m)	[ʃikím]
to have a look	i hedh një sy	[i héð ɲə sý]
fixed (look)	i ngurtë	[i ŋúrtə]
to blink (vi)	hap e mbyll sytë	[hap ɛ mbýɫ sýtə]

| to wink (vi) | luaj syrin | [lúaj sýrin] |
| to nod (in assent) | pohoj me kokë | [pohój mɛ kókə] |

sigh	psherëtimë (f)	[pʃɛrətímə]
to sigh (vi)	psherëtij	[pʃɛrətíj]
to shudder (vi)	rrëqethem	[rəcéθɛm]
gesture	gjest (m)	[ɟɛst]
to touch (one's arm, etc.)	prek	[prɛk]
to seize	kap	[kap]
(e.g., ~ by the arm)		
to tap (on the shoulder)	prek	[prɛk]

Look out!	Kujdes!	[kujdés!]
Really?	Vërtet?	[vərtét?]
Are you sure?	Je i sigurt?	[jɛ i sígurt?]
Good luck!	Paç fat!	[patʃ fat!]
I see!	E kuptova!	[ɛ kuptóva!]
What a pity!	Sa keq!	[sa kɛc!]

68. Agreement. Refusal

consent	leje (f)	[léjɛ]
to consent (vi)	lejoj	[lɛjój]
approval	miratim (m)	[miratím]
to approve (vt)	miratoj	[miratój]
refusal	refuzim (m)	[rɛfuzím]
to refuse (vi, vt)	refuzoj	[rɛfuzój]

Great!	Të lumtë!	[tə lúmtə!]
All right!	Në rregull!	[nə réguɫ!]
Okay! (I agree)	Në rregull!	[nə réguɫ!]

forbidden (adj)	i ndaluar	[i ndalúar]
it's forbidden	është e ndalúar	[əʃtə ɛ ndalúar]
it's impossible	është e pamundur	[əʃtə ɛ pámundur]
incorrect (adj)	i pasaktë	[i pasáktə]

to reject (~ a demand)	hedh poshtë	[hɛð póʃtə]
to support (cause, idea)	mbështes	[mbəʃtés]
to accept (~ an apology)	pranoj	[pranój]

to confirm (vt)	konfirmoj	[konfirmój]
confirmation	konfirmim (m)	[konfirmím]
permission	leje (f)	[léjɛ]
to permit (vt)	lejoj	[lɛjój]
decision	vendim (m)	[vɛndím]
to say nothing	nuk them asgjë	[nuk θɛm ásɟə]
(hold one's tongue)		
condition (term)	kusht (m)	[kuʃt]
excuse (pretext)	justifikim (m)	[justifikim]

| praise (compliments) | lëvdata (f) | [ləvdáta] |
| to praise (vt) | lavdëroj | [lavdərój] |

69. Success. Good luck. Failure

success	sukses (m)	[suksés]
successfully (adv)	me sukses	[mɛ suksés]
successful (adj)	i suksesshëm	[i suksésʃəm]

luck (good luck)	fat (m)	[fat]
Good luck!	Paç fat!	[patʃ fat!]
lucky (e.g., ~ day)	me fat	[mɛ fat]
lucky (fortunate)	fatlum	[fatlúm]

failure	dështim (m)	[dəʃtím]
misfortune	fatkeqësi (f)	[fatkɛcəsí]
bad luck	ters (m)	[tɛrs]
unsuccessful (adj)	i pasuksesshëm	[i pasuksésʃəm]
catastrophe	katastrofë (f)	[katastrófə]

pride	krenari (f)	[krɛnarí]
proud (adj)	krenar	[krɛnár]
to be proud	jam krenar	[jam krɛnár]

winner	fitues (m)	[fitúɛs]
to win (vi)	fitoj	[fitój]
to lose (not win)	humb	[húmb]
try	përpjekje (f)	[pərpjékjɛ]
to try (vi)	përpiqem	[pərpícɛm]
chance (opportunity)	shans (m)	[ʃans]

70. Quarrels. Negative emotions

shout (scream)	britmë (f)	[brítmə]
to shout (vi)	bërtas	[bərtás]
to start to cry out	filloj të ulërij	[fiłój tə uləríj]

quarrel	grindje (f)	[gríndjɛ]
to quarrel (vi)	grindem	[gríndɛm]
fight (squabble)	sherr (m)	[ʃɛr]
to make a scene	bëj skenë	[bəj skénə]
conflict	konflikt (m)	[konflíkt]
misunderstanding	keqkuptim (m)	[kɛckuptím]

insult	ofendim (m)	[ofɛndím]
to insult (vt)	fyej	[fýɛj]
insulted (adj)	i ofenduar	[i ofɛndúaɾ]
resentment	fyerje (f)	[fýɛɾjɛ]

| to offend (vt) | ofendoj | [ofɛndój] |
| to take offense | mbrohem | [mbróhɛm] |

indignation	indinjatë (f)	[indiɲátə]
to be indignant	zemërohem	[zɛməróhɛm]
complaint	ankesë (f)	[ankésə]
to complain (vi, vt)	ankohem	[ankóhɛm]

apology	falje (f)	[fáljɛ]
to apologize (vi)	kërkoj falje	[kərkój fáljɛ]
to beg pardon	kërkoj ndjesë	[kərkój ndjésə]

criticism	kritikë (f)	[kritíkə]
to criticize (vt)	kritikoj	[kritikój]
accusation (charge)	akuzë (f)	[akúzə]
to accuse (vt)	akuzoj	[akuzój]

revenge	hakmarrje (f)	[hakmárjɛ]
to avenge (get revenge)	hakmerrem	[hakmérɛm]
to pay back	shpaguaj	[ʃpagúaj]

disdain	përbuzje (f)	[pərbúzjɛ]
to despise (vt)	përbuz	[pərbúz]
hatred, hate	urrejtje (f)	[uréjtjɛ]
to hate (vt)	urrej	[uréj]

nervous (adj)	nervoz	[nɛrvóz]
to be nervous	nervozohem	[nɛrvozóhɛm]
angry (mad)	i zemëruar	[i zɛmərúar]
to make angry	zemëroj	[zɛmərój]

humiliation	poshtërim (m)	[poʃtərím]
to humiliate (vt)	poshtëroj	[poʃtərój]
to humiliate oneself	poshtërohem	[poʃtəróhɛm]

| shock | tronditje (f) | [tronadítjɛ] |
| to shock (vt) | trondit | [trondít] |

| trouble (e.g., serious ~) | shqetësim (m) | [ʃcɛtəsím] |
| unpleasant (adj) | i pakëndshëm | [i pakéndʃəm] |

fear (dread)	frikë (f)	[fríkə]
terrible (storm, heat)	i tmerrshëm	[i tmérʃəm]
scary (e.g., ~ story)	i frikshëm	[i fríkʃəm]
horror	horror (m)	[horór]
awful (crime, news)	i tmerrshëm	[i tmérʃəm]

to begin to tremble	filloj të dridhem	[fiłój tə dríðɛm]
to cry (weep)	qaj	[caj]
to start crying	filloj të qaj	[fiłój tə cáj]
tear	lot (m)	[lot]
fault	faj (m)	[faj]

guilt (feeling)	**faj** (m)	[faj]
dishonor (disgrace)	**turp** (m)	[turp]
protest	**protestë** (f)	[protéstə]
stress	**stres** (m)	[strɛs]
to disturb (vt)	**shqetësoj**	[ʃcɛtəsój]
to be furious	**tërbohem**	[tərbóhɛm]
mad, angry (adj)	**i inatosur**	[i inatósur]
to end (~ a relationship)	**përfundoj**	[pərfundój]
to swear (at sb)	**betohem**	[bɛtóhɛm]
to scare (become afraid)	**tremb**	[trɛmb]
to hit (strike with hand)	**qëlloj**	[cəłój]
to fight (street fight, etc.)	**grindem**	[gríndɛm]
to settle (a conflict)	**zgjidh**	[zɟið]
discontented (adj)	**i pakënaqur**	[i pakənácur]
furious (adj)	**i xhindosur**	[i dʒindósur]
It's not good!	**Nuk është mirë!**	[nuk əʃtə mírə!]
It's bad!	**Është keq!**	[əʃtə kɛc!]

Medicine

71. Diseases

sickness	sëmundje (f)	[səmúndjɛ]
to be sick	jam sëmurë	[jam səmúrə]
health	shëndet (m)	[ʃəndét]
runny nose (coryza)	rrifë (f)	[rífə]
tonsillitis	grykët (m)	[grýkət]
cold (illness)	ftohje (f)	[ftóhjɛ]
to catch a cold	ftohem	[ftóhɛm]
bronchitis	bronkit (m)	[bronkít]
pneumonia	pneumoni (f)	[pnɛumoní]
flu, influenza	grip (m)	[grip]
nearsighted (adj)	miop	[mióp]
farsighted (adj)	presbit	[prɛsbít]
strabismus (crossed eyes)	strabizëm (m)	[strabízəm]
cross-eyed (adj)	strabik	[strabík]
cataract	katarakt (m)	[katarákt]
glaucoma	glaukoma (f)	[glaukóma]
stroke	goditje (f)	[godítjɛ]
heart attack	sulm në zemër (m)	[sulm nə zémər]
myocardial infarction	infarkt miokardiak (m)	[infárkt miokardiák]
paralysis	paralizë (f)	[paralízə]
to paralyze (vt)	paralizoj	[paralizój]
allergy	alergji (f)	[alɛɾɟí]
asthma	astmë (f)	[ástmə]
diabetes	diabet (m)	[diabét]
toothache	dhimbje dhëmbi (f)	[ðímbjɛ ðə́mbi]
caries	karies (m)	[kariés]
diarrhea	diarre (f)	[diaré]
constipation	kapsllëk (m)	[kapsɫə́k]
stomach upset	dispepsi (f)	[dispɛpsí]
food poisoning	helmim (m)	[hɛlmím]
to get food poisoning	helmohem nga ushqimi	[hɛlmóhɛm ŋa uʃcími]
arthritis	artrit (m)	[artrít]
rickets	rakit (m)	[rakít]
rheumatism	reumatizëm (m)	[rɛumatízəm]

atherosclerosis	arteriosklerozë (f)	[artɛriosklɛrózə]
gastritis	gastrit (m)	[gastrít]
appendicitis	apendicit (m)	[apɛnditsít]
cholecystitis	kolecistit (m)	[kolɛtsistít]
ulcer	ulcerë (f)	[ultsérə]

measles	fruth (m)	[fruθ]
rubella (German measles)	rubeola (f)	[rubɛóla]
jaundice	verdhëza (f)	[vérðəza]
hepatitis	hepatit (m)	[hɛpatít]

schizophrenia	skizofreni (f)	[skizofrɛní]
rabies (hydrophobia)	sëmundje e tërbimit (f)	[səmúndjɛ ɛ tərbímit]
neurosis	neurozë (f)	[nɛurózə]
concussion	tronditje (f)	[trondítjɛ]

cancer	kancer (m)	[kantsér]
sclerosis	sklerozë (f)	[sklɛrózə]
multiple sclerosis	sklerozë e shumëfishtë (f)	[sklɛrózə ɛ ʃuməfíʃtə]

alcoholism	alkoolizëm (m)	[alkoolizəm]
alcoholic (n)	alkoolik (m)	[alkoolík]
syphilis	sifiliz (m)	[sifilíz]
AIDS	SIDA (f)	[sída]

tumor	tumor (m)	[tumór]
malignant (adj)	malinj	[malíɲ]
benign (adj)	beninj	[bɛníɲ]

fever	ethe (f)	[éθɛ]
malaria	malarie (f)	[malaríɛ]
gangrene	gangrenë (f)	[gaɲrénə]
seasickness	sëmundje deti (f)	[səmúndjɛ déti]
epilepsy	epilepsi (f)	[ɛpilɛpsí]

epidemic	epidemi (f)	[ɛpidɛmí]
typhus	tifo (f)	[tífo]
tuberculosis	tuberkuloz (f)	[tubɛrkulóz]
cholera	kolerë (f)	[kolérə]
plague (bubonic ~)	murtaja (f)	[murtája]

72. Symptoms. Treatments. Part 1

symptom	simptomë (f)	[simptómə]
temperature	temperaturë (f)	[tɛmpɛratúrə]
high temperature (fever)	temperaturë e lartë (f)	[tɛmpɛratúrə ɛ lártə]
pulse (heartbeat)	puls (m)	[puls]

| dizziness (vertigo) | marrje mendsh (m) | [márjɛ méndʃ] |
| hot (adj) | i nxehtë | [i ndzéhtə] |

| shivering | drithërima (f) | [driθəríma] |
| pale (e.g., ~ face) | i zbehur | [i zbéhur] |

cough	kollë (f)	[kóɫə]
to cough (vi)	kollitem	[koɫítɛm]
to sneeze (vi)	teshtij	[tɛʃtíj]
faint	të fikët (f)	[tə fíkət]
to faint (vi)	bie të fikët	[bíɛ tə fíkət]

bruise (hématome)	mavijosje (f)	[mavijósjɛ]
bump (lump)	gungë (f)	[gúŋə]
to bang (bump)	godas	[godás]
contusion (bruise)	lëndim (m)	[ləndím]
to get a bruise	lëndohem	[ləndóhɛm]

to limp (vi)	çaloj	[tʃalój]
dislocation	dislokim (m)	[dislokím]
to dislocate (vt)	del nga vendi	[dɛl ŋa véndi]
fracture	thyerje (f)	[θýɛrjɛ]
to have a fracture	thyej	[θýɛj]

cut (e.g., paper ~)	e prerë (f)	[ɛ prérə]
to cut oneself	pres veten	[prɛs vétɛn]
bleeding	rrjedhje gjaku (f)	[rjéðjɛ ɟáku]

| burn (injury) | djegie (f) | [djégiɛ] |
| to get burned | digjem | [díɟɛm] |

to prick (vt)	shpoj	[ʃpoj]
to prick oneself	shpohem	[ʃpóhɛm]
to injure (vt)	dëmtoj	[dəmtój]
injury	dëmtim (m)	[dəmtím]
wound	plagë (f)	[plágə]
trauma	traumë (f)	[traúmə]

to be delirious	fol përçart	[fól pərtʃárt]
to stutter (vi)	belbëzoj	[bɛlbəzój]
sunstroke	pikë e diellit (f)	[píkə ɛ diéɫit]

73. Symptoms. Treatments. Part 2

| pain, ache | dhimbje (f) | [ðímbjɛ] |
| splinter (in foot, etc.) | cifël (f) | [tsífəl] |

sweat (perspiration)	djersë (f)	[djérsə]
to sweat (perspire)	djersij	[djɛrsij]
vomiting	të vjella (f)	[tə vjéɫa]
convulsions	konvulsione (f)	[konvulsiónɛ]
pregnant (adj)	shtatzënë	[ʃtatzénə]
to be born	lind	[lind]

delivery, labor	lindje (f)	[líndjɛ]
to deliver (~ a baby)	sjell në jetë	[sjɛɫ nə jétə]
abortion	abort (m)	[abórt]

breathing, respiration	frymëmarrje (f)	[fryməmárjɛ]
in-breath (inhalation)	mbajtje e frymës (f)	[mbájtjɛ ɛ frýməs]
out-breath (exhalation)	lëshim i frymës (m)	[ləʃím i frýməs]
to exhale (breathe out)	nxjerr frymën	[ndzjér frýmən]
to inhale (vi)	marr frymë	[mar frýmə]

disabled person	invalid (m)	[invalíd]
cripple	i gjymtuar (m)	[i ɟymtúar]
drug addict	narkoman (m)	[narkomán]

deaf (adj)	shurdh	[ʃurð]
mute (adj)	memec	[mɛméts]
deaf mute (adj)	shurdh-memec	[ʃurð-mɛméts]

mad, insane (adj)	i marrë	[i márə]
madman (demented person)	i çmendur (m)	[i tʃméndur]
madwoman	e çmendur (f)	[ɛ tʃméndur]
to go insane	çmendem	[tʃméndɛm]

gene	gen (m)	[gɛn]
immunity	imunitet (m)	[imunitét]
hereditary (adj)	e trashëguar	[ɛ traʃəgúar]
congenital (adj)	e lindur	[ɛ líndur]

virus	virus (m)	[virús]
microbe	mikrob (m)	[mikrób]
bacterium	bakterie (f)	[baktériɛ]
infection	infeksion (m)	[infɛksión]

74. Symptoms. Treatments. Part 3

| hospital | spital (m) | [spitál] |
| patient | pacient (m) | [patsiént] |

diagnosis	diagnozë (f)	[diagnózə]
cure	kurë (f)	[kúrə]
medical treatment	trajtim mjekësor (m)	[trajtím mjɛkəsór]
to get treatment	kurohem	[kuróhɛm]
to treat (~ a patient)	kuroj	[kurój]
to nurse (look after)	kujdesem	[kujdésɛm]
care (nursing ~)	kujdes (m)	[kujdés]

operation, surgery	operacion (m)	[opɛratsión]
to bandage (head, limb)	fashoj	[faʃój]
bandaging	fashim (m)	[faʃím]

vaccination	vaksinim (m)	[vaksiním]
to vaccinate (vt)	vaksinoj	[vaksinój]
injection, shot	injeksion (m)	[iɲɛksión]
to give an injection	bëj injeksion	[bəj iɲɛksíon]

attack	atak (m)	[aták]
amputation	amputim (m)	[amputím]
to amputate (vt)	amputoj	[amputój]
coma	komë (f)	[kómə]
to be in a coma	jam në komë	[jam nə kómə]
intensive care	kujdes intensiv (m)	[kujdés intɛnsív]

to recover (~ from flu)	shërohem	[ʃəróhɛm]
condition (patient's ~)	gjendje (f)	[ɟéndjɛ]
consciousness	vetëdije (f)	[vɛtədíjɛ]
memory (faculty)	kujtesë (f)	[kujtésə]

to pull out (tooth)	heq	[hɛc]
filling	mbushje (f)	[mbúʃjɛ]
to fill (a tooth)	mbush	[mbúʃ]

| hypnosis | hipnozë (f) | [hipnózə] |
| to hypnotize (vt) | hipnotizim | [hipnotizím] |

75. Doctors

doctor	mjek (m)	[mjék]
nurse	infermiere (f)	[infɛrmiérɛ]
personal doctor	mjek personal (m)	[mjék pɛrsonál]

dentist	dentist (m)	[dɛntíst]
eye doctor	okulist (m)	[okulíst]
internist	mjek i përgjithshëm (m)	[mjék i pərɟíθʃəm]
surgeon	kirurg (m)	[kirúrg]

psychiatrist	psikiatër (m)	[psikiátər]
pediatrician	pediatër (m)	[pɛdiátər]
psychologist	psikolog (m)	[psikológ]
gynecologist	gjinekolog (m)	[ɟinɛkológ]
cardiologist	kardiolog (m)	[kardiológ]

76. Medicine. Drugs. Accessories

medicine, drug	ilaç (m)	[ilátʃ]
remedy	mjekim (m)	[mjɛkím]
to prescribe (vt)	shkruaj recetë	[ʃkrúaj rɛtsétə]
prescription	recetë (f)	[rɛtsétə]
tablet, pill	pilulë (f)	[pilúlə]

ointment	**krem** (m)	[krɛm]
ampule	**ampulë** (f)	[ampúlə]
mixture, solution	**përzierje** (f)	[pərzíɛrjɛ]
syrup	**shurup** (m)	[ʃurúp]
capsule	**pilulë** (f)	[pilúlə]
powder	**pudër** (f)	[púdər]
gauze bandage	**fashë garze** (f)	[faʃə gárzɛ]
cotton wool	**pambuk** (m)	[pambúk]
iodine	**jod** (m)	[jod]
Band-Aid	**leukoplast** (m)	[lɛukoplást]
eyedropper	**pikatore** (f)	[pikatórɛ]
thermometer	**termometër** (m)	[tɛrmométər]
syringe	**shiringë** (f)	[ʃiríŋə]
wheelchair	**karrocë me rrota** (f)	[karótsə mɛ róta]
crutches	**paterica** (f)	[patɛrítsa]
painkiller	**qetësues** (m)	[cɛtəsúɛs]
laxative	**laksativ** (m)	[laksatív]
spirits (ethanol)	**alkool dezinfektues** (m)	[alkoól dɛzinfɛktúɛs]
medicinal herbs	**bimë mjekësore** (f)	[bímə mjɛkəsórɛ]
herbal (~ tea)	**çaj bimor**	[tʃáj bimór]

77. Smoking. Tobacco products

tobacco	**duhan** (m)	[duhán]
cigarette	**cigare** (f)	[tsigárɛ]
cigar	**puro** (f)	[púro]
pipe	**llullë** (f)	[ɬúɬə]
pack (of cigarettes)	**pako cigaresh** (m)	[páko tsigárɛʃ]
matches	**shkrepëse** (pl)	[ʃkrépəsɛ]
matchbox	**kuti shkrepësesh** (f)	[kutí ʃkrépəsɛʃ]
lighter	**çakmak** (m)	[tʃakmák]
ashtray	**taketuke** (f)	[takɛtúkɛ]
cigarette case	**kuti cigaresh** (f)	[kutí tsigárɛʃ]
cigarette holder	**cigarishte** (f)	[tsigaríʃtɛ]
filter (cigarette tip)	**filtër** (m)	[fíltər]
to smoke (vi, vt)	**pi duhan**	[pi duhán]
to light a cigarette	**ndez një cigare**	[ndɛz ɲə tsigárɛ]
smoking	**pirja e duhanit** (f)	[pírja ɛ duhánit]
smoker	**duhanpirës** (m)	[duhanpírəs]
stub, butt (of cigarette)	**bishti i cigares** (m)	[bíʃti i tsigárɛs]
smoke, fumes	**tym** (m)	[tym]
ash	**hi** (m)	[hi]

HUMAN HABITAT

City

78. City. Life in the city

city, town	qytet (m)	[cytét]
capital city	kryeqytet (m)	[kryɛcytét]
village	fshat (m)	[fʃát]
city map	hartë e qytetit (f)	[hártə ɛ cytétit]
downtown	qendër e qytetit (f)	[céndər ɛ cytétit]
suburb	periferi (f)	[pɛrifɛrí]
suburban (adj)	periferik	[pɛrifɛrík]
outskirts	periferia (f)	[pɛrifɛría]
environs (suburbs)	periferia (f)	[pɛrifɛría]
city block	bllok pallatesh (m)	[bɫók paɫátɛʃ]
residential block (area)	bllok banimi (m)	[bɫók baními]
traffic	trafik (m)	[trafík]
traffic lights	semafor (m)	[sɛmafór]
public transportation	transport publik (m)	[transpórt publík]
intersection	kryqëzim (m)	[krycəzím]
crosswalk	kalim për këmbësorë (m)	[kalím pər kəmbəsórə]
pedestrian underpass	nënkalim për këmbësorë (m)	[nənkalím pər kəmbəsórə]
to cross (~ the street)	kapërcej	[kapərtséj]
pedestrian	këmbësor (m)	[kəmbəsór]
sidewalk	trotuar (m)	[trotuár]
bridge	urë (f)	[úrə]
embankment (river walk)	breg lumi (m)	[brɛg lúmi]
fountain	shatërvan (m)	[ʃatərván]
allée (garden walkway)	rrugëz (m)	[rúgəz]
park	park (m)	[park]
boulevard	bulevard (m)	[bulɛvárd]
square	shesh (m)	[ʃɛʃ]
avenue (wide street)	bulevard (m)	[bulɛvárd]
street	rrugë (f)	[rúgə]
side street	rrugë dytësore (f)	[rúgə dytəsórɛ]
dead end	rrugë pa krye (f)	[rúgə pa krýɛ]
house	shtëpi (f)	[ʃtəpí]

building	**ndërtesë** (f)	[ndərtésə]
skyscraper	**qiellgërvishtës** (m)	[ciɛɫgərvíʃtəs]
facade	**fasadë** (f)	[fasádə]
roof	**çati** (f)	[tʃatí]
window	**dritare** (f)	[dritárɛ]
arch	**hark** (m)	[hárk]
column	**kolonë** (f)	[kolónə]
corner	**kënd** (m)	[kénd]
store window	**vitrinë** (f)	[vitrínə]
signboard (store sign, etc.)	**tabelë** (f)	[tabélə]
poster (e.g., playbill)	**poster** (m)	[postér]
advertising poster	**afishe reklamuese** (f)	[afíʃɛ rɛklamúɛsɛ]
billboard	**tabelë reklamash** (f)	[tabélə rɛklámaʃ]
garbage, trash	**plehra** (f)	[pléhra]
trash can (public ~)	**kosh plehrash** (m)	[koʃ pléhraʃ]
to litter (vi)	**hedh mbeturina**	[hɛð mbɛturína]
garbage dump	**deponi plehrash** (f)	[dɛponí pléhraʃ]
phone booth	**kabinë telefonike** (f)	[kabínə tɛlɛfoníkɛ]
lamppost	**shtyllë dritash** (f)	[ʃtýlə drítaʃ]
bench (park ~)	**stol** (m)	[stol]
police officer	**polic** (m)	[políts]
police	**polici** (f)	[politsí]
beggar	**lypës** (m)	[lýpəs]
homeless (n)	**i pastrehë** (m)	[i pastréhə]

79. Urban institutions

store	**dyqan** (m)	[dycán]
drugstore, pharmacy	**farmaci** (f)	[farmatsí]
eyeglass store	**optikë** (f)	[optíkə]
shopping mall	**qendër tregtare** (f)	[céndər trɛgtárɛ]
supermarket	**supermarket** (m)	[supɛrmarkét]
bakery	**furrë** (f)	[fúrə]
baker	**furrtar** (m)	[furtár]
pastry shop	**pastiçeri** (f)	[pastitʃɛrí]
grocery store	**dyqan ushqimor** (m)	[dycán uʃcimór]
butcher shop	**dyqan mishi** (m)	[dycán míʃi]
produce store	**dyqan fruta-perimesh** (m)	[dycán frúta-pɛrímɛʃ]
market	**treg** (m)	[trɛg]
coffee house	**kafene** (f)	[kafɛné]
restaurant	**restorant** (m)	[rɛstoránt]
pub, bar	**pab** (m), **pijetore** (f)	[pab], [pijɛtórɛ]

pizzeria	piceri (f)	[pitsɛrí]
hair salon	parukeri (f)	[parukɛrí]
post office	zyrë postare (f)	[zýrə postárɛ]
dry cleaners	pastrim kimik (m)	[pastrím kimík]
photo studio	studio fotografike (f)	[stúdio fotografíkɛ]

shoe store	dyqan këpucësh (m)	[dycán kəpútsəʃ]
bookstore	librari (f)	[librarí]
sporting goods store	dyqan me mallra sportivë (m)	[dycán mɛ máɫra sportívə]

clothes repair shop	rrobaqepësi (f)	[robacɛpəsí]
formal wear rental	dyqan veshjesh me qira (m)	[dycán véʃjɛʃ mɛ cirá]
video rental store	dyqan videosh me qira (m)	[dycán vídɛoʃ mɛ cirá]

circus	cirk (m)	[tsírk]
zoo	kopsht zoologjik (m)	[kópʃt zooloɟík]
movie theater	kinema (f)	[kinɛmá]
museum	muze (m)	[muzé]
library	bibliotekë (f)	[bibliotékə]

theater	teatër (m)	[tɛátər]
opera (opera house)	opera (f)	[opéra]
nightclub	klub nate (m)	[klúb nátɛ]
casino	kazino (f)	[kazíno]

mosque	xhami (f)	[dʒamí]
synagogue	sinagogë (f)	[sinagógə]
cathedral	katedrale (f)	[katɛdrálɛ]
temple	tempull (m)	[témpuɫ]
church	kishë (f)	[kíʃə]

college	kolegj (m)	[koléɟ]
university	universitet (m)	[univɛrsitét]
school	shkollë (f)	[ʃkóɫə]

prefecture	prefekturë (f)	[prɛfɛktúrə]
city hall	bashki (f)	[baʃkí]
hotel	hotel (m)	[hotél]
bank	bankë (f)	[bánkə]

embassy	ambasadë (f)	[ambasádə]
travel agency	agjenci udhëtimesh (f)	[aɟɛntsí uðətímɛʃ]
information office	zyrë informacioni (f)	[zýrə informatsióni]
currency exchange	këmbim valutor (m)	[kəmbím valutór]

subway	metro (f)	[mɛtró]
hospital	spital (m)	[spitál]
gas station	pikë karburanti (f)	[píkə karburánti]
parking lot	parking (m)	[parkíŋ]

80. Signs

signboard (store sign, etc.)	tabelë (f)	[tabélə]
notice (door sign, etc.)	njoftim (m)	[ɲoftím]
poster	poster (m)	[postér]
direction sign	tabelë drejtuese (f)	[tabélə drɛjtúɛsɛ]
arrow (sign)	shigjetë (f)	[ʃiɟétə]
caution	kujdes (m)	[kujdés]
warning sign	shenjë paralajmëruese (f)	[ʃéɲə paralajmərúɛsɛ]
to warn (vt)	paralajmëroj	[paralajmərój]
rest day (weekly ~)	ditë pushimi (f)	[dítə puʃími]
timetable (schedule)	orar (m)	[orár]
opening hours	orari i punës (m)	[orári i púnəs]
WELCOME!	MIRË SE VINI!	[mírə sɛ víni!]
ENTRANCE	HYRJE	[hýrjɛ]
EXIT	DALJE	[dáljɛ]
PUSH	SHTY	[ʃty]
PULL	TËRHIQ	[tərhíc]
OPEN	HAPUR	[hápuɾ]
CLOSED	MBYLLUR	[mbýɫuɾ]
WOMEN	GRA	[gra]
MEN	BURRA	[búra]
DISCOUNTS	ZBRITJE	[zbrítjɛ]
SALE	ULJE	[úljɛ]
NEW!	TË REJA!	[tə réja!]
FREE	FALAS	[fálas]
ATTENTION!	KUJDES!	[kujdés!]
NO VACANCIES	NUK KA VENDE TË LIRA	[nuk ka véndɛ tə líra]
RESERVED	E REZERVUAR	[ɛ rɛzɛrvúaɾ]
ADMINISTRATION	ADMINISTRATA	[administráta]
STAFF ONLY	VETËM PËR STAFIN	[vétəm pər stáfin]
BEWARE OF THE DOG!	RUHUNI NGA QENI!	[rúhuni ŋa céni!]
NO SMOKING	NDALOHET DUHANI	[ndalóhɛt duháni]
DO NOT TOUCH!	MOS PREK!	[mos prék!]
DANGEROUS	TË RREZIKSHME	[tə rɛzíkʃmɛ]
DANGER	RREZIK	[rɛzík]
HIGH VOLTAGE	TENSION I LARTË	[tɛnsión i lártə]
NO SWIMMING!	NUK LEJOHET NOTI!	[nuk lɛjóhɛt nóti!]
OUT OF ORDER	E PRISHUR	[ɛ príʃuɾ]
FLAMMABLE	LËNDË DJEGËSE	[ləndə djégəsɛ]
FORBIDDEN	E NDALUAR	[ɛ ndalúaɾ]

| NO TRESPASSING! | NDALOHET HYRJA | [ndalóhɛt hýrja] |
| WET PAINT | BOJË E FRESKËT | [bójə ɛ fréskət] |

81. Urban transportation

bus	autobus (m)	[autobús]
streetcar	tramvaj (m)	[tramváj]
trolley bus	autobus tramvaj (m)	[autobús tramváj]
route (of bus, etc.)	itinerar (m)	[itinɛrár]
number (e.g., bus ~)	numër (m)	[númər]

to go by ...	udhëtoj me ...	[uðətój mɛ ...]
to get on (~ the bus)	hip	[hip]
to get off ...	zbres ...	[zbrɛs ...]

stop (e.g., bus ~)	stacion (m)	[statsión]
next stop	stacioni tjetër (m)	[statsióni tjétər]
terminus	terminal (m)	[tɛrminál]
schedule	orar (m)	[orár]
to wait (vt)	pres	[prɛs]

ticket	biletë (f)	[bilétə]
fare	çmim bilete (m)	[tʃmím bilétɛ]
cashier (ticket seller)	shitës biletash (m)	[ʃítəs bilétaʃ]
ticket inspection	kontroll biletash (m)	[kontrół bilétaʃ]
ticket inspector	kontrollues biletash (m)	[kontrołúɛs bilétaʃ]

to be late (for ...)	vonohem	[vonóhɛm]
to miss (~ the train, etc.)	humbas	[humbás]
to be in a hurry	nxitoj	[ndzitój]

taxi, cab	taksi (m)	[táksi]
taxi driver	shofer taksie (m)	[ʃofér taksíɛ]
by taxi	me taksi	[mɛ táksi]
taxi stand	stacion taksish (m)	[statsión táksiʃ]
to call a taxi	thërras taksi	[θərás táksi]
to take a taxi	marr taksi	[mar táksi]

traffic	trafik (m)	[trafík]
traffic jam	bllokim trafiku (m)	[bɫokím trafíku]
rush hour	orë e trafikut të rëndë (f)	[órə ɛ trafikut tə rəndə]
to park (vi)	parkoj	[parkój]
to park (vt)	parkim	[parkím]
parking lot	parking (m)	[parkíŋ]

subway	metro (f)	[mɛtró]
station	stacion (m)	[statsión]
to take the subway	shkoj me metro	[ʃkoj mɛ métró]
train	tren (m)	[trɛn]
train station	stacion treni (m)	[statsión tréni]

82. Sightseeing

monument	**monument** (m)	[monumént]
fortress	**kala** (f)	[kalá]
palace	**pallat** (m)	[pałát]
castle	**kështjellë** (f)	[kəʃtjéłə]
tower	**kullë** (f)	[kúłə]
mausoleum	**mauzoleum** (m)	[mauzolɛúm]
architecture	**arkitekturë** (f)	[arkitɛktúrə]
medieval (adj)	**mesjetare**	[mɛsjɛtárɛ]
ancient (adj)	**e lashtë**	[ɛ láʃtə]
national (adj)	**kombëtare**	[kombətárɛ]
famous (monument, etc.)	**i famshëm**	[i fámʃəm]
tourist	**turist** (m)	[turíst]
guide (person)	**udhërrëfyes** (m)	[uðərəfýɛs]
excursion, sightseeing tour	**ekskursion** (m)	[ɛkskursión]
to show (vt)	**tregoj**	[trɛgój]
to tell (vt)	**dëftoj**	[dəftój]
to find (vt)	**gjej**	[ɟéj]
to get lost (lose one's way)	**humbas**	[humbás]
map (e.g., subway ~)	**hartë** (f)	[hártə]
map (e.g., city ~)	**hartë** (f)	[hártə]
souvenir, gift	**suvenir** (m)	[suvɛnír]
gift shop	**dyqan dhuratash** (m)	[dycán ðúrátaʃ]
to take pictures	**bëj foto**	[bəj fóto]
to have one's picture taken	**bëj fotografi**	[bəj fotografí]

83. Shopping

to buy (purchase)	**blej**	[blɛj]
purchase	**blerje** (f)	[blérjɛ]
to go shopping	**shkoj për pazar**	[ʃkoj pər pazár]
shopping	**pazar** (m)	[pazár]
to be open (ab. store)	**hapur**	[hápur]
to be closed	**mbyllur**	[mbýłur]
footwear, shoes	**këpucë** (f)	[kəpútsə]
clothes, clothing	**veshje** (f)	[véʃjɛ]
cosmetics	**kozmetikë** (f)	[kozmɛtíkə]
food products	**mallra ushqimore** (f)	[máłra uʃcimórɛ]
gift, present	**dhuratë** (f)	[ðurátə]
salesman	**shitës** (m)	[ʃítəs]
saleswoman	**shitëse** (f)	[ʃítəsɛ]

check out, cash desk	arkë (f)	[árkə]
mirror	pasqyrë (f)	[pascýrə]
counter (store ~)	banak (m)	[bának]
fitting room	dhomë prove (f)	[ðómə próvɛ]
to try on	provoj	[provój]
to fit (ab. dress, etc.)	më rri mirë	[mə ri mírə]
to like (I like …)	pëlqej	[pəlcéj]
price	çmim (m)	[tʃmím]
price tag	etiketa e çmimit (f)	[ɛtikéta ɛ tʃmímit]
to cost (vt)	kushton	[kuʃtón]
How much?	Sa?	[sa?]
discount	ulje (f)	[úljɛ]
inexpensive (adj)	jo e shtrenjtë	[jo ɛ ʃtréɲtə]
cheap (adj)	e lirë	[ɛ lírə]
expensive (adj)	i shtrenjtë	[i ʃtréɲtə]
It's expensive	Është e shtrenjtë	[əʃtə ɛ ʃtréɲtə]
rental (n)	qiramarrje (f)	[ciramárjɛ]
to rent (~ a tuxedo)	marr me qira	[mar mɛ cirá]
credit (trade credit)	kredit (m)	[krɛdít]
on credit (adv)	me kredi	[mɛ krɛdí]

84. Money

money	para (f)	[pará]
currency exchange	këmbim valutor (m)	[kəmbím valutór]
exchange rate	kurs këmbimi (m)	[kurs kəmbími]
ATM	bankomat (m)	[bankomát]
coin	monedhë (f)	[monéðə]
dollar	dollar (m)	[doɫár]
euro	euro (f)	[éuro]
lira	lirë (f)	[lírə]
Deutschmark	Marka gjermane (f)	[márka ɟɛrmánɛ]
franc	franga (f)	[fráŋa]
pound sterling	sterlina angleze (f)	[stɛrɫína aŋlézɛ]
yen	jen (m)	[jén]
debt	borxh (m)	[bórdʒ]
debtor	debitor (m)	[dɛbitór]
to lend (money)	jap hua	[jap huá]
to borrow (vi, vt)	marr hua	[mar huá]
bank	bankë (f)	[bánkə]
account	llogari (f)	[ɫogarí]
to deposit (vt)	depozitoj	[dɛpozitój]

| to deposit into the account | depozitoj në llogari | [dɛpozitój nə łogarí] |
| to withdraw (vt) | tërheq | [tərhéc] |

credit card	kartë krediti (f)	[kártə krɛdíti]
cash	kesh (m)	[kɛʃ]
check	çek (m)	[tʃɛk]
to write a check	lëshoj një çek	[ləʃój ɲə tʃék]
checkbook	bllok çeqesh (m)	[błók tʃécɛʃ]

wallet	portofol (m)	[portofól]
change purse	kuletë (f)	[kulétə]
safe	kasafortë (f)	[kasafórtə]

heir	trashëgimtar (m)	[traʃəgimtár]
inheritance	trashëgimi (f)	[traʃəgimí]
fortune (wealth)	pasuri (f)	[pasurí]

lease	qira (f)	[cirá]
rent (money)	qiraja (f)	[cirája]
to rent (sth from sb)	marr me qira	[mar mɛ cirá]

price	çmim (m)	[tʃmím]
cost	kosto (f)	[kósto]
sum	shumë (f)	[ʃúmə]

to spend (vt)	shpenzoj	[ʃpɛnzój]
expenses	shpenzime (f)	[ʃpɛnzímɛ]
to economize (vi, vt)	kursej	[kurséj]
economical	ekonomik	[ɛkonomík]

to pay (vi, vt)	paguaj	[pagúaj]
payment	pagesë (f)	[pagésə]
change (give the ~)	kusur (m)	[kusúr]

tax	taksë (f)	[táksə]
fine	gjobë (f)	[ɟóbə]
to fine (vt)	vendos gjobë	[vɛndós ɟóbə]

85. Post. Postal service

post office	zyrë postare (f)	[zýrə postárɛ]
mail (letters, etc.)	postë (f)	[póstə]
mailman	postier (m)	[postiér]
opening hours	orari i punës (m)	[orári i púnəs]

letter	letër (f)	[létər]
registered letter	letër rekomande (f)	[létər rɛkomándɛ]
postcard	kartolinë (f)	[kartolínə]
telegram	telegram (m)	[tɛlɛgrám]
package (parcel)	pako (f)	[páko]

money transfer	transfer parash (m)	[transfér paráʃ]
to receive (vt)	pranoj	[pranój]
to send (vt)	dërgoj	[dərgój]
sending	dërgesë (f)	[dərgésə]

address	adresë (f)	[adrésə]
ZIP code	kodi postar (m)	[kódi postár]
sender	dërguesi (m)	[dərgúɛsi]
receiver	pranues (m)	[pranúɛs]

| name (first name) | emër (m) | [émər] |
| surname (last name) | mbiemër (m) | [mbiémər] |

postage rate	tarifë postare (f)	[tarifə postárɛ]
standard (adj)	standard	[standárd]
economical (adj)	ekonomike	[ɛkonomíkɛ]

weight	peshë (f)	[péʃə]
to weigh (~ letters)	peshoj	[pɛʃój]
envelope	zarf (m)	[zarf]
postage stamp	pullë postare (f)	[pútə postárɛ]
to stamp an envelope	vendos pullën postare	[vɛndós pútən postárɛ]

Dwelling. House. Home

86. House. Dwelling

house	shtëpi (f)	[ʃtəpí]
at home (adv)	në shtëpi	[nə ʃtəpí]
yard	oborr (m)	[obór]
fence (iron ~)	gardh (m)	[garð]
brick (n)	tullë (f)	[túłə]
brick (as adj)	me tulla	[mɛ túła]
stone (n)	gur (m)	[gur]
stone (as adj)	guror	[gurór]
concrete (n)	çimento (f)	[tʃiménto]
concrete (as adj)	prej çimentoje	[prɛj tʃiméntojɛ]
new (new-built)	i ri	[i rí]
old (adj)	i vjetër	[i vjétər]
decrepit (house)	e vjetruar	[ɛ vjɛtrúar]
modern (adj)	moderne	[modérnɛ]
multistory (adj)	shumëkatëshe	[ʃuməkátəʃɛ]
tall (~ building)	e lartë	[ɛ lártə]
floor, story	kat (m)	[kat]
single-story (adj)	njëkatëshe	[ɲəkátəʃɛ]
1st floor	përdhese (f)	[pərðésɛ]
top floor	kati i fundit (m)	[káti i fúndit]
roof	çati (f)	[tʃatí]
chimney	oxhak (m)	[odʒák]
roof tiles	tjegulla (f)	[tjéguła]
tiled (adj)	me tjegulla	[mɛ tjéguła]
attic (storage place)	papafingo (f)	[papafíŋo]
window	dritare (f)	[dritárɛ]
glass	xham (m)	[dʒam]
window ledge	prag dritareje (m)	[prag dritárɛjɛ]
shutters	grila (f)	[gríla]
wall	mur (m)	[mur]
balcony	ballkon (m)	[bałkón]
downspout	ulluk (m)	[ułúk]
upstairs (to be ~)	lart	[lart]
to go upstairs	ngjitem lart	[ɲjitém lárt]

| to come down (the stairs) | zbres | [zbrɛs] |
| to move (to new premises) | lëviz | [ləvíz] |

87. House. Entrance. Lift

entrance	hyrje (f)	[hýrjɛ]
stairs (stairway)	shkallë (f)	[ʃkáɬə]
steps	shkallë (f)	[ʃkáɬə]
banister	parmak (m)	[parmák]
lobby (hotel ~)	holl (m)	[hoɬ]

mailbox	kuti postare (f)	[kutí postárɛ]
garbage can	kazan mbeturinash (m)	[kazán mbɛturínaʃ]
trash chute	ashensor mbeturinash (m)	[aʃɛnsór mbɛturínaʃ]

elevator	ashensor (m)	[aʃɛnsór]
freight elevator	ashensor mallrash (m)	[aʃɛnsór máɬraʃ]
elevator cage	kabinë ashensori (f)	[kabínə aʃɛnsóri]
to take the elevator	marr ashensorin	[mar aʃɛnsórin]

apartment	apartament (m)	[apartamént]
residents (~ of a building)	banorë (pl)	[banórə]
neighbor (masc.)	komshi (m)	[komʃí]
neighbor (fem.)	komshike (f)	[komʃíkɛ]
neighbors	komshinj (pl)	[komʃíɲ]

88. House. Electricity

electricity	elektricitet (m)	[ɛlɛktritsitét]
light bulb	poç (m)	[potʃ]
switch	çelës drite (m)	[tʃéləs drítɛ]
fuse (plug fuse)	siguresë (f)	[sigurésə]

cable, wire (electric ~)	kabllo (f)	[kábɬo]
wiring	rrjet elektrik (m)	[rjét ɛlɛktrík]
electricity meter	njehsor elektrik (m)	[ɲɛhsór ɛlɛktrík]
readings	matjet (pl)	[mátjɛt]

89. House. Doors. Locks

door	derë (f)	[dérə]
gate (vehicle ~)	portik (m)	[portík]
handle, doorknob	dorezë (f)	[dorézə]
to unlock (unbolt)	zhbllokoj	[ʒbɬokój]
to open (vt)	hap	[hap]

to close (vt)	**mbyll**	[mbyɫ]
key	**çelës** (m)	[tʃéləs]
bunch (of keys)	**tufë çelësash** (f)	[túfə tʃéləsaʃ]
to creak (door, etc.)	**kërcet**	[kərtsét]
creak	**kërcitje** (f)	[kərtsítjɛ]
hinge (door ~)	**menteshë** (f)	[mɛntéʃə]
doormat	**tapet hyrës** (m)	[tapét hýrəs]
door lock	**kyç** (m)	[kytʃ]
keyhole	**vrimë e çelësit** (f)	[vrímə ɛ tʃéləsit]
crossbar (sliding bar)	**shul** (m)	[ʃul]
door latch	**shul** (m)	[ʃul]
padlock	**dry** (m)	[dry]
to ring (~ the door bell)	**i bie ziles**	[i bíɛ zíɫɛs]
ringing (sound)	**tingulli i ziles** (m)	[tíŋuɫi i zíɫɛs]
doorbell	**zile** (f)	[zíɫɛ]
doorbell button	**çelësi i ziles** (m)	[tʃéləsi i zíɫɛs]
knock (at the door)	**trokitje** (f)	[trokítjɛ]
to knock (vi)	**trokas**	[trokás]
code	**kod** (m)	[kod]
combination lock	**kod** (m)	[kod]
intercom	**interkom** (m)	[intɛrkóm]
number (on the door)	**numër** (m)	[númər]
doorplate	**pllakë e emrit** (f)	[pɫákə ɛ émrit]
peephole	**vrimë përgjimi** (f)	[vrímə pərɟími]

90. Country house

village	**fshat** (m)	[fʃát]
vegetable garden	**kopsht zarzavatesh** (m)	[kópʃt zarzavátɛʃ]
fence	**gardh** (m)	[garð]
picket fence	**gardh kunjash**	[garð kúɲaʃ]
wicket gate	**portik** (m)	[portík]
granary	**hambar** (m)	[hambár]
root cellar	**qilar** (m)	[cilár]
shed (garden ~)	**kasolle** (f)	[kasóɫɛ]
water well	**pus** (m)	[pus]
stove (wood-fired ~)	**sobë** (f)	[sóbə]
to stoke the stove	**mbush sobën**	[mbúʃ sóbən]
firewood	**dru për zjarr** (m)	[dru pər zjár]
log (firewood)	**dru** (m)	[dru]
veranda	**verandë** (f)	[vɛrándə]
deck (terrace)	**ballkon** (m)	[baɫkón]
stoop (front steps)	**prag i derës** (m)	[prag i dérəs]
swing (hanging seat)	**kolovajzë** (f)	[kolovájzə]

91. Villa. Mansion

country house	vilë (f)	[vílə]
villa (seaside ~)	vilë (f)	[vílə]
wing (~ of a building)	krah (m)	[krah]

garden	kopsht (m)	[kopʃt]
park	park (m)	[park]
conservatory (greenhouse)	serrë (f)	[sérə]
to look after (garden, etc.)	përkujdesem	[pərkujdésɛm]

swimming pool	pishinë (f)	[piʃínə]
gym (home gym)	palestër (f)	[paléstər]
tennis court	fushë tenisi (f)	[fúʃə tɛnísi]
home theater (room)	sallon teatri (m)	[sałón tɛátri]
garage	garazh (m)	[garáʒ]

private property	pronë private (f)	[prónə privátɛ]
private land	tokë private (f)	[tókə privátɛ]

warning (caution)	paralajmërim (m)	[paralajmərím]
warning sign	shenjë paralajmëruese (f)	[ʃéɲə paralajmərúɛsɛ]

security	sigurim (m)	[sigurím]
security guard	roje sigurimi (m)	[rójɛ sigurími]
burglar alarm	alarm (m)	[alárm]

92. Castle. Palace

castle	kështjellë (f)	[kəʃtjéłə]
palace	pallat (m)	[paɫát]
fortress	kala (f)	[kalá]

wall (round castle)	mur rrethues (m)	[mur rɛθúɛs]
tower	kullë (f)	[kúłə]
keep, donjon	kulla e parë (f)	[kúła ɛ párə]

portcullis	portë me hekura (f)	[pórtə mɛ hékura]
underground passage	nënkalim (m)	[nənkalím]
moat	kanal (m)	[kanál]

chain	zinxhir (m)	[zindʒír]
arrow loop	frëngji (f)	[frəɲí]

magnificent (adj)	e mrekullueshme	[ɛ mrɛkułúɛʃmɛ]
majestic (adj)	madhështore	[maðəʃtórɛ]

impregnable (adj)	e padepërtueshme	[ɛ padɛpərtúɛʃmɛ]
medieval (adj)	mesjetare	[mɛsjɛtárɛ]

93. Apartment

apartment	apartament (m)	[apartamént]
room	dhomë (f)	[ðómə]
bedroom	dhomë gjumi (f)	[ðómə ɟúmi]
dining room	dhomë ngrënie (f)	[ðómə ŋrəniɛ]
living room	dhomë ndeje (f)	[ðómə ndéjɛ]
study (home office)	dhomë pune (f)	[ðómə púnɛ]
entry room	hyrje (f)	[hýrjɛ]
bathroom (room with a bath or shower)	banjo (f)	[báɲo]
half bath	tualet (m)	[tualét]
ceiling	tavan (m)	[taván]
floor	dysheme (f)	[dyʃɛmé]
corner	qoshe (f)	[cóʃɛ]

94. Apartment. Cleaning

to clean (vi, vt)	pastroj	[pastrój]
to put away (to stow)	vendos	[vɛndós]
dust	pluhur (m)	[plúhur]
dusty (adj)	e pluhurosur	[ɛ pluhurósur]
to dust (vt)	marr pluhurat	[mar plúhurat]
vacuum cleaner	fshesë elektrike (f)	[fʃésə ɛlɛktríkɛ]
to vacuum (vt)	thith pluhurin	[θiθ plúhurin]
to sweep (vi, vt)	fshij	[fʃij]
sweepings	plehra (f)	[pléhra]
order	rregull (m)	[réguɫ]
disorder, mess	rrëmujë (f)	[rəmújə]
mop	shtupë (f)	[ʃtúpə]
dust cloth	leckë (f)	[létskə]
short broom	fshesë (f)	[fʃésə]
dustpan	kaci (f)	[katsí]

95. Furniture. Interior

furniture	orendi (f)	[orɛndí]
table	tryezë (f)	[tryézə]
chair	karrige (f)	[karígɛ]
bed	shtrat (m)	[ʃtrat]
couch, sofa	divan (m)	[diván]
armchair	kolltuk (m)	[koɫtúk]

| bookcase | raft librash (m) | [ráft líbraʃ] |
| shelf | sergjen (m) | [sɛɾjén] |

wardrobe	gardërobë (f)	[gardəróbə]
coat rack (wall-mounted ~)	varëse (f)	[várəsɛ]
coat stand	varëse xhaketash (f)	[várəsɛ dʒakétaʃ]

| bureau, dresser | komodë (f) | [komódə] |
| coffee table | tryezë e ulët (f) | [tryézə ɛ úlət] |

mirror	pasqyrë (f)	[pascýrə]
carpet	qilim (m)	[cilím]
rug, small carpet	tapet (m)	[tapét]

fireplace	oxhak (m)	[odʒák]
candle	qiri (m)	[círi]
candlestick	shandan (m)	[ʃandán]

drapes	perde (f)	[pérdɛ]
wallpaper	tapiceri (f)	[tapitsɛrí]
blinds (jalousie)	grila (f)	[gríla]

table lamp	llambë tavoline (f)	[ɫámbə tavolínɛ]
wall lamp (sconce)	llambadar muri (m)	[ɫambadár múri]
floor lamp	llambadar (m)	[ɫambadár]
chandelier	llambadar (m)	[ɫambadár]

leg (of chair, table)	këmbë (f)	[kémbə]
armrest	mbështetëse krahu (f)	[mbəʃtétəsɛ kráhu]
back (backrest)	mbështetëse (f)	[mbəʃtétəsɛ]
drawer	sirtar (m)	[sirtár]

96. Bedding

bedclothes	çarçafë (pl)	[tʃartʃáfə]
pillow	jastëk (m)	[jasték]
pillowcase	këllëf jastëku (m)	[kəɫəf jastéku]
duvet, comforter	jorgan (m)	[jorgán]
sheet	çarçaf (m)	[tʃartʃáf]
bedspread	mbulesë (f)	[mbulésə]

97. Kitchen

kitchen	kuzhinë (f)	[kuʒínə]
gas	gaz (m)	[gaz]
gas stove (range)	sobë me gaz (f)	[sóbə mɛ gaz]
electric stove	sobë elektrike (f)	[sóbə ɛlɛktríkɛ]
oven	furrë (f)	[fúrə]

microwave oven	mikrovalë (f)	[mikroválə]
refrigerator	frigorifer (m)	[frigorifér]
freezer	frigorifer (m)	[frigorifér]
dishwasher	pjatalarëse (f)	[pjataláresɛ]

meat grinder	grirëse mishi (f)	[grírəsɛ míʃi]
juicer	shtrydhëse frutash (f)	[ʃtrýðəsɛ frútaʃ]
toaster	toster (m)	[tostér]
mixer	mikser (m)	[miksér]

coffee machine	makinë kafeje (f)	[makínə kaféjɛ]
coffee pot	kafetierë (f)	[kafɛtiérə]
coffee grinder	mulli kafeje (f)	[muɫí káfɛjɛ]

kettle	çajnik (m)	[tʃajník]
teapot	çajnik (m)	[tʃajník]
lid	kapak (m)	[kapák]
tea strainer	sitë çaji (f)	[sítə tʃáji]

spoon	lugë (f)	[lúgə]
teaspoon	lugë çaji (f)	[lúgə tʃáji]
soup spoon	lugë gjelle (f)	[lúgə ɟéɫɛ]
fork	pirun (m)	[pirún]
knife	thikë (f)	[θíkə]

tableware (dishes)	enë kuzhine (f)	[énə kuʒínɛ]
plate (dinner ~)	pjatë (f)	[pjátə]
saucer	pjatë filxhani (f)	[pjátə fildʒáni]

shot glass	potir (m)	[potír]
glass (tumbler)	gotë (f)	[gótə]
cup	filxhan (m)	[fildʒán]

sugar bowl	tas për sheqer (m)	[tas pər ʃɛcér]
salt shaker	kripore (f)	[kripórɛ]
pepper shaker	enë piperi (f)	[énə pipéri]
butter dish	pjatë gjalpi (f)	[pjátə ɟálpi]

stock pot (soup pot)	tenxhere (f)	[tɛndʒérɛ]
frying pan (skillet)	tigan (m)	[tigán]
ladle	garuzhdë (f)	[garúʒdə]
colander	kullesë (f)	[kuɫésə]
tray (serving ~)	tabaka (f)	[tabaká]

bottle	shishe (f)	[ʃíʃɛ]
jar (glass)	kavanoz (m)	[kavanóz]
can	kanoçe (f)	[kanótʃɛ]

bottle opener	hapëse shishesh (f)	[hapəsé ʃíʃɛʃ]
can opener	hapëse kanoçesh (f)	[hapəsé kanótʃɛʃ]
corkscrew	turjelë tapash (f)	[turjélə tápaʃ]
filter	filtër (m)	[fíltər]

to filter (vt)	filtroj	[filtrój]
trash, garbage (food waste, etc.)	pleh (m)	[plɛh]
trash can (kitchen ~)	kosh plehrash (m)	[koʃ pléhraʃ]

98. Bathroom

bathroom	banjo (f)	[báɲo]
water	ujë (m)	[újə]
faucet	rubinet (m)	[rubinét]
hot water	ujë i nxehtë (f)	[újə i ndzéhtə]
cold water	ujë i ftohtë (f)	[újə i ftóhtə]

toothpaste	pastë dhëmbësh (f)	[pástə ðə́mbəʃ]
to brush one's teeth	laj dhëmbët	[laj ðə́mbət]
toothbrush	furçë dhëmbësh (f)	[fúrtʃə ðə́mbəʃ]

to shave (vi)	rruhem	[rúhɛm]
shaving foam	shkumë rroje (f)	[ʃkumə rójɛ]
razor	brisk (m)	[brísk]

to wash (one's hands, etc.)	laj duart	[laj dúart]
to take a bath	lahem	[láhɛm]
shower	dush (m)	[duʃ]
to take a shower	bëj dush	[bəj dúʃ]

bathtub	vaskë (f)	[váskə]
toilet (toilet bowl)	tualet (m)	[tualét]
sink (washbasin)	lavaman (m)	[lavamán]

soap	sapun (m)	[sapún]
soap dish	pjatë sapuni (f)	[pjátə sapúni]

sponge	sfungjer (m)	[sfuɲɟér]
shampoo	shampo (f)	[ʃampó]
towel	peshqir (m)	[pɛʃcír]
bathrobe	peshqir trupi (m)	[pɛʃcír trúpi]

laundry (laundering)	larje (f)	[lárjɛ]
washing machine	makinë larëse (f)	[makinə lárəsɛ]
to do the laundry	laj rroba	[laj róba]
laundry detergent	detergjent (m)	[dɛtɛrɟént]

99. Household appliances

TV set	televizor (m)	[tɛlɛvizór]
tape recorder	inçizues me shirit (m)	[intʃizúɛs mɛ ʃirít]
VCR (video recorder)	video regjistrues (m)	[vídɛo rɛɟistrúɛs]

| radio | radio (f) | [rádio] |
| player (CD, MP3, etc.) | kasetofon (m) | [kasɛtofón] |

video projector	projektor (m)	[projɛktór]
home movie theater	kinema shtëpie (f)	[kinɛmá ʃtəpíɛ]
DVD player	DVD player (m)	[dividí plɛjər]
amplifier	amplifikator (m)	[amplifikatór]
video game console	konsol video loje (m)	[konsól vídɛo lójɛ]

video camera	videokamerë (f)	[vidɛokamérə]
camera (photo)	aparat fotografik (m)	[aparát fotografík]
digital camera	kamerë digjitale (f)	[kamérə diɟitálɛ]

vacuum cleaner	fshesë elektrike (f)	[fʃésə ɛlɛktríkɛ]
iron (e.g., steam ~)	hekur (m)	[hékur]
ironing board	tryezë për hekurosje (f)	[tryézə pər hɛkurósjɛ]

telephone	telefon (m)	[tɛlɛfón]
cell phone	celular (m)	[tsɛlulár]
typewriter	makinë shkrimi (f)	[makínə ʃkrími]
sewing machine	makinë qepëse (f)	[makínə cépəsɛ]

microphone	mikrofon (m)	[mikrofón]
headphones	kufje (f)	[kúfjɛ]
remote control (TV)	telekomandë (f)	[tɛlɛkomándə]

CD, compact disc	CD (f)	[tsɛdé]
cassette, tape	kasetë (f)	[kasétə]
vinyl record	pllakë gramafoni (f)	[pɫákə gramafóni]

100. Repairs. Renovation

renovations	renovim (m)	[rɛnovím]
to renovate (vt)	rinovoj	[rinovój]
to repair, to fix (vt)	riparoj	[riparój]
to put in order	rregulloj	[rɛguɫój]
to redo (do again)	ribëj	[ribéj]

paint	bojë (f)	[bójə]
to paint (~ a wall)	lyej	[lýɛj]
house painter	bojaxhi (m)	[bojadʒí]
paintbrush	furçë (f)	[fúrtʃə]

| whitewash | gëlqere (f) | [gəlcérɛ] |
| to whitewash (vt) | lyej me gëlqere | [lýɛj mɛ gəlcérɛ] |

wallpaper	tapiceri (f)	[tapitsɛrí]
to wallpaper (vt)	vendos tapiceri	[vɛndós tapitsɛrí]
varnish	llak (m)	[ɫak]
to varnish (vt)	lustroj	[lustrój]

101. Plumbing

water	ujë (m)	[újə]
hot water	ujë i nxehtë (f)	[újə i ndzéhtə]
cold water	ujë i ftohtë (f)	[újə i ftóhtə]
faucet	rubinet (m)	[rubinét]

drop (of water)	pikë uji (f)	[píkə úji]
to drip (vi)	pikon	[pikón]
to leak (ab. pipe)	rrjedh	[rjéð]
leak (pipe ~)	rrjedhje (f)	[rjéðjɛ]
puddle	pellg (m)	[pɛłg]

pipe	gyp (m)	[gyp]
valve (e.g., ball ~)	valvulë (f)	[valvúlə]
to be clogged up	bllokohet	[błokóhɛt]

tools	vegla (pl)	[végla]
adjustable wrench	çelës anglez (m)	[tʃéləs aŋléz]
to unscrew (lid, filter, etc.)	zhvidhos	[ʒviðós]
to screw (tighten)	vidhos	[viðós]

to unclog (vt)	zhbllokoj	[ʒbłokój]
plumber	hidraulik (m)	[hidraulík]
basement	qilar (m)	[cilár]
sewerage (system)	kanalizim (m)	[kanalizím]

102. Fire. Conflagration

fire (accident)	zjarr (m)	[zjar]
flame	flakë (f)	[flákə]
spark	shkëndijë (f)	[ʃkəndíjə]
smoke (from fire)	tym (m)	[tym]
torch (flaming stick)	pishtar (m)	[piʃtár]
campfire	zjarr kampingu (m)	[zjar kampíŋu]

gas, gasoline	benzinë (f)	[bɛnzínə]
kerosene (type of fuel)	vajgur (m)	[vajgúr]
flammable (adj)	djegëse	[djégesɛ]
explosive (adj)	shpërthyese	[ʃpərθýɛsɛ]
NO SMOKING	NDALOHET DUHANI	[ndalóhɛt duháni]

safety	siguri (f)	[sigurí]
danger	rrezik (m)	[rɛzík]
dangerous (adj)	i rrezikshëm	[i rɛzíkʃəm]

to catch fire	merr flakë	[mɛr flákə]
explosion	shpërthim (m)	[ʃpərθím]
to set fire	vë flakën	[və flákən]

arsonist	**zjarrvënës** (m)	[zjarvénəs]
arson	**zjarrvënie e qëllimshme** (f)	[zjarvéniε ε cəłímʃmε]
to blaze (vi)	**flakëron**	[flakərón]
to burn (be on fire)	**digjet**	[díɟεt]
to burn down	**u dogj**	[u doɟ]
to call the fire department	**telefonoj zjarrfikësit**	[tεlεfonój zjarfíkəsit]
firefighter, fireman	**zjarrfikës** (m)	[zjarfíkəs]
fire truck	**kamion zjarrfikës** (m)	[kamión zjarfíkəs]
fire department	**zjarrfikës** (m)	[zjarfíkəs]
fire truck ladder	**shkallë e zjarrfikëses** (f)	[ʃkáłə ε zjarfíkəsεs]
fire hose	**pompë e ujit** (f)	[pómpə ε újit]
fire extinguisher	**bombolë kundër zjarrit** (f)	[bombólə kúndər zjárit]
helmet	**helmetë** (f)	[hεlmétə]
siren	**alarm** (m)	[alárm]
to cry (for help)	**bërtas**	[bərtás]
to call for help	**thërras për ndihmë**	[θərás pər ndíhmə]
rescuer	**shpëtimtar** (m)	[ʃpətimtár]
to rescue (vt)	**shpëtoj**	[ʃpətój]
to arrive (vi)	**arrij**	[aríj]
to extinguish (vt)	**shuaj**	[ʃúaj]
water	**ujë** (m)	[újə]
sand	**rërë** (f)	[rə́rə]
ruins (destruction)	**gërmadhë** (f)	[gərmáðə]
to collapse (building, etc.)	**shembet**	[ʃémbεt]
to fall down (vi)	**rrëzohem**	[rəzóhεm]
to cave in (ceiling, floor)	**shembet**	[ʃémbεt]
piece of debris	**mbetje** (f)	[mbétjε]
ash	**hi** (m)	[hi]
to suffocate (die)	**asfiksim**	[asfiksím]
to be killed (perish)	**vdes**	[vdεs]

HUMAN ACTIVITIES

Job. Business. Part 1

103. Office. Working in the office

office (company ~)	**zyrë** (f)	[zýrə]
office (of director, etc.)	**zyrë** (f)	[zýrə]
reception desk	**recepsion** (m)	[rɛtsɛpsión]
secretary	**sekretar** (m)	[sɛkrɛtár]
secretary (fem.)	**sekretare** (f)	[sɛkrɛtárɛ]
director	**drejtor** (m)	[drɛjtór]
manager	**menaxher** (m)	[mɛnadʒér]
accountant	**kontabilist** (m)	[kontabilíst]
employee	**punonjës** (m)	[punóɲəs]
furniture	**orendi** (f)	[orɛndí]
desk	**tavolinë pune** (f)	[tavolínə púnɛ]
desk chair	**karrige pune** (f)	[karígɛ púnɛ]
drawer unit	**njësi sirtarësh** (f)	[ɲəsí sirtárəʃ]
coat stand	**varëse xhaketash** (f)	[várəsɛ dʒakétaʃ]
computer	**kompjuter** (m)	[kompjutér]
printer	**printer** (m)	[printér]
fax machine	**aparat faksi** (m)	[aparát fáksi]
photocopier	**fotokopje** (f)	[fotokópjɛ]
paper	**letër** (f)	[létər]
office supplies	**pajisje zyre** (f)	[pajísjɛ zýrɛ]
mouse pad	**shtroje e mausit** (f)	[ʃtrójɛ ɛ máusit]
sheet (of paper)	**fletë** (f)	[flétə]
binder	**dosje** (f)	[dósjɛ]
catalog	**katalog** (m)	[katalóg]
phone directory	**numerator telefonik** (m)	[numɛratór tɛlɛfoník]
documentation	**dokumentacion** (m)	[dokumɛntatsión]
brochure	**broshurë** (f)	[broʃúrə]
(e.g., 12 pages ~)		
leaflet (promotional ~)	**fletëpalosje** (f)	[flɛtəpalósjɛ]
sample	**mostër** (f)	[móstər]
training meeting	**takim trajnimi** (m)	[takím trajními]
meeting (of managers)	**takim** (m)	[takím]
lunch time	**pushim dreke** (m)	[puʃim drékɛ]

to make a copy	bëj fotokopje	[bəj fotokópjɛ]
to make multiple copies	shumëfishoj	[ʃuməfiʃój]
to receive a fax	marr faks	[mar fáks]
to send a fax	dërgoj faks	[dərgój fáks]

to call (by phone)	telefonoj	[tɛlɛfonój]
to answer (vt)	përgjigjem	[pərɟiɟɛm]
to put through	kaloj linjën	[kalój líɲən]

to arrange, to set up	lë takim	[lə takím]
to demonstrate (vt)	tregoj	[trɛgój]
to be absent	mungoj	[muɲój]
absence	mungesë (f)	[muɲésə]

104. Business processes. Part 1

business	biznes (m)	[biznés]
occupation	profesion (m)	[profɛsión]

firm	firmë (f)	[fírmə]
company	kompani (f)	[kompaní]
corporation	korporatë (f)	[korporátə]
enterprise	ndërmarrje (f)	[ndərmárjɛ]
agency	agjenci (f)	[aɟɛntsí]

agreement (contract)	marrëveshje (f)	[marəvéʃjɛ]
contract	kontratë (f)	[kontrátə]
deal	marrëveshje (f)	[marəvéʃjɛ]
order (to place an ~)	porosi (f)	[porosí]
terms (of the contract)	kushte (f)	[kúʃtɛ]

wholesale (adv)	me shumicë	[mɛ ʃumítsə]
wholesale (adj)	me shumicë	[mɛ ʃumítsə]
wholesale (n)	me shumicë (f)	[mɛ ʃumítsə]
retail (adj)	me pakicë	[mɛ pakítsə]
retail (n)	me pakicë (f)	[mɛ pakítsə]

competitor	konkurrent (m)	[konkurént]
competition	konkurrencë (f)	[konkuréntsə]
to compete (vi)	konkurroj	[konkurój]

partner (associate)	ortak (m)	[orták]
partnership	partneritet (m)	[partnɛritét]

crisis	krizë (f)	[krízə]
bankruptcy	falimentim (m)	[falimɛntím]
to go bankrupt	falimentoj	[falimɛntój]
difficulty	vështirësi (f)	[vəʃtirəsí]
problem	problem (m)	[problém]
catastrophe	katastrofë (f)	[katastrófə]

economy	**ekonomi** (f)	[ɛkonomí]
economic (~ growth)	**ekonomik**	[ɛkonomík]
economic recession	**recesion ekonomik** (m)	[rɛtsɛsión ɛkonomík]

goal (aim)	**qëllim** (m)	[cətím]
task	**detyrë** (f)	[dɛtýrə]

to trade (vi)	**tregtoj**	[trɛgtój]
network (distribution ~)	**rrjet** (m)	[rjét]
inventory (stock)	**inventar** (m)	[invɛntárʲ]
range (assortment)	**gamë** (f)	[gámə]

leader (leading company)	**lider** (m)	[lidérʲ]
large (~ company)	**e madhe**	[ɛ máðɛ]
monopoly	**monopol** (m)	[monopól]

theory	**teori** (f)	[tɛorí]
practice	**praktikë** (f)	[praktíkə]
experience (in my ~)	**përvojë** (f)	[pərvójə]
trend (tendency)	**trend** (m)	[trɛnd]
development	**zhvillim** (m)	[ʒviłím]

105. Business processes. Part 2

profit (foregone ~)	**fitim** (m)	[fitím]
profitable (~ deal)	**fitimprurës**	[fitimprúrəs]

delegation (group)	**delegacion** (m)	[dɛlɛgatsión]
salary	**pagë** (f)	[págə]
to correct (an error)	**korrigjoj**	[koriʝój]
business trip	**udhëtim pune** (m)	[uðətím púnɛ]
commission	**komision** (m)	[komisión]

to control (vt)	**kontrolloj**	[kontrołój]
conference	**konferencë** (f)	[konfɛréntsə]
license	**licencë** (f)	[litséntsə]
reliable (~ partner)	**i besueshëm**	[i bɛsúɛʃəm]

initiative (undertaking)	**nismë** (f)	[nísmə]
norm (standard)	**normë** (f)	[nórmə]
circumstance	**rrethanë** (f)	[rɛθánə]
duty (of employee)	**detyrë** (f)	[dɛtýrə]

organization (company)	**organizatë** (f)	[organizátə]
organization (process)	**organizativ** (m)	[organizatív]
organized (adj)	**i organizuar**	[i organizúarʲ]
cancellation	**anulim** (m)	[anulím]
to cancel (call off)	**anuloj**	[anulój]
report (official ~)	**raport** (m)	[rapórt]
patent	**patentë** (f)	[paténtə]

to patent (obtain patent)	patentoj	[patɛntój]
to plan (vt)	planifikoj	[planifikój]

bonus (money)	bonus (m)	[bonús]
professional (adj)	profesional	[profɛsionál]
procedure	procedurë (f)	[protsɛdúrə]

to examine (contract, etc.)	shqyrtoj	[ʃcyrtój]
calculation	llogaritje (f)	[ɫogarítjɛ]
reputation	reputacion (m)	[rɛputatsión]
risk	rrezik (m)	[rɛzík]

to manage, to run	drejtoj	[drɛjtój]
information (report)	informacion (m)	[informatsión]
property	pronë (f)	[prónə]
union	bashkim (m)	[baʃkím]

life insurance	sigurim jete (m)	[sigurím jétɛ]
to insure (vt)	siguroj	[sigurój]
insurance	sigurim (m)	[sigurím]

auction (~ sale)	ankand (m)	[ankánd]
to notify (inform)	njoftoj	[ɲoftój]
management (process)	menaxhim (m)	[mɛnadʒím]
service (~ industry)	shërbim (m)	[ʃərbím]

forum	forum (m)	[forúm]
to function (vi)	funksionoj	[funksionój]
stage (phase)	fazë (f)	[fázə]
legal (~ services)	ligjor	[liɟór]
lawyer (legal advisor)	avokat (m)	[avokát]

106. Production. Works

plant	uzinë (f)	[uzínə]
factory	fabrikë (f)	[fabríkə]
workshop	punëtori (f)	[punətorí]
works, production site	punishte (f)	[puníʃtɛ]

industry (manufacturing)	industri (f)	[industrí]
industrial (adj)	industrial	[industriál]
heavy industry	industri e rëndë (f)	[industrí ɛ rəndə]
light industry	industri e lehtë (f)	[industrí ɛ léhtə]

products	produkt (m)	[prodúkt]
to produce (vt)	prodhoj	[proðój]
raw materials	lëndë e parë (f)	[lə́ndə ɛ párə]

foreman (construction ~)	përgjegjës (m)	[pərɟéɟəs]
workers team (crew)	skuadër (f)	[skuádər]

worker	punëtor (m)	[punǝtór]
working day	ditë pune (f)	[dítǝ púnɛ]
pause (rest break)	pushim (m)	[puʃím]
meeting	mbledhje (f)	[mbléðjɛ]
to discuss (vt)	diskutoj	[diskutój]

plan	plan (m)	[plan]
to fulfill the plan	përmbush planin	[pǝrmbúʃ plánin]
rate of output	normë prodhimi (f)	[nórmǝ proðími]
quality	cilësi (f)	[tsilǝsí]
control (checking)	kontroll (m)	[kontróɬ]
quality control	kontroll cilësie (m)	[kontróɬ tsilǝsíɛ]

workplace safety	siguri në punë (f)	[sigurí nǝ púnǝ]
discipline	disiplinë (f)	[disiplínǝ]
violation	thyerje rregullash (f)	[θýɛrjɛ réguɬaʃ]
(of safety rules, etc.)		
to violate (rules)	thyej rregullat	[θýɛj réguɬat]

strike	grevë (f)	[grévǝ]
striker	grevist (m)	[grɛvíst]
to be on strike	jam në grevë	[jam nǝ grévǝ]
labor union	sindikatë punëtorësh (f)	[sindikátǝ punǝtórǝʃ]

to invent (machine, etc.)	shpik	[ʃpik]
invention	shpikje (f)	[ʃpíkjɛ]
research	kërkim (m)	[kǝrkím]
to improve (make better)	përmirësoj	[pǝrmirǝsój]
technology	teknologji (f)	[tɛknoloɟí]
technical drawing	vizatim teknik (m)	[vizatím tɛkník]

load, cargo	ngarkesë (f)	[ŋarkésǝ]
loader (person)	ngarkues (m)	[ŋarkúɛs]
to load (vehicle, etc.)	ngarkoj	[ŋarkój]
loading (process)	ngarkimi	[ŋarkími]
to unload (vi, vt)	shkarkoj	[ʃkarkój]
unloading	shkarkim (m)	[ʃkarkím]

transportation	transport (m)	[transpórt]
transportation company	agjenci transporti (f)	[aɟɛntsí transpórti]
to transport (vt)	transportoj	[transportój]

freight car	vagon mallrash (m)	[vagón máɬraʃ]
tank (e.g., oil ~)	cisternë (f)	[tsistérnǝ]
truck	kamion (m)	[kamión]

| machine tool | makineri veglash (f) | [makinɛrí vɛgláʃ] |
| mechanism | mekanizëm (m) | [mɛkanízǝm] |

industrial waste	mbetje industriale (f)	[mbétjɛ industriálɛ]
packing (process)	paketim (m)	[pakɛtím]
to pack (vt)	paketoj	[pakɛtój]

107. Contract. Agreement

contract	kontratë (f)	[kontrátə]
agreement	marrëveshje (f)	[marəvéʃɛ]
addendum	shtojcë (f)	[ʃtójtsə]

to sign a contract	nënshkruaj një kontratë	[nənʃkrúaj ɲə kontrátə]
signature	nënshkrim (m)	[nənʃkrím]
to sign (vt)	nënshkruaj	[nənʃkrúaj]
seal (stamp)	vulë (f)	[vúlə]

subject of the contract	objekt i kontratës (m)	[objékt i kontrátəs]
clause	kusht (m)	[kuʃt]
parties (in contract)	palët (m)	[pálət]
legal address	adresa zyrtare (f)	[adrésa zyrtárɛ]

to violate the contract	mosrespektim kontrate	[mosrɛspɛktím kontrátɛ]
commitment (obligation)	detyrim (m)	[dɛtyrím]
responsibility	përgjegjësi (f)	[pərɟɛɟəsí]
force majeure	forcë madhore (f)	[fórtsə maðórɛ]
dispute	mosmarrëveshje (f)	[mosmarəvéʃɛ]
penalties	ndëshkime (pl)	[ndəʃkímɛ]

108. Import & Export

import	import (m)	[impórt]
importer	importues (m)	[importúɛs]
to import (vt)	importoj	[importój]
import (as adj.)	i importuar	[i importúar]

export (exportation)	eksport (m)	[ɛksport]
exporter	eksportues (m)	[ɛksportúɛs]
to export (vi, vt)	eksportoj	[ɛksportój]
export (as adj.)	i eksportuar	[i ɛksportúar]

goods (merchandise)	mallra (pl)	[máɫra]
consignment, lot	ngarkesë (f)	[ŋarkésə]

weight	peshë (f)	[péʃə]
volume	vëllim (m)	[vəɫím]
cubic meter	metër kub (m)	[métər kúb]

manufacturer	prodhues (m)	[proðúɛs]
transportation company	agjenci transporti (f)	[aɟɛntsí transpórti]
container	kontejner (m)	[kontɛjnér]

border	kufi (m)	[kufí]
customs	doganë (f)	[dogánə]
customs duty	taksë doganore (f)	[táksə doganórɛ]

customs officer	doganier (m)	[doganiér]
smuggling	trafikim (m)	[trafikím]
contraband (smuggled goods)	kontrabandë (f)	[kontrabándə]

109. Finances

stock (share)	stok (m)	[stok]
bond (certificate)	certifikatë valutore (f)	[tsɛrtifikátə valutórɛ]
promissory note	letër me vlerë (f)	[létər mɛ vlérə]

stock exchange	bursë (f)	[búrsə]
stock price	çmimi i stokut (m)	[tʃmími i stókut]

to go down (become cheaper)	ulet	[úlɛt]
to go up (become more expensive)	rritet	[rítɛt]

share	kuotë (f)	[kuótə]
controlling interest	përqindje kontrolluese (f)	[pərcíndjɛ kontroɫúɛsɛ]

investment	investim (m)	[invɛstím]
to invest (vt)	investoj	[invɛstój]
percent	përqindje (f)	[pərcíndjɛ]
interest (on investment)	interes (m)	[intɛrés]

profit	fitim (m)	[fitím]
profitable (adj)	fitimprurës	[fitimprúrəs]
tax	taksë (f)	[táksə]

currency (foreign ~)	valutë (f)	[valútə]
national (adj)	kombëtare	[kombətárɛ]
exchange (currency ~)	këmbim valute (m)	[kəmbím valútɛ]

accountant	kontabilist (m)	[kontabilíst]
accounting	kontabilitet (m)	[kontabilitét]

bankruptcy	falimentim (m)	[falimɛntím]
collapse, crash	kolaps (m)	[koláps]
ruin	rrënim (m)	[rəním]
to be ruined (financially)	rrënohem	[rənóhɛm]
inflation	inflacion (m)	[inflatsión]
devaluation	zhvlerësim (m)	[ʒvlɛrəsím]

capital	kapital (m)	[kapitál]
income	të ardhura (f)	[tə árðura]
turnover	qarkullim (m)	[carkuɫím]
resources	burime (f)	[burímɛ]
monetary resources	burime monetare (f)	[burímɛ monɛtárɛ]

| overhead | shpenzime bazë (f) | [ʃpɛnzímɛ bázə] |
| to reduce (expenses) | zvogëloj | [zvogəlój] |

110. Marketing

marketing	marketing (m)	[markɛtíŋ]
market	treg (m)	[trɛg]
market segment	segment tregu (m)	[sɛgmént trégu]
product	produkt (m)	[prodúkt]
goods (merchandise)	mallra (pl)	[máɬra]

brand	markë (f)	[márkə]
trademark	markë tregtare (f)	[márkə trɛgtárɛ]
logotype	logo (f)	[lógo]
logo	logo (f)	[lógo]

demand	kërkesë (f)	[kərkésə]
supply	furnizim (m)	[furnizím]
need	nevojë (f)	[nɛvójə]
consumer	konsumator (m)	[konsumatór]

analysis	analizë (f)	[analízə]
to analyze (vt)	analizoj	[analizój]
positioning	vendosje (f)	[vɛndósjɛ]
to position (vt)	vendos	[vɛndós]

price	çmim (m)	[tʃmím]
pricing policy	politikë e çmimeve (f)	[politíkə ɛ tʃmímɛvɛ]
price formation	formim i çmimit (m)	[formím i tʃmímit]

111. Advertising

advertising	reklamë (f)	[rɛklámə]
to advertise (vt)	reklamoj	[rɛklamój]
budget	buxhet (m)	[budʒét]

ad, advertisement	reklamë (f)	[rɛklámə]
TV advertising	reklamë televizive (f)	[rɛklámə tɛlɛvizívɛ]
radio advertising	reklamë në radio (f)	[rɛklámə nə rádio]
outdoor advertising	reklamë ambientale (f)	[rɛklámə ambiɛntálɛ]

mass media	masmedia (f)	[masmédia]
periodical (n)	botim periodik (m)	[botím pɛriodík]
image (public appearance)	imazh (m)	[imáʒ]

slogan	slogan (m)	[slogán]
motto (maxim)	moto (f)	[móto]
campaign	fushatë (f)	[fuʃátə]

advertising campaign	fushatë reklamuese (f)	[fuʃátə rɛklamúɛsɛ]
target group	grup i synuar (m)	[grup i synúar]

business card	kartëvizitë (f)	[kartəvizítə]
leaflet (promotional ~)	fletëpalosje (f)	[flɛtəpalósjɛ]
brochure	broshurë (f)	[broʃúrə]
(e.g., 12 pages ~)		
pamphlet	pamflet (m)	[pamflét]
newsletter	buletin (m)	[bulɛtín]

signboard (store sign, etc.)	tabelë (f)	[tabélə]
poster	poster (m)	[postér]
billboard	tabelë reklamash (f)	[tabélə rɛklámaʃ]

112. Banking

bank	bankë (f)	[bánkə]
branch (of bank, etc.)	degë (f)	[dégə]

bank clerk, consultant	punonjës banke (m)	[punóɲəs bánkɛ]
manager (director)	drejtor (m)	[drɛjtór]

bank account	llogari bankare (f)	[ɬogarí bankárɛ]
account number	numër llogarie (m)	[númər ɬogaríɛ]
checking account	llogari rrjedhëse (f)	[ɬogarí rjéðəsɛ]
savings account	llogari kursimesh (f)	[ɬogarí kursímɛʃ]

to open an account	hap një llogari	[hap ɲə ɬogarí]
to close the account	mbyll një llogari	[mbýɬ ɲə ɬogarí]
to deposit into the account	depozitoj në llogari	[dɛpozitój nə ɬogarí]
to withdraw (vt)	tërheq	[tərhéc]

deposit	depozitë (f)	[dɛpozítə]
to make a deposit	kryej një depozitim	[krýɛj ɲə dɛpozitím]
wire transfer	transfer bankar (m)	[transfér bankár]
to wire, to transfer	transferoj para	[transfɛrój pará]

sum	shumë (f)	[ʃúmə]
How much?	Sa?	[sa?]

signature	nënshkrim (m)	[nənʃkrím]
to sign (vt)	nënshkruaj	[nənʃkrúaj]

credit card	kartë krediti (f)	[kártə krɛdíti]
code (PIN code)	kodi PIN (m)	[kódi pin]
credit card number	numri i kartës	[númri i kártəs
	së kreditit (m)	sə krɛdítit]

ATM	bankomat (m)	[bankomát]
check	çek (m)	[tʃɛk]
to write a check	lëshoj një çek	[ləʃój ɲə tʃék]

checkbook	bllok çeqesh (m)	[błók tʃécɛʃ]
loan (bank ~)	kredi (f)	[krɛdí]
to apply for a loan	aplikoj për kredi	[aplikój pər krɛdí]
to get a loan	marr kredi	[mar krɛdí]
to give a loan	jap kredi	[jap krɛdí]
guarantee	garanci (f)	[garantsí]

113. Telephone. Phone conversation

telephone	telefon (m)	[tɛlɛfón]
cell phone	celular (m)	[tsɛlulár]
answering machine	sekretari telefonike (f)	[sɛkrɛtarí tɛlɛfoníkɛ]

| to call (by phone) | telefonoj | [tɛlɛfonój] |
| phone call | telefonatë (f) | [tɛlɛfonátə] |

to dial a number	i bie numrit	[i bíɛ númrit]
Hello!	Përshëndetje!	[pərʃəndétjɛ!]
to ask (vt)	pyes	[pýɛs]
to answer (vi, vt)	përgjigjem	[pərɟíɟɛm]

to hear (vt)	dëgjoj	[dəɟój]
well (adv)	mirë	[mírə]
not well (adv)	jo mirë	[jo mírə]
noises (interference)	zhurmë (f)	[ʒúrmə]

receiver	marrës (m)	[márəs]
to pick up (~ the phone)	ngre telefonin	[ŋré tɛlɛfónin]
to hang up (~ the phone)	mbyll telefonin	[mbýł tɛlɛfónin]

busy (engaged)	i zënë	[i zónə]
to ring (ab. phone)	bie zilja	[bíɛ zílja]
telephone book	numerator telefonik (m)	[numɛratór tɛlɛfoník]

local (adj)	lokale	[lokálɛ]
local call	thirrje lokale (f)	[θírjɛ lokálɛ]
long distance (~ call)	distancë e largët	[distántsə ɛ lárgət]
long-distance call	thirrje në distancë (f)	[θírjɛ nə distántsə]
international (adj)	ndërkombëtar	[ndərkombətár]
international call	thirrje ndërkombëtare (f)	[θírjɛ ndərkombətárɛ]

114. Cell phone

cell phone	celular (m)	[tsɛlulár]
display	ekran (m)	[ɛkrán]
button	buton (m)	[butón]
SIM card	karta SIM (m)	[kárta sim]
battery	bateri (f)	[batɛrí]

| to be dead (battery) | e shkarkuar | [ɛ ʃkarkúaɾ] |
| charger | karikues (m) | [karikúɛs] |

menu	menu (f)	[mɛnú]
settings	parametra (f)	[paramétra]
tune (melody)	melodi (f)	[mɛlodí]
to select (vt)	përzgjedh	[pərzɟéð]

calculator	makinë llogaritëse (f)	[makínə ɫogarítəsɛ]
voice mail	postë zanore (f)	[póstə zanórɛ]
alarm clock	alarm (m)	[alárm]
contacts	kontakte (pl)	[kontáktɛ]

| SMS (text message) | SMS (m) | [ɛsɛmɛs] |
| subscriber | abonent (m) | [abonént] |

115. Stationery

| ballpoint pen | stilolaps (m) | [stiloláps] |
| fountain pen | stilograf (m) | [stilográf] |

pencil	laps (m)	[láps]
highlighter	shënjues (m)	[ʃəɲúɛs]
felt-tip pen	tushë me bojë (f)	[túʃə mɛ bójə]

| notepad | bllok shënimesh (m) | [bɫók ʃənímɛʃ] |
| agenda (diary) | agjendë (f) | [aɟéndə] |

ruler	vizore (f)	[vizórɛ]
calculator	makinë llogaritëse (f)	[makínə ɫogarítəsɛ]
eraser	gomë (f)	[gómə]
thumbtack	pineskë (f)	[pinéskə]
paper clip	kapëse fletësh (f)	[kápəsɛ flétəʃ]

glue	ngjitës (m)	[nɟítəs]
stapler	ngjitës metalik (m)	[nɟítəs mɛtalík]
hole punch	hapës vrimash (m)	[hápəs vrímaʃ]
pencil sharpener	mprehëse lapsash (m)	[mpréhəsɛ lápsaʃ]

116. Various kinds of documents

account (report)	raport (m)	[rapórt]
agreement	marrëveshje (f)	[marəvéʃjɛ]
application form	aplikacion (m)	[aplikatsión]
authentic (adj)	autentike	[autɛntíkɛ]
badge (identity tag)	kartë identifikimi (f)	[kártə idɛntifikími]
business card	kartëvizitë (f)	[kartəvizítə]
certificate (~ of quality)	certifikatë (f)	[tsɛrtifikátə]

check (e.g., draw a ~)	**çek** (m)	[tʃɛk]
check (in restaurant)	**llogari** (f)	[ɫogarí]
constitution	**kushtetutë** (f)	[kuʃtɛtútə]
contract (agreement)	**kontratë** (f)	[kontrátə]
copy	**kopje** (f)	[kópjɛ]
copy (of contract, etc.)	**kopje** (f)	[kópjɛ]
customs declaration	**deklarim doganor** (m)	[dɛklarím doganór]
document	**dokument** (m)	[dokumént]
driver's license	**patentë shoferi** (f)	[paténtə ʃoféri]
addendum	**shtojcë** (f)	[ʃtójtsə]
form	**formular** (m)	[formulár]
ID card (e.g., FBI ~)	**letërnjoftim** (m)	[lɛtərɲoftím]
inquiry (request)	**kërkesë** (f)	[kərkésə]
invitation card	**ftesë** (f)	[ftésə]
invoice	**faturë** (f)	[fatúrə]
law	**ligj** (m)	[liɟ]
letter (mail)	**letër** (f)	[létər]
letterhead	**kryeradhë** (f)	[kryɛráðə]
list (of names, etc.)	**listë** (f)	[lístə]
manuscript	**dorëshkrim** (m)	[dorəʃkrím]
newsletter	**buletin** (m)	[bulɛtín]
note (short letter)	**shënim** (m)	[ʃəním]
pass (for worker, visitor)	**lejekalim** (m)	[lɛjɛkalím]
passport	**pasaportë** (f)	[pasapórtə]
permit	**leje** (f)	[léjɛ]
résumé	**resume** (f)	[rɛsumé]
debt note, IOU	**shënim borxhi** (m)	[ʃəním bórdʒi]
receipt (for purchase)	**faturë** (f)	[fatúrə]
sales slip, receipt	**faturë shitjesh** (f)	[fatúrə ʃítjɛʃ]
report (mil.)	**raport** (m)	[rapórt]
to show (ID, etc.)	**tregoj**	[trɛgój]
to sign (vt)	**nënshkruaj**	[nənʃkrúaj]
signature	**nënshkrim** (m)	[nənʃkrím]
seal (stamp)	**vulë** (f)	[vúlə]
text	**tekst** (m)	[tɛkst]
ticket (for entry)	**biletë** (f)	[bilétə]
to cross out	**fshij**	[fʃij]
to fill out (~ a form)	**plotësoj**	[plotəsój]
waybill (shipping invoice)	**faturë dërgese** (f)	[fatúrə dərgésɛ]
will (testament)	**testament** (m)	[tɛstamént]

117. Kinds of business

accounting services	kontabilitet (m)	[kontabilitét]
advertising	reklamë (f)	[rɛklámə]
advertising agency	agjenci reklamash (f)	[aɟɛntsí rɛklámaʃ]
air-conditioners	kondicioner (m)	[konditsionér]
airline	kompani ajrore (f)	[kompaní ajrórɛ]
alcoholic beverages	pije alkoolike (pl)	[píjɛ alkoólikɛ]
antiques (antique dealers)	antikitete (pl)	[antikitétɛ]
art gallery (contemporary ~)	galeri e artit (f)	[galɛrí ɛ ártit]
audit services	shërbime auditimi (pl)	[ʃərbíme auditími]
banking industry	industri bankare (f)	[industrí bankárɛ]
bar	lokal (m)	[lokál]
beauty parlor	sallon bukurie (m)	[saⱡón bukuríɛ]
bookstore	librari (f)	[librarí]
brewery	birrari (f)	[birarí]
business center	qendër biznesi (f)	[céndər biznési]
business school	shkollë biznesi (f)	[ʃkóⱡə biznési]
casino	kazino (f)	[kazíno]
construction	ndërtim (m)	[ndərtím]
consulting	konsulencë (f)	[konsuléntsə]
dental clinic	klinikë dentare (f)	[kliníkə dɛntárɛ]
design	dizajn (m)	[dizájn]
drugstore, pharmacy	farmaci (f)	[farmatsí]
dry cleaners	pastrim kimik (m)	[pastrím kimík]
employment agency	agjenci punësimi (f)	[aɟɛntsí punəsími]
financial services	shërbime financiare (pl)	[ʃərbímɛ finantsiárɛ]
food products	mallra ushqimore (f)	[máⱡra uʃcimórɛ]
funeral home	agjenci funeralesh (f)	[aɟɛntsí funɛrálɛʃ]
furniture (e.g., house ~)	orendi (f)	[orɛndí]
clothing, garment	rroba (f)	[róba]
hotel	hotel (m)	[hotél]
ice-cream	akullore (f)	[akuⱡórɛ]
industry (manufacturing)	industri (f)	[industrí]
insurance	sigurim (m)	[sigurím]
Internet	internet (m)	[intɛrnét]
investments (finance)	investim (m)	[invɛstím]
jeweler	argjendar (m)	[arɟɛndár]
jewelry	bizhuteri (f)	[biʒutɛrí]
laundry (shop)	lavanteri (f)	[lavantɛrí]
legal advisor	këshilltar ligjor (m)	[kəʃiⱡtár liɟór]
light industry	industri e lehtë (f)	[industrí ɛ léhtə]
magazine	revistë (f)	[rɛvístə]

mail order selling	shitje me katalog (f)	[ʃítjɛ mɛ katalóg]
medicine	mjekësi (f)	[mjɛkəsí]
movie theater	kinema (f)	[kinɛmá]
museum	muze (m)	[muzé]

news agency	agjenci lajmesh (f)	[aɟɛntsí lájmɛʃ]
newspaper	gazetë (f)	[gazétə]
nightclub	klub nate (m)	[klúb nátɛ]

oil (petroleum)	naftë (f)	[náftə]
courier services	shërbime postare (f)	[ʃərbímɛ postárɛ]
pharmaceutics	industria farmaceutike (f)	[industría farmatsɛutíkɛ]
printing (industry)	shtyp (m)	[ʃtyp]
publishing house	shtëpi botuese (f)	[ʃtəpí botúɛsɛ]

radio (~ station)	radio (f)	[rádio]
real estate	patundshmëri (f)	[patundʃmərí]
restaurant	restorant (m)	[rɛstoránt]

security company	kompani sigurimi (f)	[kompaní sigurími]
sports	sport (m)	[sport]
stock exchange	bursë (f)	[búrsə]
store	dyqan (m)	[dycán]
supermarket	supermarket (m)	[supɛrmarkét]
swimming pool (public ~)	pishinë (f)	[piʃínə]

tailor shop	rrobaqepësi (f)	[robacɛpəsí]
television	televizor (m)	[tɛlɛvizór]
theater	teatër (m)	[tɛátər]
trade (commerce)	tregti (f)	[trɛgtí]
transportation	transport (m)	[transpórt]
travel	udhëtim (m)	[uðətím]

veterinarian	veteriner (m)	[vɛtɛrinér]
warehouse	magazinë (f)	[magazínə]
waste collection	mbledhja e mbeturinave (f)	[mbléðja ɛ mbɛturínavɛ]

Job. Business. Part 2

118. Show. Exhibition

exhibition, show	ekspozitë (f)	[ɛkspozítə]
trade show	panair (m)	[panaír]
participation	pjesëmarrje (f)	[pjɛsəmárjɛ]
to participate (vi)	marr pjesë	[mar pjésə]
participant (exhibitor)	pjesëmarrës (m)	[pjɛsəmárəs]
director	drejtor (m)	[drɛjtór]
organizers' office	zyra drejtuese (f)	[zýra drɛjtúɛsɛ]
organizer	organizator (m)	[organizatór]
to organize (vt)	organizoj	[organizój]
participation form	kërkesë për pjesëmarrje (f)	[kərkésə pər pjɛsəmárjɛ]
to fill out (vt)	plotësoj	[plotəsój]
details	hollësi (pl)	[hoɬəsí]
information	informacion (m)	[informatsión]
price (cost, rate)	çmim (m)	[tʃmím]
including	përfshirë	[pərfʃírə]
to include (vt)	përfshij	[pərfʃíj]
to pay (vi, vt)	paguaj	[pagúaj]
registration fee	taksa e regjistrimit (f)	[táksa ɛ rɛɟistrímit]
entrance	hyrje (f)	[hýrjɛ]
pavilion, hall	pavijon (m)	[pavijón]
to register (vt)	regjistroj	[rɛɟistrój]
badge (identity tag)	kartë identifikimi (f)	[kártə idɛntifikími]
booth, stand	kioskë (f)	[kióskə]
to reserve, to book	rezervoj	[rɛzɛrvój]
display case	vitrinë (f)	[vitrínə]
spotlight	dritë (f)	[drítə]
design	dizajn (m)	[dizájn]
to place (put, set)	vendos	[vɛndós]
to be placed	vendosur	[vɛndósur]
distributor	distributor (m)	[distributór]
supplier	furnitor (m)	[furnitór]
to supply (vt)	furnizoj	[furnizój]
country	shtet (m)	[ʃtɛt]

foreign (adj)	huaj	[húaj]
product	produkt (m)	[prodúkt]

association	shoqatë (f)	[ʃocátə]
conference hall	sallë konference (f)	[sátə konfɛréntsɛ]
congress	kongres (m)	[koŋrés]
contest (competition)	konkurs (m)	[konkúrs]

visitor (attendee)	vizitor (m)	[vizitór]
to visit (attend)	vizitoj	[vizitój]
customer	klient (m)	[kliént]

119. Mass Media

newspaper	gazetë (f)	[gazétə]
magazine	revistë (f)	[rɛvístə]
press (printed media)	shtyp (m)	[ʃtyp]
radio	radio (f)	[rádio]
radio station	radio stacion (m)	[rádio statsión]
television	televizor (m)	[tɛlɛvizór]

presenter, host	prezantues (m)	[prɛzantúɛs]
newscaster	prezantues lajmesh (m)	[prɛzantúɛs lájmɛʃ]
commentator	komentues (m)	[komɛntúɛs]

journalist	gazetar (m)	[gazɛtár]
correspondent (reporter)	reporter (m)	[rɛportér]
press photographer	fotograf gazetar (m)	[fotográf gazɛtár]
reporter	reporter (m)	[rɛportér]

editor	redaktor (m)	[rɛdaktór]
editor-in-chief	kryeredaktor (m)	[kryɛrɛdaktór]

to subscribe (to ...)	abonohem	[abonóhɛm]
subscription	abonim (m)	[aboním]
subscriber	abonent (m)	[abonént]
to read (vi, vt)	lexoj	[lɛdzój]
reader	lexues (m)	[lɛdzúɛs]

circulation (of newspaper)	qarkullim (m)	[carkułím]
monthly (adj)	mujore	[mujórɛ]
weekly (adj)	javor	[javór]
issue (edition)	edicion (m)	[ɛditsión]
new (~ issue)	i ri	[i rí]

headline	kryeradhë (f)	[kryɛráðə]
short article	artikull i shkurtër (m)	[artíkuł i ʃkúrtər]
column (regular article)	rubrikë (f)	[rubríkə]
article	artikull (m)	[artíkuł]
page	faqe (f)	[fácɛ]

reportage, report	reportazh (m)	[rɛportáʒ]
event (happening)	ceremoni (f)	[tsɛrɛmoní]
sensation (news)	ndjesi (f)	[ndjɛsí]
scandal	skandal (m)	[skandál]
scandalous (adj)	skandaloz	[skandalóz]
great (~ scandal)	i madh	[i máð]

show (e.g., cooking ~)	emision (m)	[ɛmisión]
interview	intervistë (f)	[intɛrvístə]
live broadcast	lidhje direkte (f)	[líðjɛ diréktɛ]
channel	kanal (m)	[kanál]

120. Agriculture

agriculture	agrikulturë (f)	[agrikultúrə]
peasant (masc.)	fshatar (m)	[fʃatár]
peasant (fem.)	fshatare (f)	[fʃatárɛ]
farmer	fermer (m)	[fɛrmér]

| tractor (farm ~) | traktor (m) | [traktór] |
| combine, harvester | autokombajnë (f) | [autokombájnə] |

plow	plug (m)	[plug]
to plow (vi, vt)	lëroj	[lərój]
plowland	tokë bujqësore (f)	[tókə bujcəsórɛ]
furrow (in field)	brazdë (f)	[brázdə]

to sow (vi, vt)	mbjell	[mbjéɬ]
seeder	mbjellës (m)	[mbjéɬəs]
sowing (process)	mbjellje (f)	[mbjéɬjɛ]

| scythe | kosë (f) | [kósə] |
| to mow, to scythe | kosit | [kosít] |

| spade (tool) | lopatë (f) | [lopátə] |
| to till (vt) | lëroj | [lərój] |

hoe	shat (m)	[ʃat]
to hoe, to weed	prashis	[praʃís]
weed (plant)	bar i keq (m)	[bar i kɛc]

watering can	vaditës (m)	[vadítəs]
to water (plants)	ujis	[ujís]
watering (act)	vaditje (f)	[vadítjɛ]

| pitchfork | sfurk (m) | [sfúrk] |
| rake | grabujë (f) | [grabújə] |

| fertilizer | pleh (m) | [plɛh] |
| to fertilize (vt) | hedh pleh | [hɛð pléh] |

manure (fertilizer)	pleh kafshësh (m)	[plɛh káfʃəʃ]
field	fushë (f)	[fúʃə]
meadow	lëndinë (f)	[ləndínə]
vegetable garden	kopsht zarzavatesh (m)	[kópʃt zarzavátɛʃ]
orchard (e.g., apple ~)	kopsht frutor (m)	[kópʃt frutór]

to graze (vt)	kullos	[kuɫós]
herder (herdsman)	bari (m)	[bari]
pasture	kullota (f)	[kuɫóta]

| cattle breeding | mbarështim bagëtish (m) | [mbarəʃtím bagətíʃ] |
| sheep farming | rritje e deleve (f) | [rítjɛ ɛ délɛvɛ] |

plantation	plantacion (m)	[plantatsión]
row (garden bed ~s)	rresht (m)	[réʃt]
hothouse	serë (f)	[sérə]

| drought (lack of rain) | thatësirë (f) | [θatəsírə] |
| dry (~ summer) | e thatë | [ɛ θátə] |

grain	drithë (m)	[dríθə]
cereal crops	drithëra (pl)	[dríθəra]
to harvest, to gather	korr	[kor]

miller (person)	mullixhi (m)	[muɫidʒí]
mill (e.g., gristmill)	mulli (m)	[muɫí]
to grind (grain)	bluaj	[blúaj]
flour	miell (m)	[míɛɫ]
straw	kashtë (f)	[káʃtə]

121. Building. Building process

construction site	kantier ndërtimi (m)	[kantiér ndərtími]
to build (vt)	ndërtoj	[ndərtój]
construction worker	punëtor ndërtimi (m)	[punətór ndərtími]

project	projekt (m)	[projékt]
architect	arkitekt (m)	[arkitékt]
worker	punëtor (m)	[punətór]

foundation (of a building)	themel (m)	[θɛmél]
roof	çati (f)	[tʃatí]
foundation pile	shtyllë themeli (f)	[ʃtýɫə θɛméli]
wall	mur (m)	[mur]

| reinforcing bars | shufra përforcuese (pl) | [ʃúfra pərfortsúɛsɛ] |
| scaffolding | skela (f) | [skéla] |

| concrete | beton (m) | [bɛtón] |
| granite | granit (m) | [granít] |

| stone | gur (m) | [guɾ] |
| brick | tullë (f) | [túɬə] |

sand	rërë (f)	[rə́rə]
cement	çimento (f)	[tʃiménto]
plaster (for walls)	suva (f)	[súva]
to plaster (vt)	suvatoj	[suvatój]

paint	bojë (f)	[bójə]
to paint (~ a wall)	lyej	[lýɛj]
barrel	fuçi (f)	[futʃí]

crane	vinç (m)	[vintʃ]
to lift, to hoist (vt)	ngreh	[ŋɾéh]
to lower (vt)	ul	[ul]

bulldozer	buldozer (m)	[buldozéɾ]
excavator	ekskavator (m)	[ɛkskavatóɾ]
scoop, bucket	goja e ekskavatorit (f)	[gója ɛ ɛkskavatórit]
to dig (excavate)	gërmoj	[gərmój]
hard hat	helmetë (f)	[hɛlmétə]

122. Science. Research. Scientists

science	shkencë (f)	[ʃkéntsə]
scientific (adj)	shkencore	[ʃkɛntsóɾɛ]
scientist	shkencëtar (m)	[ʃkɛntsətáɾ]
theory	teori (f)	[tɛorí]

axiom	aksiomë (f)	[aksiómə]
analysis	analizë (f)	[analízə]
to analyze (vt)	analizoj	[analizój]
argument (strong ~)	argument (m)	[argumént]
substance (matter)	substancë (f)	[substántsə]

hypothesis	hipotezë (f)	[hipotézə]
dilemma	dilemë (f)	[dilémə]
dissertation	disertacion (m)	[disɛrtatsión]
dogma	dogma (f)	[dógma]

doctrine	doktrinë (f)	[doktrínə]
research	kërkim (m)	[kərkím]
to research (vt)	kërkoj	[kərkój]
tests (laboratory ~)	analizë (f)	[analízə]
laboratory	laborator (m)	[laboratóɾ]

method	metodë (f)	[mɛtódə]
molecule	molekulë (f)	[molɛkúlə]
monitoring	monitorim (m)	[monitorím]
discovery (act, event)	zbulim (m)	[zbulím]

postulate	postulat (m)	[postulát]
principle	parim (m)	[parím]
forecast	parashikim (m)	[paraʃikím]
to forecast (vt)	parashikoj	[paraʃikój]

synthesis	sintezë (f)	[sintézə]
trend (tendency)	trend (m)	[trɛnd]
theorem	teoremë (f)	[tɛorémə]

teachings	mësim (m)	[məsím]
fact	fakt (m)	[fakt]
expedition	ekspeditë (f)	[ɛkspɛdítə]
experiment	eksperiment (m)	[ɛkspɛrimént]

academician	akademik (m)	[akadɛmík]
bachelor (e.g., ~ of Arts)	baçelor (m)	[bátʃɛlor]
doctor (PhD)	doktor shkencash (m)	[doktór ʃkéntsaʃ]
Associate Professor	Profesor i Asociuar (m)	[profɛsór i asotsiúar]
Master (e.g., ~ of Arts)	Master (m)	[mastér]
professor	profesor (m)	[profɛsór]

Professions and occupations

123. Job search. Dismissal

job	punë (f)	[púnə]
staff (work force)	staf (m)	[staf]
personnel	personel (m)	[pɛrsonél]
career	karrierë (f)	[kariérə]
prospects (chances)	mundësi (f)	[mundəsí]
skills (mastery)	aftësi (f)	[aftəsí]
selection (screening)	përzgjedhje (f)	[pərzɟéðjɛ]
employment agency	agjenci punësimi (f)	[aɟɛntsí punəsími]
résumé	resume (f)	[rɛsumé]
job interview	intervistë punësimi (f)	[intɛrvístə punəsími]
vacancy, opening	vend i lirë pune (m)	[vɛnd i lírə púnɛ]
salary, pay	rrogë (f)	[rógə]
fixed salary	rrogë fikse (f)	[rógə fíksɛ]
pay, compensation	pagesë (f)	[pagésə]
position (job)	post (m)	[post]
duty (of employee)	detyrë (f)	[dɛtýrə]
range of duties	lista e detyrave (f)	[lísta ɛ dɛtýravɛ]
busy (I'm ~)	i zënë	[i zə́nə]
to fire (dismiss)	pushoj nga puna	[puʃój ŋa púna]
dismissal	pushim nga puna (m)	[puʃím ŋa púna]
unemployment	papunësi (m)	[papunəsí]
unemployed (n)	i papunë (m)	[i papúnə]
retirement	pension (m)	[pɛnsión]
to retire (from job)	dal në pension	[dál nə pɛnsión]

124. Business people

director	drejtor (m)	[drɛjtór]
manager (director)	drejtor (m)	[drɛjtór]
boss	bos (m)	[bos]
superior	epror (m)	[ɛprór]
superiors	eprorët (pl)	[ɛprórət]
president	president (m)	[prɛsidént]

chairman	kryetar (m)	[kryɛtár]
deputy (substitute)	zëvendës (m)	[zəvéndəs]
assistant	ndihmës (m)	[ndíhməs]
secretary	sekretar (m)	[sɛkrɛtár]
personal assistant	ndihmës personal (m)	[ndíhməs pɛrsonál]

businessman	biznesmen (m)	[biznɛsmén]
entrepreneur	sipërmarrës (m)	[sipərmárəs]
founder	themelues (m)	[θɛmɛlúɛs]
to found (vt)	themeloj	[θɛmɛlój]

incorporator	bashkëthemelues (m)	[baʃkəθɛmɛlúɛs]
partner	partner (m)	[partnér]
stockholder	aksioner (m)	[aksionér]

millionaire	milioner (m)	[milionér]
billionaire	bilioner (m)	[bilionér]
owner, proprietor	pronar (m)	[pronár]
landowner	pronar tokash (m)	[pronár tókaʃ]

client	klient (m)	[kliént]
regular client	klient i rregullt (m)	[kliént i régułt]
buyer (customer)	blerës (m)	[blérəs]
visitor	vizitor (m)	[vizitór]

professional (n)	profesionist (m)	[profɛsioníst]
expert	ekspert (m)	[ɛkspért]
specialist	specialist (m)	[spɛtsialíst]

| banker | bankier (m) | [bankiér] |
| broker | komisioner (m) | [komisionér] |

cashier, teller	arkëtar (m)	[arkətár]
accountant	kontabilist (m)	[kontabilíst]
security guard	roje sigurimi (m)	[rójɛ sigurími]

investor	investitor (m)	[invɛstitór]
debtor	debitor (m)	[dɛbitór]
creditor	kreditor (m)	[krɛditór]
borrower	huamarrës (m)	[huamárəs]

| importer | importues (m) | [importúɛs] |
| exporter | eksportues (m) | [ɛksportúɛs] |

manufacturer	prodhues (m)	[proðúɛs]
distributor	distributor (m)	[distributór]
middleman	ndërmjetës (m)	[ndərmjétəs]

consultant	këshilltar (m)	[kəʃiłtár]
sales representative	përfaqësues i shitjeve (m)	[pərfacəsúɛs i ʃitjévɛ]
agent	agjent (m)	[aɟént]
insurance agent	agjent sigurimesh (m)	[aɟént sigurímɛʃ]

125. Service professions

cook	kuzhinier (m)	[kuʒiniér]
chef (kitchen chef)	shef kuzhine (m)	[ʃɛf kuʒínɛ]
baker	furrtar (m)	[furtár]
bartender	banakier (m)	[banakiér]
waiter	kamerier (m)	[kamɛriér]
waitress	kameriere (f)	[kamɛriérɛ]
lawyer, attorney	avokat (m)	[avokát]
lawyer (legal expert)	jurist (m)	[juríst]
notary public	noter (m)	[notér]
electrician	elektricist (m)	[ɛlɛktritsíst]
plumber	hidraulik (m)	[hidraulík]
carpenter	marangoz (m)	[maraŋóz]
masseur	masazhist (m)	[masaʒíst]
masseuse	masazhiste (f)	[masaʒístɛ]
doctor	mjek (m)	[mjék]
taxi driver	shofer taksie (m)	[ʃofér taksíɛ]
driver	shofer (m)	[ʃofér]
delivery man	postier (m)	[postiér]
chambermaid	pastruese (f)	[pastrúɛsɛ]
security guard	roje sigurimi (m)	[rójɛ sigurími]
flight attendant (fem.)	stjuardesë (f)	[stjuardésə]
schoolteacher	mësues (m)	[məsúɛs]
librarian	punonjës biblioteke (m)	[punóɲəs bibliotékɛ]
translator	përkthyes (m)	[pərkθýɛs]
interpreter	përkthyes (m)	[pərkθýɛs]
guide	udhërrëfyes (m)	[uðərəfýɛs]
hairdresser	parukiere (f)	[parukiérɛ]
mailman	postier (m)	[postiér]
salesman (store staff)	shitës (m)	[ʃítəs]
gardener	kopshtar (m)	[kopʃtár]
domestic servant	shërbëtor (m)	[ʃərbətór]
maid (female servant)	shërbëtore (f)	[ʃərbətórɛ]
cleaner (cleaning lady)	pastruese (f)	[pastrúɛsɛ]

126. Military professions and ranks

private	ushtar (m)	[uʃtár]
sergeant	rreshter (m)	[rɛʃtér]

| lieutenant | toger (m) | [togér] |
| captain | kapiten (m) | [kapitén] |

major	major (m)	[majór]
colonel	kolonel (m)	[kolonél]
general	gjeneral (m)	[ɟɛnɛrál]
marshal	marshall (m)	[marʃáɫ]
admiral	admiral (m)	[admirál]

military (n)	ushtri (f)	[uʃtrí]
soldier	ushtar (m)	[uʃtár]
officer	oficer (m)	[ofitsér]
commander	komandant (m)	[komandánt]

border guard	roje kufiri (m)	[rójɛ kufíri]
radio operator	radist (m)	[radíst]
scout (searcher)	eksplorues (m)	[ɛksplorúɛs]
pioneer (sapper)	xhenier (m)	[dʒɛniér]
marksman	shënjues (m)	[ʃəɲúɛs]
navigator	navigues (m)	[navigúɛs]

127. Officials. Priests

| king | mbret (m) | [mbrét] |
| queen | mbretëreshë (f) | [mbrɛtəréʃə] |

| prince | princ (m) | [prints] |
| princess | princeshë (f) | [printséʃə] |

| czar | car (m) | [tsár] |
| czarina | carina (f) | [tsarína] |

president	president (m)	[prɛsidént]
Secretary (minister)	ministër (m)	[minístər]
prime minister	kryeministër (m)	[kryɛminístər]
senator	senator (m)	[sɛnatór]

diplomat	diplomat (m)	[diplomát]
consul	konsull (m)	[kónsuɫ]
ambassador	ambasador (m)	[ambasadór]
counselor (diplomatic officer)	këshilltar diplomatik (m)	[kəʃiɫtár diplomatík]

| official, functionary (civil servant) | zyrtar (m) | [zyrtár] |

prefect	prefekt (m)	[prɛfékt]
mayor	kryetar komune (m)	[kryɛtár komúnɛ]
judge	gjykatës (m)	[ɟykátəs]
prosecutor (e.g., district attorney)	prokuror (m)	[prokurór]

missionary	misionar (m)	[misionár]
monk	murg (m)	[murg]
abbot	abat (m)	[abát]
rabbi	rabin (m)	[rabín]

vizier	vezir (m)	[vɛzír]
shah	shah (m)	[ʃah]
sheikh	sheik (m)	[ʃéik]

128. Agricultural professions

beekeeper	bletar (m)	[blɛtár]
herder, shepherd	bari (m)	[barí]
agronomist	agronom (m)	[agronóm]
cattle breeder	rritës bagëtish (m)	[rítəs bagətíʃ]
veterinarian	veteriner (m)	[vɛtɛrinér]

farmer	fermer (m)	[fɛrmér]
winemaker	prodhues verërash (m)	[proðúɛs vérəraʃ]
zoologist	zoolog (m)	[zoológ]
cowboy	lopar (m)	[lopár]

129. Art professions

actor	aktor (m)	[aktór]
actress	aktore (f)	[aktórɛ]

singer (masc.)	këngëtar (m)	[kəŋətár]
singer (fem.)	këngëtare (f)	[kəŋətárɛ]

dancer (masc.)	valltar (m)	[vałtár]
dancer (fem.)	valltare (f)	[vałtárɛ]

performer (masc.)	artist (m)	[artíst]
performer (fem.)	artiste (f)	[artístɛ]

musician	muzikant (m)	[muzikánt]
pianist	pianist (m)	[pianíst]
guitar player	kitarist (m)	[kitaríst]

conductor (orchestra ~)	dirigjent (m)	[diriɟént]
composer	kompozitor (m)	[kompozitór]
impresario	organizator (m)	[organizatór]

film director	regjisor (m)	[rɛɟisór]
producer	producent (m)	[produtsént]
scriptwriter	skenarist (m)	[skɛnaríst]
critic	kritik (m)	[kritík]

writer	shkrimtar (m)	[ʃkrimtár]
poet	poet (m)	[poét]
sculptor	skulptor (m)	[skulptór]
artist (painter)	piktor (m)	[piktór]

juggler	zhongler (m)	[ʒoŋlér]
clown	kloun (m)	[kloún]
acrobat	akrobat (m)	[akrobát]
magician	magjistar (m)	[maɉistár]

130. Various professions

doctor	mjek (m)	[mjék]
nurse	infermiere (f)	[infɛrmiérɛ]
psychiatrist	psikiatër (m)	[psikiátər]
dentist	dentist (m)	[dɛntíst]
surgeon	kirurg (m)	[kirúrg]

astronaut	astronaut (m)	[astronaút]
astronomer	astronom (m)	[astronóm]
pilot	pilot (m)	[pilót]

driver (of taxi, etc.)	shofer (m)	[ʃofér]
engineer (train driver)	makinist (m)	[makiníst]
mechanic	mekanik (m)	[mɛkaník]

miner	minator (m)	[minatór]
worker	punëtor (m)	[punətór]
locksmith	bravandreqës (m)	[bravandrécəs]
joiner (carpenter)	marangoz (m)	[maraŋóz]
turner (lathe operator)	tornitor (m)	[tornitór]
construction worker	punëtor ndërtimi (m)	[punətór ndərtími]
welder	saldator (m)	[saldatór]

professor (title)	profesor (m)	[profɛsór]
architect	arkitekt (m)	[arkitékt]
historian	historian (m)	[historián]
scientist	shkencëtar (m)	[ʃkɛntsətár]
physicist	fizikant (m)	[fizikánt]
chemist (scientist)	kimist (m)	[kimíst]

archeologist	arkeolog (m)	[arkɛológ]
geologist	gjeolog (m)	[ɟɛológ]
researcher (scientist)	studiues (m)	[studiúɛs]

| babysitter | dado (f) | [dádo] |
| teacher, educator | mësues (m) | [məsúɛs] |

| editor | redaktor (m) | [rɛdaktór] |
| editor-in-chief | kryeredaktor (m) | [kryɛrɛdaktór] |

| correspondent | korrespondent (m) | [korɛspondént] |
| typist (fem.) | daktilografiste (f) | [daktilografístɛ] |

designer	projektues (m)	[projɛktúɛs]
computer expert	ekspert kompjuterësh (m)	[ɛkspért kompjutérəʃ]
programmer	programues (m)	[programúɛs]
engineer (designer)	inxhinier (m)	[indʒiniér]

sailor	marinar (m)	[marinár]
seaman	marinar (m)	[marinár]
rescuer	shpëtimtar (m)	[ʃpətimtár]

fireman	zjarrfikës (m)	[zjarfíkəs]
police officer	polic (m)	[políts]
watchman	roje (f)	[rójɛ]
detective	detektiv (m)	[dɛtɛktív]

customs officer	doganier (m)	[doganiér]
bodyguard	truprojë (f)	[truprójə]
prison guard	gardian burgu (m)	[gardián búrgu]
inspector	inspektor (m)	[inspɛktór]

sportsman	sportist (m)	[sportíst]
trainer, coach	trajner (m)	[trajnér]
butcher	kasap (m)	[kasáp]
cobbler (shoe repairer)	këpucëtar (m)	[kəputsətár]
merchant	tregtar (m)	[trɛgtár]
loader (person)	ngarkues (m)	[ŋarkúɛs]

| fashion designer | stilist (m) | [stilíst] |
| model (fem.) | modele (f) | [modélɛ] |

131. Occupations. Social status

| schoolboy | nxënës (m) | [ndzə́nəs] |
| student (college ~) | student (m) | [studént] |

philosopher	filozof (m)	[filozóf]
economist	ekonomist (m)	[ɛkonomíst]
inventor	shpikës (m)	[ʃpíkəs]

unemployed (n)	i papunë (m)	[i papúnə]
retiree	pensionist (m)	[pɛnsioníst]
spy, secret agent	spiun (m)	[spiún]

prisoner	i burgosur (m)	[i burgósur]
striker	grevist (m)	[grɛvíst]
bureaucrat	burokrat (m)	[burokrát]
traveler (globetrotter)	udhëtar (m)	[uðətár]
gay, homosexual (n)	homoseksual (m)	[homosɛksuál]

hacker	**haker** (m)	[hakér]
hippie	**hipik** (m)	[hipík]
bandit	**bandit** (m)	[bandít]
hit man, killer	**vrasës** (m)	[vrásəs]
drug addict	**narkoman** (m)	[narkomán]
drug dealer	**trafikant droge** (m)	[trafikánt drógɛ]
prostitute (fem.)	**prostitutë** (f)	[prostitútə]
pimp	**tutor** (m)	[tutór]
sorcerer	**magjistar** (m)	[maɟistár]
sorceress (evil ~)	**shtrigë** (f)	[ʃtrígə]
pirate	**pirat** (m)	[pirát]
slave	**skllav** (m)	[skɫav]
samurai	**samurai** (m)	[samurái]
savage (primitive)	**i egër** (m)	[i égər]

Sports

132. Kinds of sports. Sportspersons

sportsman	**sportist** (m)	[sportíst]
kind of sports	**lloj sporti** (m)	[łoj spórti]
basketball	**basketboll** (m)	[baskɛtbół]
basketball player	**basketbollist** (m)	[baskɛtbołíst]
baseball	**bejsboll** (m)	[bɛjsbół]
baseball player	**lojtar bejsbolli** (m)	[lojtár bɛjsbółi]
soccer	**futboll** (m)	[futbół]
soccer player	**futbollist** (m)	[futbołíst]
goalkeeper	**portier** (m)	[portiér]
hockey	**hokej** (m)	[hokéj]
hockey player	**lojtar hokeji** (m)	[lojtár hokéji]
volleyball	**volejboll** (m)	[volɛjbół]
volleyball player	**volejbollist** (m)	[volɛjbołíst]
boxing	**boks** (m)	[boks]
boxer	**boksier** (m)	[boksiér]
wrestling	**mundje** (f)	[múndjɛ]
wrestler	**mundës** (m)	[múndəs]
karate	**karate** (f)	[karátɛ]
karate fighter	**karateist** (m)	[karatɛíst]
judo	**xhudo** (f)	[dʒúdo]
judo athlete	**xhudist** (m)	[dʒudíst]
tennis	**tenis** (m)	[tɛnís]
tennis player	**tenist** (m)	[tɛníst]
swimming	**not** (m)	[not]
swimmer	**notar** (m)	[notár]
fencing	**skerma** (f)	[skérma]
fencer	**skermist** (m)	[skɛrmíst]
chess	**shah** (m)	[ʃah]
chess player	**shahist** (m)	[ʃahíst]

alpinism	alpinizëm (m)	[alpinízəm]
alpinist	alpinist (m)	[alpiníst]
running	vrapim (m)	[vrapím]
runner	vrapues (m)	[vrapúɛs]
athletics	atletikë (f)	[atlɛtíkə]
athlete	atlet (m)	[atlét]
horseback riding	kalërim (m)	[kalərím]
horse rider	kalorës (m)	[kalórəs]
figure skating	patinazh (m)	[patináʒ]
figure skater (masc.)	patinator (m)	[patinatór]
figure skater (fem.)	patinatore (f)	[patinatórɛ]
powerlifting	peshëngritje (f)	[pɛʃəŋrítjɛ]
powerlifter	peshëngritës (m)	[pɛʃəŋrítəs]
car racing	garë me makina (f)	[gárə mɛ makína]
racer (driver)	shofer garash (m)	[ʃofér gáraʃ]
cycling	çiklizëm (m)	[tʃiklízəm]
cyclist	çiklist (m)	[tʃiklíst]
broad jump	kërcim së gjati (m)	[kərtsím sə ɟáti]
pole vault	kërcim së larti (m)	[kərtsím sə lárti]
jumper	kërcyes (m)	[kərtsýɛs]

133. Kinds of sports. Miscellaneous

football	futboll amerikan (m)	[futbóɫ amɛrikán]
badminton	badminton (m)	[bádminton]
biathlon	biatlon (m)	[biatlón]
billiards	bilardo (f)	[bilárdo]
bobsled	bobsled (m)	[bobsléd]
bodybuilding	bodybuilding (m)	[bodybuildíŋ]
water polo	vaterpol (m)	[vatɛrpól]
handball	hendboll (m)	[hɛndbóɫ]
golf	golf (m)	[golf]
rowing, crew	kanotazh (m)	[kanotáʒ]
scuba diving	zhytje (f)	[ʒýtjɛ]
cross-country skiing	skijim nordik (m)	[skijím nordík]
table tennis (ping-pong)	ping pong (m)	[piŋ póŋ]
sailing	lundrim me vela (m)	[lundrím mɛ véla]
rally racing	garë rally (f)	[gárə ráɫy]
rugby	ragbi (m)	[rágbi]

| snowboarding | snoubord (m) | [snoubórd] |
| archery | gjuajtje me hark (f) | [ɰúajtjɛ mɛ hárk] |

134. Gym

| barbell | peshë (f) | [péʃə] |
| dumbbells | gira (f) | [gíra] |

training machine	makinë trajnimi (f)	[makínə trajními]
exercise bicycle	biçikletë ushtrimesh (f)	[bitʃiklétə uʃtrímɛʃ]
treadmill	makinë vrapi (f)	[makínə vrápi]

horizontal bar	tra horizontal (m)	[tra horizontál]
parallel bars	trarë paralele (pl)	[trárə paralélɛ]
vault (vaulting horse)	kaluç (m)	[kalútʃ]
mat (exercise ~)	tapet gjimnastike (m)	[tapét ɰimnastíkɛ]

jump rope	litar kërcimi (m)	[litár kərtsími]
aerobics	aerobik (m)	[aɛrobík]
yoga	joga (f)	[jóga]

135. Hockey

hockey	hokej (m)	[hokéj]
hockey player	lojtar hokeji (m)	[lojtár hokéji]
to play hockey	luaj hokej	[lúaj hokéj]
ice	akull (m)	[ákuɫ]

puck	top hokeji (m)	[top hokéji]
hockey stick	shkop hokeji (m)	[ʃkop hokéji]
ice skates	patina akulli (pl)	[patína ákuɫi]

board (ice hockey rink ~)	fushë hokeji (f)	[fúʃə hokéji]
shot	gjuajtje (f)	[ɰúajtjɛ]
goaltender	portier (m)	[portiér]
goal (score)	gol (m)	[gol]
to score a goal	shënoj gol	[ʃənój gol]

period	pjesë (f)	[pjésə]
second period	pjesa e dytë	[pjésa ɛ dýtə]
substitutes bench	stol i rezervave (m)	[stol i rɛzérvavɛ]

136. Soccer

| soccer | futboll (m) | [futbóɫ] |
| soccer player | futbollist (m) | [futboɫíst] |

to play soccer	luaj futboll	[lúaj futbóɫ]
major league	liga e parë (f)	[líga ɛ párə]
soccer club	klub futbolli (m)	[klúb futbóɫi]
coach	trajner (m)	[trajnér]
owner, proprietor	pronar (m)	[pronár]

team	skuadër (f)	[skuádər]
team captain	kapiteni i skuadrës (m)	[kapiténi i skuádrəs]
player	lojtar (m)	[lojtár]
substitute	zëvendësues (m)	[zəvɛndəsúɛs]

forward	sulmues (m)	[sulmúɛs]
center forward	qendërsulmues (m)	[cɛndərsulmúɛs]
scorer	golashënues (m)	[golaʃənúɛs]
defender, back	mbrojtës (m)	[mbrójtəs]
midfielder, halfback	mesfushor (m)	[mɛsfuʃór]

match	ndeshje (f)	[ndéʃjɛ]
to meet (vi, vt)	takoj	[takój]
final	finale	[finálɛ]
semi-final	gjysmë-finale (f)	[ɟýsmə-finálɛ]
championship	kampionat (m)	[kampionát]

period, half	pjesë (f)	[pjésə]
first period	pjesa e parë (f)	[pjésa ɛ párə]
half-time	pushim (m)	[puʃím]

goal	gol (m)	[gol]
goalkeeper	portier (m)	[portiér]
goalpost	shtyllë (f)	[ʃtýɫə]
crossbar	traversa (f)	[travérsa]
net	rrjetë (f)	[rjétə]
to concede a goal	pësoj gol	[pəsój gol]

ball	top (m)	[top]
pass	pas (m)	[pas]
kick	goditje (f)	[godítjɛ]
to kick (~ the ball)	godas	[godás]
free kick (direct ~)	goditje e lirë (f)	[godítjɛ ɛ lírə]
corner kick	goditje nga këndi (f)	[godítjɛ ŋa kəndi]

attack	sulm (m)	[sulm]
counterattack	kundërsulm (m)	[kundərsúlm]
combination	kombinim (m)	[kombiním]

referee	arbitër (m)	[arbítər]
to blow the whistle	i bie bilbilit	[i bíɛ bilbílit]
whistle (sound)	bilbil (m)	[bilbíl]
foul, misconduct	faull (m)	[faúɫ]
to commit a foul	faulloj	[fauɫój]
to send off	nxjerr nga loja	[ndzjér ŋa lója]
yellow card	karton i verdhë (m)	[kartón i vérðə]

red card	karton i kuq (m)	[kartón i kúc]
disqualification	diskualifikim (m)	[diskualifikím]
to disqualify (vt)	diskualifikoj	[diskualifikój]

penalty kick	goditje dënimi (f)	[godítjɛ dəními]
wall	mur (m)	[mur]
to score (vi, vt)	shënoj	[ʃənój]
goal (score)	gol (m)	[gol]
to score a goal	shënoj gol	[ʃənój gol]

substitution	zëvendësim (m)	[zəvɛndəsím]
to replace (a player)	zëvendësoj	[zəvɛndəsój]
rules	rregullat (pl)	[réguɫat]
tactics	taktikë (f)	[taktíkə]

stadium	stadium (m)	[stadiúm]
stand (bleachers)	tribunë (f)	[tribúnə]
fan, supporter	tifoz (m)	[tifóz]
to shout (vi)	bërtas	[bərtás]

scoreboard	tabela e rezultateve (f)	[tabéla ɛ rɛzultátɛvɛ]
score	rezultat (m)	[rɛzultát]

defeat	humbje (f)	[húmbjɛ]
to lose (not win)	humb	[húmb]
tie	barazim (m)	[barazím]
to tie (vi)	barazoj	[barazój]

victory	fitore (f)	[fitórɛ]
to win (vi, vt)	fitoj	[fitój]

champion	kampion (m)	[kampión]
best (adj)	më i miri	[mə i míri]
to congratulate (vt)	përgëzoj	[pərgəzój]

commentator	komentues (m)	[komɛntúɛs]
to commentate (vt)	komentoj	[komɛntój]
broadcast	transmetim (m)	[transmɛtím]

137. Alpine skiing

skis	ski (pl)	[ski]
to ski (vi)	bëj ski	[bəj skí]

mountain-ski resort	resort malor për ski (m)	[rɛsórt malór pər skí]
ski lift	ashensor për ski (m)	[aʃɛnsór pər skí]

ski poles	heshta skish (pl)	[héʃta skíʃ]
slope	shpat (m)	[ʃpat]
slalom	slalom (m)	[slalóm]

138. Tennis. Golf

golf	golf (m)	[golf]
golf club	klub golfi (m)	[klúb gólfi]
golfer	golfist (m)	[golfíst]
hole	vrimë (f)	[vrímə]
club	shkop golfi (m)	[ʃkop gólfi]
golf trolley	karrocë golfi (f)	[karótsə gólfi]
tennis	tenis (m)	[tɛnís]
tennis court	fushë tenisi (f)	[fúʃə tɛnísi]
serve	servim (m)	[sɛrvím]
to serve (vt)	servoj	[sɛrvój]
racket	reket (m)	[rɛkét]
net	rrjetë (f)	[rjétə]
ball	top (m)	[top]

139. Chess

chess	shah (m)	[ʃah]
chessmen	figura shahu (pl)	[figúra ʃáhu]
chess player	shahist (m)	[ʃahíst]
chessboard	fushë shahu (f)	[fúʃə ʃáhu]
chessman	figurë shahu (f)	[figúrə ʃáhu]
White (white pieces)	të bardhat (pl)	[tə bárðat]
Black (black pieces)	të zezat (pl)	[tə zézat]
pawn	ushtar (m)	[uʃtár]
bishop	oficer (m)	[ofitsér]
knight	kalorës (m)	[kalórəs]
rook	top (m)	[top]
queen	mbretëreshë (f)	[mbrɛtəréʃə]
king	mbret (m)	[mbrét]
move	lëvizje (f)	[ləvízjɛ]
to move (vi, vt)	lëviz	[ləvíz]
to sacrifice (vt)	sakrifikoj	[sakrifikój]
castling	rokadë (f)	[rokádə]
check	shah (m)	[ʃah]
checkmate	shah mat (m)	[ʃah mat]
chess tournament	turne shahu (m)	[turné ʃáhu]
Grand Master	Mjeshtër i Madh (m)	[mjéʃtər i máð]
combination	kombinim (m)	[kombiním]
game (in chess)	lojë (f)	[lójə]
checkers	damë (f)	[dámə]

140. Boxing

boxing	**boks** (m)	[boks]
fight (bout)	**ndeshje** (f)	[ndéʃjɛ]
boxing match	**ndeshje boksi** (f)	[ndéʃjɛ bóksi]
round (in boxing)	**raund** (m)	[ráund]
ring	**ring** (m)	[riŋ]
gong	**gong** (m)	[goŋ]
punch	**goditje** (f)	[godítjɛ]
knockdown	**nokdaun** (m)	[nokdáun]
knockout	**nokaut** (m)	[nokaút]
to knock out	**hedh nokaut**	[hɛð nokaút]
boxing glove	**dorezë boksi** (f)	[dorézə bóksi]
referee	**arbitër** (m)	[arbítər]
lightweight	**peshë e lehtë** (f)	[péʃə ɛ léhtə]
middleweight	**peshë e mesme** (f)	[péʃə ɛ mésmɛ]
heavyweight	**peshë e rëndë** (f)	[péʃə ɛ rəndə]

141. Sports. Miscellaneous

Olympic Games	**Lojërat Olimpike** (pl)	[lójərat olimpíkɛ]
winner	**fitues** (m)	[fitúɛs]
to be winning	**duke fituar**	[dúkɛ fitúar]
to win (vi)	**fitoj**	[fitój]
leader	**lider** (m)	[lidér]
to lead (vi)	**udhëheq**	[uðəhéc]
first place	**vendi i parë**	[véndi i párə]
second place	**vendi i dytë**	[véndi i dýtə]
third place	**vendi i tretë**	[véndi i trétə]
medal	**medalje** (f)	[mɛdáljɛ]
trophy	**trofe** (f)	[trofé]
prize cup (trophy)	**kupë** (f)	[kúpə]
prize (in game)	**çmim** (m)	[tʃmím]
main prize	**çmimi i parë** (m)	[tʃmími i párə]
record	**rekord** (m)	[rɛkórd]
to set a record	**vendos rekord**	[vɛndós rɛkórd]
final	**finale**	[finálɛ]
final (adj)	**finale**	[finálɛ]
champion	**kampion** (m)	[kampión]
championship	**kampionat** (m)	[kampionát]

stadium	**stadium** (m)	[stadiúm]
stand (bleachers)	**tribunë** (f)	[tribúnə]
fan, supporter	**tifoz** (m)	[tifóz]
opponent, rival	**kundërshtar** (m)	[kundərʃtár]
start (start line)	**start** (m)	[start]
finish line	**cak** (m)	[tsák]
defeat	**humbje** (f)	[húmbjɛ]
to lose (not win)	**humb**	[húmb]
referee	**arbitër** (m)	[arbítər]
jury (judges)	**juri** (f)	[jurí]
score	**rezultat** (m)	[rɛzultát]
tie	**barazim** (m)	[barazím]
to tie (vi)	**barazoj**	[barazój]
point	**pikë** (f)	[píkə]
result (final score)	**rezultat** (m)	[rɛzultát]
period	**pjesë** (f)	[pjésə]
half-time	**pushim** (m)	[puʃím]
doping	**doping** (m)	[dopíŋ]
to penalize (vt)	**penalizoj**	[pɛnalizój]
to disqualify (vt)	**diskualifikoj**	[diskualifikój]
apparatus	**aparat** (m)	[aparát]
javelin	**hedhje e shtizës** (f)	[héðjɛ ɛ ʃtízəs]
shot (metal ball)	**gjyle** (f)	[ɟýlɛ]
ball (snooker, etc.)	**bile** (f)	[bílɛ]
aim (target)	**shënjestër** (f)	[ʃənéstər]
target	**shënjestër** (f)	[ʃənéstər]
to shoot (vi)	**qëlloj**	[cəɫój]
accurate (~ shot)	**e saktë**	[ɛ sáktə]
trainer, coach	**trajner** (m)	[trajnér]
to train (sb)	**stërvit**	[stərvít]
to train (vi)	**stërvitem**	[stərvítɛm]
training	**trajnim** (m)	[trajním]
gym	**palestër** (f)	[paléstər]
exercise (physical)	**ushtrime** (f)	[uʃtrímɛ]
warm-up (athlete ~)	**ngrohje** (f)	[ŋróhjɛ]

Education

142. School

school	**shkollë** (f)	[ʃkótə]
principal (headmaster)	**drejtor shkolle** (m)	[drɛjtór ʃkótɛ]
pupil (boy)	**nxënës** (m)	[ndzə́nəs]
pupil (girl)	**nxënëse** (f)	[ndzə́nəsɛ]
schoolboy	**nxënës** (m)	[ndzə́nəs]
schoolgirl	**nxënëse** (f)	[ndzə́nəsɛ]
to teach (sb)	**jap mësim**	[jap məsím]
to learn (language, etc.)	**mësoj**	[məsój]
to learn by heart	**mësoj përmendësh**	[məsój pərméndəʃ]
to learn (~ to count, etc.)	**mësoj**	[məsój]
to be in school	**jam në shkollë**	[jam nə ʃkótə]
to go to school	**shkoj në shkollë**	[ʃkoj nə ʃkótə]
alphabet	**alfabet** (m)	[alfabét]
subject (at school)	**lëndë** (f)	[lə́ndə]
classroom	**klasë** (f)	[klásə]
lesson	**mësim** (m)	[məsím]
recess	**pushim** (m)	[puʃím]
school bell	**zile e shkollës** (f)	[zílɛ ɛ ʃkótəs]
school desk	**bankë e shkollës** (f)	[bánkə ɛ ʃkótəs]
chalkboard	**tabelë e zezë** (f)	[tabélə ɛ zézə]
grade	**notë** (f)	[nótə]
good grade	**notë e mirë** (f)	[nótə ɛ mírə]
bad grade	**notë e keqe** (f)	[nótə ɛ kécɛ]
to give a grade	**vendos notë**	[vɛndós nótə]
mistake, error	**gabim** (m)	[gabím]
to make mistakes	**bëj gabime**	[bəj gabímɛ]
to correct (an error)	**korrigjoj**	[koriɟój]
cheat sheet	**kopje** (f)	[kópjɛ]
homework	**detyrë shtëpie** (f)	[dɛtýrə ʃtəpíɛ]
exercise (in education)	**ushtrim** (m)	[uʃtrím]
to be present	**jam prezent**	[jam prɛzént]
to be absent	**mungoj**	[muŋój]
to miss school	**mungoj në shkollë**	[muŋój nə ʃkótə]

to punish (vt)	ndëshkoj	[ndəʃkój]
punishment	ndëshkim (m)	[ndəʃkím]
conduct (behavior)	sjellje (f)	[sjétjɛ]

report card	dëftesë (f)	[dəftésə]
pencil	laps (m)	[láps]
eraser	gomë (f)	[gómə]
chalk	shkumës (m)	[ʃkúməs]
pencil case	portofol lapsash (m)	[portofól lápsaʃ]

schoolbag	çantë shkolle (f)	[tʃántə ʃkótɛ]
pen	stilolaps (m)	[stiloláps]
school notebook	fletore (f)	[flɛtórɛ]
textbook	tekst mësimor (m)	[tɛkst məsimór]
drafting compass	kompas (m)	[kompás]

| to make technical drawings | vizatoj | [vizatój] |
| technical drawing | vizatim teknik (m) | [vizatím tɛkník] |

poem	poezi (f)	[poɛzí]
by heart (adv)	përmendësh	[pərméndəʃ]
to learn by heart	mësoj përmendësh	[məsój pərméndəʃ]

school vacation	pushimet e shkollës (m)	[puʃímɛt ɛ ʃkótəs]
to be on vacation	jam me pushime	[jam mɛ puʃímɛ]
to spend one's vacation	kaloj pushimet	[kalój puʃímɛt]

test (written math ~)	test (m)	[tɛst]
essay (composition)	ese (f)	[ɛsé]
dictation	diktim (m)	[diktím]
exam (examination)	provim (m)	[provím]
to take an exam	kam provim	[kam provím]
experiment (e.g., chemistry ~)	eksperiment (m)	[ɛkspɛrimént]

143. College. University

academy	akademi (f)	[akadɛmí]
university	universitet (m)	[univɛrsitét]
faculty (e.g., ~ of Medicine)	fakultet (m)	[fakultét]

student (masc.)	student (m)	[studént]
student (fem.)	studente (f)	[studéntɛ]
lecturer (teacher)	pedagog (m)	[pɛdagóg]

lecture hall, room	auditor (m)	[auditór]
graduate	i diplomuar (m)	[i diplomúar]
diploma	diplomë (f)	[diplómə]

dissertation	disertacion (m)	[disɛrtatsión]
study (report)	studim (m)	[studím]
laboratory	laborator (m)	[laboratór]

lecture	leksion (m)	[lɛksión]
coursemate	shok kursi (m)	[ʃok kúrsi]
scholarship	bursë (f)	[búrsə]
academic degree	diplomë akademike (f)	[diplómə akadɛmíkɛ]

144. Sciences. Disciplines

mathematics	matematikë (f)	[matɛmatíkə]
algebra	algjebër (f)	[aḷébər]
geometry	gjeometri (f)	[ɟɛomɛtrí]

astronomy	astronomi (f)	[astronomí]
biology	biologji (f)	[bioloɟí]
geography	gjeografi (f)	[ɟɛografí]
geology	gjeologji (f)	[ɟɛoloɟí]
history	histori (f)	[historí]

medicine	mjekësi (f)	[mjɛkəsí]
pedagogy	pedagogji (f)	[pɛdagoɟí]
law	drejtësi (f)	[drɛjtəsí]

physics	fizikë (f)	[fizíkə]
chemistry	kimi (f)	[kimí]
philosophy	filozofi (f)	[filozofí]
psychology	psikologji (f)	[psikoloɟí]

145. Writing system. Orthography

grammar	gramatikë (f)	[gramatíkə]
vocabulary	fjalor (m)	[fjalór]
phonetics	fonetikë (f)	[fonɛtíkə]

noun	emër (m)	[émər]
adjective	mbiemër (m)	[mbiémər]
verb	folje (f)	[fóljɛ]
adverb	ndajfolje (f)	[ndajfóljɛ]

pronoun	përemër (m)	[pərémər]
interjection	pasthirrmë (f)	[pasθírmə]
preposition	parafjalë (f)	[parafjálə]

root	rrënjë (f)	[rə́ɲə]
ending	fundore (f)	[fundórɛ]
prefix	parashtesë (f)	[paraʃtésə]

| syllable | rrokje (f) | [rókjɛ] |
| suffix | prapashtesë (f) | [prapaʃtésə] |

| stress mark | theks (m) | [θɛks] |
| apostrophe | apostrof (m) | [apostróf] |

period, dot	pikë (f)	[píkə]
comma	presje (f)	[présjɛ]
semicolon	pikëpresje (f)	[pikəprésjɛ]
colon	dy pika (f)	[dy píka]
ellipsis	tre pika (f)	[trɛ píka]

| question mark | pikëpyetje (f) | [pikəpýɛtjɛ] |
| exclamation point | pikëçuditje (f) | [pikətʃudítjɛ] |

quotation marks	thonjëza (f)	[θóɲəza]
in quotation marks	në thonjëza	[nə θóɲəza]
parenthesis	kllapa (f)	[kɫápa]
in parenthesis	brenda kllapave	[brénda kɫápavɛ]

hyphen	vizë ndarëse (f)	[vízə ndárəsɛ]
dash	vizë (f)	[vízə]
space (between words)	hapësirë (f)	[hapəsírə]

| letter | shkronjë (f) | [ʃkróɲə] |
| capital letter | shkronjë e madhe (f) | [ʃkróɲə ɛ máðɛ] |

| vowel (n) | zanore (f) | [zanórɛ] |
| consonant (n) | bashkëtingëllore (f) | [baʃkətiŋətórɛ] |

sentence	fjali (f)	[fjalí]
subject	kryefjalë (f)	[kryɛfjálə]
predicate	kallëzues (m)	[kaɫəzúɛs]

line	rresht (m)	[réʃt]
on a new line	rresht i ri	[réʃt i rí]
paragraph	paragraf (m)	[paragráf]

word	fjalë (f)	[fjálə]
group of words	grup fjalësh (m)	[grup fjáləʃ]
expression	shprehje (f)	[ʃpréhjɛ]
synonym	sinonim (m)	[sinoním]
antonym	antonim (m)	[antoním]

rule	rregull (m)	[réguɫ]
exception	përjashtim (m)	[pərjaʃtím]
correct (adj)	saktë	[sáktə]

conjugation	lakim (m)	[lakím]
declension	rasë	[rásə]
nominal case	rasë emërore (f)	[rásə ɛmərórɛ]
question	pyetje (f)	[pýɛtjɛ]

| to underline (vt) | nënvijëzoj | [nənvijəzój] |
| dotted line | vijë me ndërprerje (f) | [víjə mɛ ndərprérjɛ] |

146. Foreign languages

language	gjuhë (f)	[ɟúhə]
foreign (adj)	huaj	[húaj]
foreign language	gjuhë e huaj (f)	[ɟúhə ɛ húaj]
to study (vt)	studioj	[studiój]
to learn (language, etc.)	mësoj	[məsój]

to read (vi, vt)	lexoj	[lɛdzój]
to speak (vi, vt)	flas	[flas]
to understand (vt)	kuptoj	[kuptój]
to write (vt)	shkruaj	[ʃkrúaj]

fast (adv)	shpejt	[ʃpɛjt]
slowly (adv)	ngadalë	[ŋadálə]
fluently (adv)	rrjedhshëm	[rjéðʃəm]

rules	rregullat (pl)	[réguɫat]
grammar	gramatikë (f)	[gramatíkə]
vocabulary	fjalor (m)	[fjalór]
phonetics	fonetikë (f)	[fonɛtíkə]

textbook	tekst mësimor (m)	[tɛkst məsimór]
dictionary	fjalor (m)	[fjalór]
teach-yourself book	libër i mësimit autodidakt (m)	[líbər i məsímit autodidákt]
phrasebook	libër frazeologjik (m)	[líbər frazɛoloɟík]

cassette, tape	kasetë (f)	[kasétə]
videotape	videokasetë (f)	[vidɛokasétə]
CD, compact disc	CD (f)	[tsɛdé]
DVD	DVD (m)	[dividí]

alphabet	alfabet (m)	[alfabét]
to spell (vt)	gërmëzoj	[gərməzój]
pronunciation	shqiptim (m)	[ʃciptím]

accent	aksent (m)	[aksént]
with an accent	me aksent	[mɛ aksént]
without an accent	pa aksent	[pa aksént]

| word | fjalë (f) | [fjálə] |
| meaning | kuptim (m) | [kuptím] |

course (e.g., a French ~)	kurs (m)	[kurs]
to sign up	regjistrohem	[rɛɟistróhɛm]
teacher	mësues (m)	[məsúɛs]

translation (process)	përkthim (m)	[pərkθím]
translation (text, etc.)	përkthim (m)	[pərkθím]
translator	përkthyes (m)	[pərkθýɛs]
interpreter	përkthyes (m)	[pərkθýɛs]
polyglot	poliglot (m)	[poliglót]
memory	kujtesë (f)	[kujtésə]

147. Fairy tale characters

Santa Claus	Santa Klaus (m)	[sánta kláus]
Cinderella	Hirushja (f)	[hirúʃja]
mermaid	sirenë (f)	[sirénə]
Neptune	Neptuni (m)	[nɛptúni]
magician, wizard	magjistar (m)	[maɟistár]
fairy	zanë (f)	[zánə]
magic (adj)	magjike	[maɟíkɛ]
magic wand	shkop magjik (m)	[ʃkop maɟík]
fairy tale	përrallë (f)	[pəráɫə]
miracle	mrekulli (f)	[mrɛkuɫí]
dwarf	xhuxh (m)	[dʒudʒ]
to turn into ...	shndërrohem ...	[ʃndəróhɛm ...]
ghost	fantazmë (f)	[fantázmə]
phantom	fantazmë (f)	[fantázmə]
monster	bishë (f)	[bíʃə]
dragon	dragua (m)	[dragúa]
giant	gjigant (m)	[ɟigánt]

148. Zodiac Signs

Aries	Dashi (m)	[dáʃi]
Taurus	Demi (m)	[démi]
Gemini	Binjakët (pl)	[biɲákət]
Cancer	Gaforrja (f)	[gafórja]
Leo	Luani (m)	[luáni]
Virgo	Virgjëresha (f)	[virɲəréʃa]
Libra	Peshorja (f)	[pɛʃórja]
Scorpio	Akrepi (m)	[akrépi]
Sagittarius	Shigjetari (m)	[ʃiɟɛtári]
Capricorn	Bricjapi (m)	[britsjápi]
Aquarius	Ujori (m)	[ujóri]
Pisces	Peshqit (pl)	[péʃcit]
character	karakter (m)	[karaktér]
character traits	tipare të karakterit (pl)	[típárɛ tə karaktérit]

behavior	**sjellje** (f)	[sjéɫjɛ]
to tell fortunes	**parashikoj fatin**	[paraʃikój fátin]
fortune-teller	**lexuese e fatit** (f)	[lɛdzúɛsɛ ɛ fátit]
horoscope	**horoskop** (m)	[horoskóp]

Arts

149. Theater

theater	teatër (m)	[tɛátər]
opera	operë (f)	[opérə]
operetta	operetë (f)	[opɛrétə]
ballet	balet (m)	[balét]
theater poster	afishe teatri (f)	[afíʃɛ tɛátri]
troupe	trupë teatrale (f)	[trúpə tɛatrálɛ]
(theatrical company)		
tour	turne (f)	[turné]
to be on tour	jam në turne	[jam nə turné]
to rehearse (vi, vt)	bëj prova	[bəj próva]
rehearsal	provë (f)	[próvə]
repertoire	repertor (m)	[rɛpɛrtór]
performance	shfaqje (f)	[ʃfácjɛ]
theatrical show	shfaqje teatrale (f)	[ʃfácjɛ tɛatrálɛ]
play	dramë (f)	[drámə]
ticket	biletë (f)	[bilétə]
box office (ticket booth)	zyrë e shitjeve	[zýrə ɛ ʃítjɛvɛ
	të biletave (f)	tə bilétavɛ]
lobby, foyer	holl (m)	[hoɫ]
coat check (cloakroom)	dhoma e xhaketave (f)	[ðóma ɛ dʒakétavɛ]
coat check tag	numri i xhaketës (m)	[númri i dʒakétəs]
binoculars	dylbi (f)	[dylbí]
usher	portier (m)	[portiér]
orchestra seats	plato (f)	[plató]
balcony	ballkon (m)	[baɫkón]
dress circle	galeria e parë (f)	[galɛría ɛ párə]
box	lozhë (f)	[lóʒə]
row	rresht (m)	[réʃt]
seat	karrige (f)	[karígɛ]
audience	publiku (m)	[publíku]
spectator	spektator (m)	[spɛktatór]
to clap (vi, vt)	duartrokas	[duartrokás]
applause	duartrokitje (f)	[duartrokítjɛ]
ovation	brohoritje (f)	[brohorítjɛ]
stage	skenë (f)	[skénə]
curtain	perde (f)	[pérdɛ]

| scenery | skenografi (f) | [skɛnografí] |
| backstage | prapaskenë (f) | [prapaskénə] |

scene (e.g., the last ~)	skenë (f)	[skénə]
act	akt (m)	[ákt]
intermission	pushim (m)	[puʃím]

150. Cinema

| actor | aktor (m) | [aktór] |
| actress | aktore (f) | [aktórɛ] |

movies (industry)	kinema (f)	[kinɛmá]
movie	film (m)	[film]
episode	episod (m)	[ɛpisód]

detective movie	triller (m)	[trił́ér]
action movie	aksion (m)	[aksión]
adventure movie	aventurë (f)	[avɛntúrə]
sci-fi movie	fanta-shkencë (f)	[fánta-ʃkéntsə]
horror movie	film horror (m)	[film horór]

comedy movie	komedi (f)	[komɛdí]
melodrama	melodramë (f)	[mɛlodrámə]
drama	dramë (f)	[drámə]

fictional movie	film fiktiv (m)	[film fiktív]
documentary	dokumentar (m)	[dokumɛntár]
cartoon	film vizatimor (m)	[film vizatimór]
silent movies	filma pa zë (m)	[fílma pa zə]

role (part)	rol (m)	[rol]
leading role	rol kryesor (m)	[rol kryɛsór]
to play (vi, vt)	luaj	[lúaj]

movie star	yll kinemaje (m)	[ył kinɛmájɛ]
well-known (adj)	i njohur	[i ɲóhur]
famous (adj)	i famshëm	[i fámʃəm]
popular (adj)	popullor	[popułór]

script (screenplay)	skenar (m)	[skɛnár]
scriptwriter	skenarist (m)	[skɛnaríst]
movie director	regjisor (m)	[rɛɟisór]
producer	producent (m)	[produtsént]
assistant	ndihmës (m)	[ndíhməs]
cameraman	kameraman (m)	[kamɛramán]
stuntman	dubla (f)	[dúbla]
double (stand-in)	dubla (f)	[dúbla]
to shoot a movie	xhiroj film	[dʒirój film]
audition, screen test	provë (f)	[próvə]

shooting	xhirim (m)	[dʒirím]
movie crew	ekip kinematografik (m)	[ɛkíp kinɛmatografík]
movie set	set kinematografik (m)	[sɛt kinɛmatografík]
camera	kamerë (f)	[kamérə]

movie theater	kinema (f)	[kinɛmá]
screen (e.g., big ~)	ekran (m)	[ɛkrán]
to show a movie	shfaq film	[ʃfac film]

soundtrack	muzikë e filmit (f)	[muzíkə ɛ filmit]
special effects	efekte speciale (pl)	[ɛféktɛ spɛtsiálɛ]
subtitles	titra (pl)	[títra]
credits	lista e pjesëmarrësve (f)	[lísta ɛ pjɛsəmárəsvɛ]
translation	përkthim (m)	[pərkθím]

151. Painting

art	art (m)	[art]
fine arts	artet e bukura (pl)	[ártɛt ɛ búkura]
art gallery	galeri arti (f)	[galɛrí árti]
art exhibition	ekspozitë (f)	[ɛkspozítə]

painting (art)	pikturë (f)	[piktúrə]
graphic art	art grafik (m)	[árt grafík]
abstract art	art abstrakt (m)	[árt abstrákt]
impressionism	impresionizëm (m)	[imprɛsionízəm]

picture (painting)	pikturë (f)	[piktúrə]
drawing	vizatim (m)	[vizatím]
poster	poster (m)	[postér]

illustration (picture)	ilustrim (m)	[ilustrím]
miniature	miniaturë (f)	[miniatúrə]
copy (of painting, etc.)	kopje (f)	[kópjɛ]
reproduction	riprodhim (m)	[riproðím]

mosaic	mozaik (m)	[mozaík]
stained glass window	pikturë në dritare (f)	[piktúrə nə dritárɛ]
fresco	afresk (m)	[afrésk]
engraving	gravurë (f)	[gravúrə]

bust (sculpture)	bust (m)	[búst]
sculpture	skulpturë (f)	[skulptúrə]
statue	statujë (f)	[statújə]
plaster of Paris	allçi (f)	[aɫtʃí]
plaster (as adj)	me allçi	[mɛ aɫtʃí]

portrait	portret (m)	[portrét]
self-portrait	autoportret (m)	[autoportrét]
landscape painting	peizazh (m)	[pɛizáʒ]

still life	natyrë e qetë (f)	[natýrə ε cétə]
caricature	karikaturë (f)	[karikatúrə]
sketch	skicë (f)	[skítsə]

paint	bojë (f)	[bójə]
watercolor paint	bojë uji (f)	[bójə úji]
oil (paint)	bojë vaji (f)	[bójə váji]
pencil	laps (m)	[láps]
India ink	bojë stilografi (f)	[bójə stilográfi]
charcoal	karbon (m)	[karbón]

to draw (vi, vt)	vizatoj	[vizatój]
to paint (vi, vt)	pikturoj	[pikturój]

to pose (vi)	pozoj	[pozój]
artist's model (masc.)	model (m)	[modél]
artist's model (fem.)	modele (f)	[modélɛ]

artist (painter)	piktor (m)	[piktór]
work of art	vepër arti (f)	[vépər árti]
masterpiece	kryevepër (f)	[kryɛvépər]
studio (artist's workroom)	studio (f)	[stúdio]

canvas (cloth)	kanavacë (f)	[kanavátsə]
easel	këmbalec (m)	[kəmbaléts]
palette	paletë (f)	[palétə]

frame (picture ~, etc.)	kornizë (f)	[kornízə]
restoration	restaurim (m)	[rɛstaurím]
to restore (vt)	restauroj	[rɛstaurój]

152. Literature & Poetry

literature	letërsi (f)	[lɛtərsí]
author (writer)	autor (m)	[autór]
pseudonym	pseudonim (m)	[psɛudoním]

book	libër (m)	[líbər]
volume	vëllim (m)	[vəlím]
table of contents	tabela e përmbajtjes (f)	[tabéla ɛ pərmbájtjɛs]
page	faqe (f)	[fácɛ]
main character	personazhi kryesor (m)	[pɛrsonáʒi kryɛsór]
autograph	autograf (m)	[autográf]

short story	tregim i shkurtër (m)	[trɛgím i ʃkúrtər]
story (novella)	novelë (f)	[novélə]
novel	roman (m)	[román]
work (writing)	vepër (m)	[vépər]
fable	fabula (f)	[fábula]
detective novel	roman policesk (m)	[román politsésk]

poem (verse)	vjershë (f)	[vjérʃə]
poetry	poezi (f)	[poɛzí]
poem (epic, ballad)	poemë (f)	[poémə]
poet	poet (m)	[poét]

fiction	trillim (m)	[triɫím]
science fiction	fanta-shkencë (f)	[fánta-ʃkéntsə]
adventures	aventurë (f)	[avɛntúrə]
educational literature	letërsi edukative (f)	[lɛtərsí ɛdukatívɛ]
children's literature	letërsi për fëmijë (f)	[lɛtərsí pər fəmíjə]

153. Circus

circus	cirk (m)	[tsírk]
traveling circus	cirk udhëtues (m)	[tsírk uðətúɛs]
program	program (m)	[prográm]
performance	shfaqje (f)	[ʃfácjɛ]

| act (circus ~) | akt (m) | [ákt] |
| circus ring | arenë cirku (f) | [arénə tsírku] |

| pantomime (act) | pantomimë (f) | [pantomímə] |
| clown | kloun (m) | [kloún] |

acrobat	akrobat (m)	[akrobát]
acrobatics	akrobaci (f)	[akrobatsí]
gymnast	gjimnast (m)	[ɟimnást]
acrobatic gymnastics	gjimnastikë (f)	[ɟimnastíkə]
somersault	salto (f)	[sálto]
athlete (strongman)	atlet (m)	[atlét]
tamer (e.g., lion ~)	zbutës (m)	[zbútəs]
rider (circus horse ~)	kalorës (m)	[kalórəs]
assistant	ndihmës (m)	[ndíhməs]

stunt	akrobaci (f)	[akrobatsí]
magic trick	truk magjik (m)	[truk maɟík]
conjurer, magician	magjistar (m)	[maɟistár]

juggler	zhongler (m)	[ʒoŋlér]
to juggle (vi, vt)	luaj	[lúaj]
animal trainer	zbutës kafshësh (m)	[zbútəs káfʃəʃ]
animal training	zbutje kafshësh (f)	[zbútjɛ káfʃəʃ]
to train (animals)	stërvit	[stərvít]

154. Music. Pop music

| music | muzikë (f) | [muzíkə] |
| musician | muzikant (m) | [muzikánt] |

| musical instrument | instrument muzikor (m) | [instrumént muzikór] |
| to play ... | i bie ... | [i bíɛ ...] |

guitar	kitarë (f)	[kitárə]
violin	violinë (f)	[violínə]
cello	violonçel (m)	[violontʃél]
double bass	kontrabas (m)	[kontrabás]
harp	lira (f)	[líra]

piano	piano (f)	[piáno]
grand piano	pianoforte (f)	[pianofórtɛ]
organ	organo (f)	[orgáno]

wind instruments	instrumente frymore (pl)	[instruméntɛ frymórɛ]
oboe	oboe (f)	[obóɛ]
saxophone	saksofon (m)	[saksofón]
clarinet	klarinetë (f)	[klarinétə]
flute	flaut (m)	[flaút]
trumpet	trombë (f)	[trómbə]

accordion	fizarmonikë (f)	[fizarmoníkə]
drum	daulle (f)	[daúɫɛ]
duo	duet (m)	[duét]
trio	trio (f)	[trío]
quartet	kuartet (m)	[kuartét]
choir	kor (m)	[kor]
orchestra	orkestër (f)	[orkéstər]

pop music	muzikë pop (f)	[muzíkə pop]
rock music	muzikë rok (m)	[muzíkə rok]
rock group	grup rok (m)	[grup rók]
jazz	xhaz (m)	[dʒaz]

| idol | idhull (m) | [íðuɫ] |
| admirer, fan | admirues (m) | [admirúɛs] |

concert	koncert (m)	[kontsért]
symphony	simfoni (f)	[simfoní]
composition	kompozicion (m)	[kompozitsión]
to compose (write)	kompozoj	[kompozój]

singing (n)	këndim (m)	[kəndím]
song	këngë (f)	[kə́ŋə]
tune (melody)	melodi (f)	[mɛlodí]
rhythm	ritëm (m)	[rítəm]
blues	bluz (m)	[blúz]

sheet music	partiturë (f)	[partitúrə]
baton	shkopi i dirigjimit (m)	[ʃkopi i diriɟímit]
bow	hark (m)	[hárk]
string	tel (m)	[tɛl]
case (e.g., guitar ~)	kuti (f)	[kutí]

Rest. Entertainment. Travel

155. Trip. Travel

tourism, travel	**turizëm** (m)	[turízəm]
tourist	**turist** (m)	[turíst]
trip, voyage	**udhëtim** (m)	[uðətím]
adventure	**aventurë** (f)	[avɛntúrə]
trip, journey	**udhëtim** (m)	[uðətím]
vacation	**pushim** (m)	[puʃím]
to be on vacation	**jam me pushime**	[jam mɛ puʃímɛ]
rest	**pushim** (m)	[puʃím]
train	**tren** (m)	[trɛn]
by train	**me tren**	[mɛ trén]
airplane	**avion** (m)	[avión]
by airplane	**me avion**	[mɛ avión]
by car	**me makinë**	[mɛ makínə]
by ship	**me anije**	[mɛ aníjɛ]
luggage	**bagazh** (m)	[bagáʒ]
suitcase	**valixhe** (f)	[valídʒɛ]
luggage cart	**karrocë bagazhesh** (f)	[karótsə bagáʒɛʃ]
passport	**pasaportë** (f)	[pasapórtə]
visa	**vizë** (f)	[vízə]
ticket	**biletë** (f)	[bilétə]
air ticket	**biletë avioni** (f)	[bilétə avióni]
guidebook	**guidë turistike** (f)	[guídə turistíkɛ]
map (tourist ~)	**hartë** (f)	[hártə]
area (rural ~)	**zonë** (f)	[zónə]
place, site	**vend** (m)	[vɛnd]
exotica (n)	**ekzotikë** (f)	[ɛkzotíkə]
exotic (adj)	**ekzotik**	[ɛkzotík]
amazing (adj)	**mahnitëse**	[mahnítəsɛ]
group	**grup** (m)	[grup]
excursion, sightseeing tour	**ekskursion** (m)	[ɛkskursión]
guide (person)	**udhërrëfyes** (m)	[uðərəfýɛs]

156. Hotel

hotel, inn	hotel (m)	[hotél]
motel	motel (m)	[motél]
three-star (~ hotel)	me tre yje	[mɛ trɛ ýjɛ]
five-star	me pesë yje	[mɛ pésə ýjɛ]
to stay (in a hotel, etc.)	qëndroj	[cəndrój]
room	dhomë (f)	[ðómə]
single room	dhomë teke (f)	[ðómə tékɛ]
double room	dhomë dyshe (f)	[ðómə dýʃɛ]
to book a room	rezervoj një dhomë	[rɛzɛrvój ɲə ðómə]
half board	gjysmë-pension (m)	[ɟýsmə-pɛnsión]
full board	pension i plotë (m)	[pɛnsión i plótə]
with bath	me banjo	[mɛ báɲo]
with shower	me dush	[mɛ dúʃ]
satellite television	televizor satelitor (m)	[tɛlɛvizór satɛlitór]
air-conditioner	kondicioner (m)	[konditsionér]
towel	peshqir (m)	[pɛʃcír]
key	çelës (m)	[tʃéləs]
administrator	administrator (m)	[administratór]
chambermaid	pastruese (f)	[pastrúɛsɛ]
porter, bellboy	portier (m)	[portiér]
doorman	portier (m)	[portiér]
restaurant	restorant (m)	[rɛstoránt]
pub, bar	pab (m), pijetore (f)	[pab], [pijɛtórɛ]
breakfast	mëngjes (m)	[mənɟés]
dinner	darkë (f)	[dárkə]
buffet	bufe (f)	[bufé]
lobby	holl (m)	[hoɬ]
elevator	ashensor (m)	[aʃɛnsór]
DO NOT DISTURB	MOS SHQETËSONI	[mos ʃcɛtəsóni]
NO SMOKING	NDALOHET DUHANI	[ndalóhɛt duháni]

157. Books. Reading

book	libër (m)	[líbər]
author	autor (m)	[autór]
writer	shkrimtar (m)	[ʃkrimtár]
to write (~ a book)	shkruaj	[ʃkrúaj]
reader	lexues (m)	[lɛdzúɛs]
to read (vi, vt)	lexoj	[lɛdzój]

reading (activity)	**lexim** (m)	[lɛdzím]
silently (to oneself)	**pa zë**	[pa zə]
aloud (adv)	**me zë**	[mɛ zə]
to publish (vt)	**botoj**	[botój]
publishing (process)	**botim** (m)	[botím]
publisher	**botues** (m)	[botúɛs]
publishing house	**shtëpi botuese** (f)	[ʃtəpí botúɛsɛ]
to come out (be released)	**botohet**	[botóhɛt]
release (of a book)	**botim** (m)	[botím]
print run	**edicion** (m)	[ɛditsión]
bookstore	**librari** (f)	[librarí]
library	**bibliotekë** (f)	[bibliotékə]
story (novella)	**novelë** (f)	[novélə]
short story	**tregim i shkurtër** (m)	[trɛgím i ʃkúrtər]
novel	**roman** (m)	[román]
detective novel	**roman policesk** (m)	[román politsésk]
memoirs	**kujtime** (pl)	[kujtímɛ]
legend	**legjendë** (f)	[lɛɟéndə]
myth	**mit** (m)	[mit]
poetry, poems	**poezi** (f)	[poɛzí]
autobiography	**autobiografi** (f)	[autobiografí]
selected works	**vepra të zgjedhura** (f)	[vépra tə zɟéðura]
science fiction	**fanta-shkencë** (f)	[fánta-ʃkéntsə]
title	**titull** (m)	[títuɫ]
introduction	**hyrje** (f)	[hýrjɛ]
title page	**faqe e titullit** (f)	[fácɛ ɛ títuɫit]
chapter	**kreu** (m)	[kréu]
extract	**ekstrakt** (m)	[ɛkstrákt]
episode	**episod** (m)	[ɛpisód]
plot (storyline)	**fabul** (f)	[fábul]
contents	**përmbajtje** (f)	[pərmbájtjɛ]
table of contents	**tabela e përmbajtjes** (f)	[tabéla ɛ pərmbájtjɛs]
main character	**personazhi kryesor** (m)	[pɛrsonáʒi kryɛsór]
volume	**vëllim** (m)	[vəɫím]
cover	**kopertinë** (f)	[kopɛrtínə]
binding	**libërlidhje** (f)	[libərlíðjɛ]
bookmark	**shënjim** (m)	[ʃəɲím]
page	**faqe** (f)	[fácɛ]
to page through	**kaloj faqet**	[kalój fácɛt]
margins	**margjinat** (pl)	[marɟínat]
annotation (marginal note, etc.)	**shënim** (m)	[ʃəním]

footnote	fusnotë (f)	[fusnótə]
text	tekst (m)	[tɛkst]
type, font	lloji i shkrimit (m)	[ɫóji i ʃkrímit]
misprint, typo	gabim ortografik (m)	[gabím ortografík]

translation	përkthim (m)	[pərkθím]
to translate (vt)	përkthej	[pərkθéj]
original (n)	origjinal (m)	[oriɟinál]

famous (adj)	i famshëm	[i fámʃəm]
unknown (not famous)	i panjohur	[i paɲóhur]
interesting (adj)	interesant	[intɛrɛsánt]
bestseller	libër më i shitur (m)	[líbər mə i ʃítur]

dictionary	fjalor (m)	[fjalór]
textbook	tekst mësimor (m)	[tɛkst məsimór]
encyclopedia	enciklopedi (f)	[ɛntsiklopɛdí]

158. Hunting. Fishing

hunting	gjueti (f)	[ɟuɛtí]
to hunt (vi, vt)	dal për gjah	[dál pər ɟáh]
hunter	gjahtar (m)	[ɟahtár]

to shoot (vi)	qëlloj	[cəɫój]
rifle	pushkë (f)	[púʃkə]
bullet (shell)	fishek (m)	[fiʃék]
shot (lead balls)	plumb (m)	[plúmb]

steel trap	grackë (f)	[grátskə]
snare (for birds, etc.)	kurth (m)	[kurθ]
to fall into the steel trap	bie në grackë	[bíɛ nə grátskə]
to lay a steel trap	ngre grackë	[ŋré grátskə]

poacher	gjahtar i jashtëligjshëm (m)	[ɟahtár i jaʃtəliɟʃəm]
game (in hunting)	gjah (m)	[ɟáh]
hound dog	zagar (m)	[zagár]
safari	safari (m)	[safári]
mounted animal	kafshë e balsamosur (f)	[káfʃə ɛ balsamósur]

fisherman, angler	peshkatar (m)	[pɛʃkatár]
fishing (angling)	peshkim (m)	[pɛʃkím]
to fish (vi)	peshkoj	[pɛʃkój]

fishing rod	kallam peshkimi (m)	[kaɫám pɛʃkími]
fishing line	tojë peshkimi (f)	[tójə pɛʃkími]
hook	grep (m)	[grép]
float, bobber	tapë (f)	[tápə]
bait	karrem (m)	[karém]

to cast a line	**hedh grepin**	[hɛð grépin]
to bite (ab. fish)	**bie në grep**	[bíɛ nə grép]
catch (of fish)	**kapje peshku** (f)	[kápjɛ péʃku]
ice-hole	**vrimë në akull** (f)	[vrímə nə ákuɬ]

fishing net	**rrjetë peshkimi** (f)	[rjétə pɛʃkími]
boat	**varkë** (f)	[várkə]
to net (to fish with a net)	**peshkoj me rrjeta**	[pɛʃkój mɛ rjéta]
to cast[throw] the net	**hedh rrjetat**	[hɛð rjétat]
to haul the net in	**tërheq rrjetat**	[tərhéc rjétat]
to fall into the net	**bie në rrjetë**	[bíɛ nə rjétə]

whaler (person)	**gjuetar balenash** (m)	[ɟuɛtár balénaʃ]
whaleboat	**balenagjuajtëse** (f)	[balɛnaɟúajtəsɛ]
harpoon	**fuzhnjë** (f)	[fúʒnə]

159. Games. Billiards

billiards	**bilardo** (f)	[bilárdo]
billiard room, hall	**sallë bilardosh** (f)	[sáɬə bilárdoʃ]
ball (snooker, etc.)	**bile** (f)	[bílɛ]

to pocket a ball	**fus në vrimë**	[fús nə vrímə]
cue	**stekë** (f)	[stékə]
pocket	**xhep** (m), **vrimë** (f)	[dʒɛp], [vrímə]

160. Games. Playing cards

diamonds	**karo** (f)	[káro]
spades	**maç** (m)	[matʃ]
hearts	**kupë** (f)	[kúpə]
clubs	**spathi** (m)	[spáθi]

ace	**as** (m)	[ás]
king	**mbret** (m)	[mbrét]
queen	**mbretëreshë** (f)	[mbrɛtəréʃə]
jack, knave	**fant** (m)	[fant]

playing card	**letër** (f)	[létər]
cards	**letrat** (pl)	[létrat]
trump	**letër e fortë** (f)	[létər ɛ fórtə]
deck of cards	**set letrash** (m)	[sɛt létraʃ]

point	**pikë** (f)	[píkə]
to deal (vi, vt)	**ndaj**	[ndáj]
to shuffle (cards)	**përziej**	[pərzíɛj]
lead, turn (n)	**radha** (f)	[ráða]
cardsharp	**mashtrues** (m)	[maʃtrúɛs]

161. Casino. Roulette

casino	**kazino** (f)	[kazíno]
roulette (game)	**ruletë** (f)	[rulétə]
bet	**bast** (m)	[bast]
to place bets	**vë bast**	[və bast]
red	**e kuqe** (f)	[ɛ kúcɛ]
black	**e zezë** (f)	[ɛ zézə]
to bet on red	**vë bast në të kuqe**	[və bast nə tə kúcɛ]
to bet on black	**vë bast në të zezë**	[və bast nə tə zézə]
croupier (dealer)	**krupier** (m)	[krupiér]
to spin the wheel	**rrotulloj ruletën**	[rotułój rulétən]
rules (of game)	**rregullat** (pl)	[régułat]
chip	**fishe** (f)	[fíʃɛ]
to win (vi, vt)	**fitoj**	[fitój]
win (winnings)	**fitim** (m)	[fitím]
to lose (~ 100 dollars)	**humb**	[húmb]
loss (losses)	**humbje** (f)	[húmbjɛ]
player	**lojtar** (m)	[lojtár]
blackjack (card game)	**blackjack** (m)	[blatskjátsk]
craps (dice game)	**lojë me zare** (f)	[lójə mɛ zárɛ]
dice (a pair of ~)	**zare** (f)	[zárɛ]
slot machine	**makinë e lojërave të fatit** (f)	[makínə ɛ lojərávɛ tə fátit]

162. Rest. Games. Miscellaneous

to stroll (vi, vt)	**shëtitem**	[ʃətítɛm]
stroll (leisurely walk)	**shëtitje** (f)	[ʃətítjɛ]
car ride	**xhiro me makinë** (f)	[dʒíro mɛ makínə]
adventure	**aventurë** (f)	[avɛntúrə]
picnic	**piknik** (m)	[pikník]
game (chess, etc.)	**lojë** (f)	[lójə]
player	**lojtar** (m)	[lojtár]
game (one ~ of chess)	**një lojë** (f)	[ɲə lójə]
collector (e.g., philatelist)	**koleksionist** (m)	[kolɛksioníst]
to collect (stamps, etc.)	**koleksionoj**	[kolɛksionój]
collection	**koleksion** (m)	[kolɛksión]
crossword puzzle	**fjalëkryq** (m)	[fjaləkrýc]
racetrack (horse racing venue)	**hipodrom** (m)	[hipodróm]

disco (discotheque)	disko (f)	[dísko]
sauna	sauna (f)	[saúna]
lottery	lotari (f)	[lotarí]

camping trip	kamping (m)	[kampíŋ]
camp	kamp (m)	[kamp]
tent (for camping)	çadër kampingu (f)	[tʃádər kampíŋu]
compass	kompas (m)	[kompás]
camper	kampinist (m)	[kampiníst]

to watch (movie, etc.)	shikoj	[ʃikój]
viewer	teleshikues (m)	[tɛlɛʃikúɛs]
TV show (TV program)	program televiziv (m)	[prográm tɛlɛvizív]

163. Photography

camera (photo)	aparat fotografik (m)	[aparát fotografík]
photo, picture	foto (f)	[fóto]

photographer	fotograf (m)	[fotográf]
photo studio	studio fotografike (f)	[stúdio fotografíkɛ]
photo album	album fotografik (m)	[albúm fotografík]

camera lens	objektiv (m)	[objɛktív]
telephoto lens	teleobjektiv (m)	[tɛlɛobjɛktív]
filter	filtër (m)	[fíltər]
lens	lente (f)	[léntɛ]

optics (high-quality ~)	optikë (f)	[optíkə]
diaphragm (aperture)	diafragma (f)	[diafrágma]
exposure time (shutter speed)	koha e ekspozimit (f)	[kóha ɛ ɛkspozímit]
viewfinder	tregues i kuadrit (m)	[trɛgúɛs i kuádrit]

digital camera	kamerë digjitale (f)	[kamérə diɟitálɛ]
tripod	tripod (m)	[tripód]
flash	blic (m)	[blits]

to photograph (vt)	fotografoj	[fotografój]
to take pictures	bëj foto	[bəj fóto]
to have one's picture taken	bëj fotografi	[bəj fotografí]

focus	fokus (m)	[fokús]
to focus	fokusoj	[fokusój]
sharp, in focus (adj)	i qartë	[i cártə]
sharpness	qartësi (f)	[cartəsí]

contrast	kontrast (m)	[kontrást]
contrast (as adj)	me kontrast	[mɛ kontrást]
picture (photo)	foto (f)	[fóto]

negative (n)	negativ (m)	[nɛgatív]
film (a roll of ~)	film negativash (m)	[film nɛgatívaʃ]
frame (still)	imazh (m)	[imáʒ]
to print (photos)	printoj	[printój]

164. Beach. Swimming

beach	plazh (m)	[plaʒ]
sand	rërë (f)	[rə́rə]
deserted (beach)	plazh i shkretë	[plaʒ i ʃkrétə]

suntan	nxirje nga dielli (f)	[ndzírjɛ ŋa díɛti]
to get a tan	nxihem	[ndzíhɛm]
tan (adj)	i nxirë	[i ndzírə]
sunscreen	krem dielli (f)	[krɛm díɛti]

bikini	bikini (m)	[bikíni]
bathing suit	rrobë banje (f)	[róbə báɲɛ]
swim trunks	mbathje banjo (f)	[mbáθjɛ báɲo]

swimming pool	pishinë (f)	[piʃínə]
to swim (vi)	notoj	[notój]
shower	dush (m)	[duʃ]
to change (one's clothes)	ndërroj	[ndərój]
towel	peshqir (m)	[pɛʃcír]

boat	varkë (f)	[várkə]
motorboat	skaf (m)	[skaf]

water ski	ski ujor (m)	[ski ujór]
paddle boat	varkë me pedale (f)	[várkə mɛ pɛdálɛ]
surfing	surf (m)	[surf]
surfer	surfist (m)	[surfíst]

scuba set	komplet për skuba (f)	[komplét pər skúba]
flippers (swim fins)	këmbale noti (pl)	[kəmbálɛ nóti]
mask (diving ~)	maskë (f)	[máskə]
diver	zhytës (m)	[ʒýtəs]
to dive (vi)	zhytem	[ʒýtɛm]
underwater (adv)	nën ujë	[nən újə]

beach umbrella	çadër plazhi (f)	[tʃádər pláʒi]
sunbed (lounger)	shezlong (m)	[ʃɛzlón]
sunglasses	syze dielli (f)	[sýzɛ diɛti]
air mattress	dyshek me ajër (m)	[dyʃék mɛ ájər]

to play (amuse oneself)	loz	[loz]
to go for a swim	notoj	[notój]
beach ball	top plazhi (m)	[top pláʒi]
to inflate (vt)	fryj	[fryj]

inflatable, air (adj)	që fryhet	[cə frýhɛt]
wave	dallgë (f)	[dáɫgə]
buoy (line of ~s)	tapë (f)	[tápə]
to drown (ab. person)	mbytem	[mbýtɛm]

to save, to rescue	shpëtoj	[ʃpətój]
life vest	jelek shpëtimi (m)	[jɛlék ʃpətími]
to observe, to watch	vëzhgoj	[vəʒgój]
lifeguard	rojë bregdetare (m)	[rójə brɛgdɛtárɛ]

TECHNICAL EQUIPMENT. TRANSPORTATION

Technical equipment

165. Computer

computer	kompjuter (m)	[kompjutér]
notebook, laptop	laptop (m)	[laptóp]
to turn on	ndez	[ndɛz]
to turn off	fik	[fik]
keyboard	tastiera (f)	[tastiéra]
key	çelës (m)	[tʃéləs]
mouse	maus (m)	[máus]
mouse pad	shtroje e mausit (f)	[ʃtrójɛ ɛ máusit]
button	buton (m)	[butón]
cursor	kursor (m)	[kurʂór]
monitor	monitor (m)	[monitór]
screen	ekran (m)	[ɛkrán]
hard disk	hard disk (m)	[hárd dísk]
hard disk capacity	kapaciteti i hard diskut (m)	[kapatsitéti i hárd dískut]
memory	memorie (f)	[mɛmóriɛ]
random access memory	memorie operative (f)	[mɛmóriɛ opɛratívɛ]
file	skedë (f)	[skédə]
folder	dosje (f)	[dósjɛ]
to open (vt)	hap	[hap]
to close (vt)	mbyll	[mbyɫ]
to save (vt)	ruaj	[rúaj]
to delete (vt)	fshij	[fʃij]
to copy (vt)	kopjoj	[kopjój]
to sort (vt)	sistemoj	[sistɛmój]
to transfer (copy)	transferoj	[transfɛrój]
program	program (m)	[prográm]
software	softuer (f)	[softuér]
programmer	programues (m)	[programúɛs]
to program (vt)	programoj	[programój]
hacker	haker (m)	[hakér]

password	fjalëkalim (m)	[fjaləkalím]
virus	virus (m)	[virús]
to find, to detect	zbuloj	[zbulój]

| byte | bajt (m) | [bájt] |
| megabyte | megabajt (m) | [mɛgabájt] |

| data | të dhënat (pl) | [tə ðǝnat] |
| database | databazë (f) | [databázə] |

cable (USB, etc.)	kabllo (f)	[kábɫo]
to disconnect (vt)	shkëpus	[ʃkəpús]
to connect (sth to sth)	lidh	[lið]

166. Internet. E-mail

Internet	internet (m)	[intɛrnét]
browser	shfletues (m)	[ʃflɛtúɛs]
search engine	makineri kërkimi (f)	[makinɛrí kərkími]
provider	ofrues (m)	[ofrúɛs]

webmaster	uebmaster (m)	[uɛbmástɛr]
website	ueb-faqe (f)	[uéb-fácɛ]
webpage	ueb-faqe (f)	[uéb-fácɛ]

| address (e-mail ~) | adresë (f) | [adrésə] |
| address book | libërth adresash (m) | [líbərθ adrésaʃ] |

mailbox	kuti postare (f)	[kutí postárɛ]
mail	postë (f)	[póstə]
full (adj)	i mbushur	[i mbúʃur]

message	mesazh (m)	[mɛsáʒ]
incoming messages	mesazhe të ardhura (pl)	[mɛsáʒɛ tə árðura]
outgoing messages	mesazhe të dërguara (pl)	[mɛsáʒɛ tə dərgúara]

sender	dërguesi (m)	[dərgúɛsi]
to send (vt)	dërgoj	[dərgój]
sending (of mail)	dërgesë (f)	[dərgésə]

| receiver | pranues (m) | [pranúɛs] |
| to receive (vt) | pranoj | [pranój] |

| correspondence | korrespondencë (f) | [korɛspondéntsə] |
| to correspond (vi) | komunikim | [komunikím] |

file	skedë (f)	[skédə]
to download (vt)	shkarkoj	[ʃkarkój]
to create (vt)	krijoj	[krijój]
to delete (vt)	fshij	[fʃij]

deleted (adj)	e fshirë	[ɛ ʃʃírə]
connection (ADSL, etc.)	lidhje (f)	[líðjɛ]
speed	shpejtësi (f)	[ʃpɛjtəsí]
modem	modem (m)	[modém]
access	hyrje (f)	[hýrjɛ]
port (e.g., input ~)	port (m)	[port]

| connection (make a ~) | lidhje (f) | [líðjɛ] |
| to connect to ... (vi) | lidhem me ... | [líðɛm mɛ ...] |

| to select (vt) | përzgjedh | [pərzɟéð] |
| to search (for ...) | kërkoj ... | [kərkój ...] |

167. Electricity

electricity	elektricitet (m)	[ɛlɛktritsitét]
electric, electrical (adj)	elektrik	[ɛlɛktrík]
electric power plant	hidrocentral (m)	[hidrotsɛntrál]
energy	energji (f)	[ɛnɛrɟí]
electric power	energji elektrike (f)	[ɛnɛrɟí ɛlɛktríkɛ]

light bulb	poç (m)	[potʃ]
flashlight	llambë dore (f)	[ɫámbə dórɛ]
street light	llambë rruge (f)	[ɫámbə rúgɛ]

light	dritë (f)	[drítə]
to turn on	ndez	[ndɛz]
to turn off	fik	[fik]
to turn off the light	fik dritën	[fik drítən]

to burn out (vi)	digjet	[díɟɛt]
short circuit	qark i shkurtër (m)	[cark i ʃkúrtər]
broken wire	tel i prishur (m)	[tɛl i príʃur]
contact (electrical ~)	kontakt (m)	[kontákt]

light switch	çelës drite (m)	[tʃéləs drítɛ]
wall socket	prizë (f)	[prízə]
plug	spinë (f)	[spínə]
extension cord	zgjatues (m)	[zɟatúɛs]

fuse	siguresë (f)	[sigurésə]
cable, wire	kabllo (f)	[kábɫo]
wiring	rrjet elektrik (m)	[rjét ɛlɛktrík]

ampere	amper (m)	[ampér]
amperage	amperazh (f)	[ampɛráʒ]
volt	volt (m)	[volt]
voltage	voltazh (m)	[voltáʒ]
electrical device	aparat elektrik (m)	[aparát ɛlɛktrík]
indicator	indikator (m)	[indikatór]

electrician	elektricist (m)	[ɛlɛktritsíst]
to solder (vt)	saldoj	[saldój]
soldering iron	pajisje saldimi (f)	[pajísjɛ saldími]
electric current	korrent elektrik (m)	[korént ɛlɛktrík]

168. Tools

tool, instrument	vegël (f)	[végəl]
tools	vegla (pl)	[végla]
equipment (factory ~)	pajisje (f)	[pajísjɛ]

hammer	çekiç (m)	[tʃɛkítʃ]
screwdriver	kaçavidë (f)	[katʃavídə]
ax	sëpatë (f)	[səpátə]

saw	sharrë (f)	[ʃárə]
to saw (vt)	sharroj	[ʃarój]
plane (tool)	zdrukthues (m)	[zdrukθúɛs]
to plane (vt)	zdrukthoj	[zdrukθój]
soldering iron	pajisje saldimi (f)	[pajísjɛ saldími]
to solder (vt)	saldoj	[saldój]

file (tool)	limë (f)	[límə]
carpenter pincers	darë (f)	[dárə]
lineman's pliers	pinca (f)	[píntsa]
chisel	daltë (f)	[dáltə]

drill bit	turjelë (f)	[turjélə]
electric drill	shpuese elektrike (f)	[ʃpúɛsɛ ɛlɛktríkɛ]
to drill (vi, vt)	shpoj	[ʃpoj]

knife	thikë (f)	[θíkə]
pocket knife	thikë xhepi (f)	[θíkə dʒépi]
blade	teh (m)	[tɛh]

sharp (blade, etc.)	i mprehtë	[i mpréhtə]
dull, blunt (adj)	i topitur	[i topítur]
to get blunt (dull)	bëhet e topitur	[bəhɛt ɛ topítur]
to sharpen (vt)	mpreh	[mpréh]

bolt	vidë (f)	[vídə]
nut	dado (f)	[dádo]
thread (of a screw)	filetë e vidhës (f)	[filétə ɛ víðəs]
wood screw	vidhë druri (f)	[víðə drúri]

| nail | gozhdë (f) | [góʒdə] |
| nailhead | kokë gozhde (f) | [kókə góʒdɛ] |

| ruler (for measuring) | vizore (f) | [vizórɛ] |
| tape measure | metër (m) | [métər] |

| spirit level | nivelizues (m) | [nivɛlizúɛs] |
| magnifying glass | lente zmadhuese (f) | [léntɛ zmaðúɛsɛ] |

measuring instrument	mjet matës (m)	[mjét mátəs]
to measure (vt)	mas	[mas]
scale	gradë (f)	[grádə]
(of thermometer, etc.)		
readings	matjet (pl)	[mátjɛt]

| compressor | kompresor (m) | [komprɛsór] |
| microscope | mikroskop (m) | [mikroskóp] |

pump (e.g., water ~)	pompë (f)	[pómpə]
robot	robot (m)	[robót]
laser	laser (m)	[lasér]

wrench	çelës (m)	[tʃéləs]
adhesive tape	shirit ngjitës (m)	[ʃirit ɲítəs]
glue	ngjitës (m)	[ɲítəs]

sandpaper	letër smeril (f)	[létər smɛríl]
spring	sustë (f)	[sústə]
magnet	magnet (m)	[magnét]
gloves	dorëza (pl)	[dórəza]

rope	litar (m)	[litár]
cord	kordon (m)	[kordón]
wire (e.g., telephone ~)	tel (m)	[tɛl]
cable	kabllo (f)	[kábɫo]

sledgehammer	çekan i rëndë (m)	[tʃɛkán i rəndə]
prybar	levë (f)	[lévə]
ladder	shkallë (f)	[ʃkáɫə]
stepladder	shkallëz (f)	[ʃkáɫəz]

to screw (tighten)	vidhos	[viðós]
to unscrew (lid, filter, etc.)	zhvidhos	[ʒviðós]
to tighten	shtrëngoj	[ʃtrəŋój]
(e.g., with a clamp)		
to glue, to stick	ngjes	[ɲés]
to cut (vt)	pres	[prɛs]

malfunction (fault)	avari (f)	[avarí]
repair (mending)	riparim (m)	[riparím]
to repair, to fix (vt)	riparoj	[riparój]
to adjust (machine, etc.)	rregulloj	[rɛguɫój]

to check (to examine)	kontrolloj	[kontroɫój]
checking	kontroll (m)	[kontróɫ]
readings	matjet (pl)	[mátjɛt]
reliable, solid (machine)	e sigurt	[ɛ sígurt]
complex (adj)	komplekse	[kompléksɛ]

to rust (get rusted)	**ndryshket**	[ndrýʃkɛt]
rusty, rusted (adj)	**e ndryshkur**	[ɛ ndrýʃkur]
rust	**ndryshk** (m)	[ndrýʃk]

Transportation

169. Airplane

airplane	avion (m)	[avión]
air ticket	biletë avioni (f)	[bilétə avióni]
airline	kompani ajrore (f)	[kompaní ajrórɛ]
airport	aeroport (m)	[aɛropórt]
supersonic (adj)	supersonik	[supɛrsoník]
captain	kapiten (m)	[kapitén]
crew	ekip (m)	[ɛkíp]
pilot	pilot (m)	[pilót]
flight attendant (fem.)	stjuardesë (f)	[stjuardésə]
navigator	navigues (m)	[navigúɛs]
wings	krahë (pl)	[kráhə]
tail	bisht (m)	[biʃt]
cockpit	kabinë (f)	[kabínə]
engine	motor (m)	[motór]
undercarriage (landing gear)	karrel (m)	[karél]
turbine	turbinë (f)	[turbínə]
propeller	helikë (f)	[hɛlíkə]
black box	kuti e zezë (f)	[kutí ɛ zézə]
yoke (control column)	timon (m)	[timón]
fuel	karburant (m)	[karburánt]
safety card	udhëzime sigurie (pl)	[uðəzímɛ siguríɛ]
oxygen mask	maskë oksigjeni (f)	[máskə oksiɉéni]
uniform	uniformë (f)	[unifórmə]
life vest	jelek shpëtimi (m)	[jɛlék ʃpətími]
parachute	parashutë (f)	[paraʃútə]
takeoff	ngritje (f)	[ŋrítjɛ]
to take off (vi)	fluturon	[fluturón]
runway	pista e fluturimit (f)	[písta ɛ fluturímit]
visibility	shikueshmëri (f)	[ʃikuɛʃməri]
flight (act of flying)	fluturim (m)	[fluturím]
altitude	lartësi (f)	[lartəsí]
air pocket	xhep ajri (m)	[dʒɛp ájri]
seat	karrige (f)	[karígɛ]
headphones	kufje (f)	[kúfjɛ]

folding tray (tray table)	tabaka (f)	[tabaká]
airplane window	dritare avioni (f)	[drítárɛ avióni]
aisle	korridor (m)	[koridór]

170. Train

train	tren (m)	[trɛn]
commuter train	tren elektrik (m)	[trɛn ɛlɛktrík]
express train	tren ekspres (m)	[trɛn ɛksprés]
diesel locomotive	lokomotivë me naftë (f)	[lokomótivə mɛ náftə]
steam locomotive	lokomotivë me avull (f)	[lokomótivə mɛ ávuł]

| passenger car | vagon (m) | [vagón] |
| dining car | vagon restorant (m) | [vagón rɛstoránt] |

rails	shina (pl)	[ʃína]
railroad	hekurudhë (f)	[hɛkurúðə]
railway tie	traversë (f)	[travérsə]

platform (railway ~)	platformë (f)	[platfórmə]
track (~ 1, 2, etc.)	binar (m)	[binár]
semaphore	semafor (m)	[sɛmafór]
station	stacion (m)	[statsión]

engineer (train driver)	makinist (m)	[makiníst]
porter (of luggage)	portier (m)	[portiér]
car attendant	konduktor (m)	[konduktór]
passenger	pasagjer (m)	[pasaɟér]
conductor (ticket inspector)	konduktor (m)	[konduktór]

| corridor (in train) | korridor (m) | [koridór] |
| emergency brake | frena urgjence (f) | [fréna uɲéntsɛ] |

compartment	ndarje (f)	[ndárjɛ]
berth	kat (m)	[kat]
upper berth	kati i sipërm (m)	[káti i sípərm]
lower berth	kati i poshtëm (m)	[káti i póʃtəm]
bed linen, bedding	shtroje shtrati (pl)	[ʃtrójɛ ʃtráti]

ticket	biletë (f)	[bilétə]
schedule	orar (m)	[orár]
information display	tabelë e informatave (f)	[tabélə ɛ infoɾmátavɛ]

to leave, to depart	niset	[nísɛt]
departure (of train)	nisje (f)	[nísjɛ]
to arrive (ab. train)	arrij	[aríj]
arrival	arritje (f)	[arítjɛ]
to arrive by train	arrij me tren	[aríj mɛ trɛn]
to get on the train	hip në tren	[hip nə trén]

to get off the train	zbres nga treni	[zbrɛs ŋa tréni]
train wreck	aksident hekurudhor (m)	[aksidént hɛkuruðór]
to derail (vi)	del nga shinat	[dɛl ŋa ʃínat]

steam locomotive	lokomotivë me avull (f)	[lokomótivə mɛ ávuɫ]
stoker, fireman	mbikëqyrës i zjarrit (m)	[mbikəcýrəs i zjárit]
firebox	furrë (f)	[fúrə]
coal	qymyr (m)	[cymýr]

171. Ship

| ship | anije (f) | [aníjɛ] |
| vessel | mjet lundrues (m) | [mjét lundrúɛs] |

steamship	anije me avull (f)	[aníjɛ mɛ ávuɫ]
riverboat	anije lumi (f)	[aníjɛ lúmi]
cruise ship	krocierë (f)	[krotsiérə]
cruiser	anije luftarake (f)	[aníjɛ luftarákɛ]

yacht	jaht (m)	[jáht]
tugboat	anije rimorkiuese (f)	[aníjɛ rimorkiúɛsɛ]
barge	anije transportuese (f)	[aníjɛ transportúɛsɛ]
ferry	traget (m)	[tragét]

| sailing ship | anije me vela (f) | [aníjɛ mɛ véla] |
| brigantine | brigantinë (f) | [brigantínə] |

| ice breaker | akullthyese (f) | [akuɫθýɛsɛ] |
| submarine | nëndetëse (f) | [nəndétəsɛ] |

boat (flat-bottomed ~)	barkë (f)	[bárkə]
dinghy	gomone (f)	[gomónɛ]
lifeboat	varkë shpëtimi (f)	[várkə ʃpətími]
motorboat	skaf (m)	[skaf]

captain	kapiten (m)	[kapitén]
seaman	marinar (m)	[marinár]
sailor	marinar (m)	[marinár]
crew	ekip (m)	[ɛkíp]

boatswain	kryemarinar (m)	[kryɛmarinár]
ship's boy	djali i anijes (m)	[djáli i aníjɛs]
cook	kuzhinier (m)	[kuʒiniér]
ship's doctor	doktori i anijes (m)	[doktóri i aníjɛs]

deck	kuverta (f)	[kuvérta]
mast	direk (m)	[dirék]
sail	vela (f)	[véla]
hold	bagazh (m)	[bagáʒ]
bow (prow)	harku sipëror (m)	[hárku sipərór]

stern	pjesa e pasme (f)	[pjésa ɛ pásmɛ]
oar	rrem (m)	[rɛm]
screw propeller	helikë (f)	[hɛlíkə]

cabin	kabinë (f)	[kabínə]
wardroom	zyrë e oficerëve (m)	[zýrə ɛ ofitsérəvɛ]
engine room	salla e motorit (m)	[sáɫa ɛ motórit]
bridge	urë komanduese (f)	[úrə komandúɛsɛ]
radio room	kabina radiotelegrafike (f)	[kabína radiotɛlɛgrafíkɛ]

| wave (radio) | valë (f) | [válə] |
| logbook | libri i shënimeve (m) | [líbri i ʃənímɛvɛ] |

spyglass	dylbi (f)	[dylbí]
bell	këmbanë (f)	[kəmbánə]
flag	flamur (m)	[flamúr]

| hawser (mooring ~) | pallamar (m) | [paɫamár] |
| knot (bowline, etc.) | nyjë (f) | [nýjə] |

| deckrails | parmakë (pl) | [parmákə] |
| gangway | shkallë (f) | [ʃkáɫə] |

| anchor | spirancë (f) | [spirántsə] |
| to weigh anchor | ngre spirancën | [ŋré spirántsən] |

| to drop anchor | hedh spirancën | [hɛð spirántsən] |
| anchor chain | zinxhir i spirancës (m) | [zindʒír i spirántsəs] |

| port (harbor) | port (m) | [port] |
| quay, wharf | skelë (f) | [skélə] |

| to berth (moor) | ankoroj | [ankorój] |
| to cast off | niset | [nísɛt] |

| trip, voyage | udhëtim (m) | [uðətím] |
| cruise (sea trip) | udhëtim me krocierë (f) | [uðətím mɛ krotsiérə] |

| course (route) | kursi i udhëtimit (m) | [kúrsi i uðətímit] |
| route (itinerary) | itinerar (m) | [itinɛrár] |

fairway (safe water channel)	ujëra të lundrueshme (f)	[újəra tə lundrúɛʃmɛ]
shallows	cekëtinë (f)	[tsɛkətínə]
to run aground	bllokohet në rërë	[bɫokóhɛt nə rərə]

storm	stuhi (f)	[stuhí]
signal	sinjal (m)	[siɲál]
to sink (vi)	fundoset	[fundósɛt]
Man overboard!	Njeri në det!	[ɲɛrí nə dɛt!]
SOS (distress signal)	SOS (m)	[sos]
ring buoy	bovë shpëtuese (f)	[bóvə ʃpətúɛsɛ]

172. Airport

airport	aeroport (m)	[aɛropórt]
airplane	avion (m)	[avión]
airline	kompani ajrore (f)	[kompaní ajrórɛ]
air traffic controller	kontroll i trafikut ajror (m)	[kontrół i trafíkut ajrór]
departure	nisje (f)	[nísjɛ]
arrival	arritje (f)	[arítjɛ]
to arrive (by plane)	arrij me avion	[arij mɛ avión]
departure time	nisja (f)	[nísja]
arrival time	arritja (f)	[arítja]
to be delayed	vonesë	[vonésə]
flight delay	vonesë avioni (f)	[vonésə avióni]
information board	ekrani i informacioneve (m)	[ɛkráni i informatsiónɛvɛ]
information	informacion (m)	[informatsión]
to announce (vt)	njoftoj	[ɲoftój]
flight (e.g., next ~)	fluturim (m)	[fluturím]
customs	doganë (f)	[dogánə]
customs officer	doganier (m)	[doganiér]
customs declaration	deklarim doganor (m)	[dɛklarím doganór]
to fill out (vt)	plotësoj	[plotəsój]
to fill out the declaration	plotësoj deklaratën	[plotəsój dɛklarátən]
passport control	kontroll pasaportash (m)	[kontrół pasapórtaʃ]
luggage	bagazh (m)	[bagáʒ]
hand luggage	bagazh dore (m)	[bagáʒ dórɛ]
luggage cart	karrocë bagazhesh (f)	[karótsə bagáʒɛʃ]
landing	aterrim (m)	[atɛrím]
landing strip	pistë aterrimi (f)	[pístə atɛrími]
to land (vi)	aterroj	[atɛrój]
airstair (passenger stair)	shkallë avioni (f)	[ʃkálə avióni]
check-in	regjistrim (m)	[rɛɟistrím]
check-in counter	sportel regjistrimi (m)	[sportél rɛɟistrími]
to check-in (vi)	regjistrohem	[rɛɟistróhɛm]
boarding pass	biletë e hyrjes (f)	[bilétə ɛ hýrjɛs]
departure gate	porta e nisjes (f)	[pórta ɛ nísjɛs]
transit	transit (m)	[transít]
to wait (vt)	pres	[prɛs]
departure lounge	salla e nisjes (f)	[sáta ɛ nísjɛs]
to see off	përcjell	[pərtsjéł]
to say goodbye	përshëndetem	[pərʃəndétɛm]

173. Bicycle. Motorcycle

bicycle	**biçikletë** (f)	[bitʃiklétə]
scooter	**skuter** (m)	[skutér]
motorcycle, bike	**motoçikletë** (f)	[mototʃiklétə]
to go by bicycle	**shkoj me biçikletë**	[ʃkoj mɛ bitʃiklétə]
handlebars	**timon** (m)	[timón]
pedal	**pedale** (f)	[pɛdálɛ]
brakes	**frenat** (pl)	[frénat]
bicycle seat (saddle)	**shalë** (f)	[ʃálə]
pump	**pompë** (f)	[pómpə]
luggage rack	**mbajtëse** (f)	[mbájtəsɛ]
front lamp	**drita e përparme** (f)	[dríta ɛ pərpármɛ]
helmet	**helmetë** (f)	[hɛlmétə]
wheel	**rrotë** (f)	[rótə]
fender	**parafango** (f)	[parafáŋo]
rim	**rreth i jashtëm i rrotës** (m)	[rɛθ i jáʃtəm i rótəs]
spoke	**telat e diskut** (m)	[télat ɛ dískut]

Cars

174. Types of cars

automobile, car	makinë (f)	[makínə]
sports car	makinë sportive (f)	[makínə sportívɛ]
limousine	limuzinë (f)	[limuzínə]
off-road vehicle	fuoristradë (f)	[fuoristrádə]
convertible (n)	kabriolet (m)	[kabriolét]
minibus	furgon (m)	[furgón]
ambulance	ambulancë (f)	[ambulántsə]
snowplow	borëpastruese (f)	[borəpastrúɛsɛ]
truck	kamion (m)	[kamión]
tanker truck	autocisternë (f)	[autotsistérnə]
van (small truck)	furgon mallrash (m)	[furgón máɫraʃ]
road tractor (trailer truck)	kamionçinë (f)	[kamiontʃínə]
trailer	rimorkio (f)	[rimórkio]
comfortable (adj)	i rehatshëm	[i rɛhátʃəm]
used (adj)	i përdorur	[i pərdórur]

175. Cars. Bodywork

hood	kofano (f)	[kófano]
fender	parafango (f)	[parafáŋo]
roof	çati (f)	[tʃatí]
windshield	xham i përparmë (m)	[dʒam i pərpármə]
rear-view mirror	pasqyrë për prapa (f)	[pascýrə pər prápa]
windshield washer	larëse xhami (f)	[lárəsɛ dʒámi]
windshield wipers	fshirëse xhami (f)	[fʃírəsɛ dʒámi]
side window	xham anësor (m)	[dʒam anəsór]
window lift (power window)	levë xhami (f)	[lévə dʒámi]
antenna	antenë (f)	[anténə]
sunroof	çati diellore (f)	[tʃatí diɛɫórɛ]
bumper	parakolp (m)	[parakólp]
trunk	bagazh (m)	[bagáʒ]
roof luggage rack	bagazh mbi çati (m)	[bagáʒ mbi tʃatí]
door	derë (f)	[dérə]

door handle	doreza e derës (m)	[doréza ɛ dérəs]
door lock	kyç (m)	[kytʃ]
license plate	targë makine (f)	[tárgə makínɛ]
muffler	silenciator (m)	[silɛntsiatór]
gas tank	serbator (m)	[sɛrbatór]
tailpipe	tub shkarkimi (m)	[tub ʃkarkími]
gas, accelerator	gaz (m)	[gaz]
pedal	këmbëz (f)	[kə́mbəz]
gas pedal	pedal i gazit (m)	[pɛdál i gázit]
brake	freni (m)	[fréni]
brake pedal	pedal i frenave (m)	[pɛdál i frénavɛ]
to brake (use the brake)	frenoj	[frɛnój]
parking brake	freni i dorës (m)	[fréni i dórəs]
clutch	friksion (m)	[friksión]
clutch pedal	pedal i friksionit (m)	[pɛdál i friksiónit]
clutch disc	disk i friksionit (m)	[dísk i friksiónit]
shock absorber	amortizator (m)	[amortizatór]
wheel	rrotë (f)	[rótə]
spare tire	gomë rezervë (f)	[gómə rɛzérvə]
tire	gomë (f)	[gómə]
hubcap	mbulesë gome (f)	[mbulésə gómɛ]
driving wheels	rrota makine (f)	[róta makínɛ]
front-wheel drive (as adj)	me rrotat e përparme	[mɛ rotat ɛ pərpármɛ]
rear-wheel drive (as adj)	me rrotat e pasme	[mɛ rótat ɛ pásmɛ]
all-wheel drive (as adj)	me të gjitha rrotat	[mɛ tə ɟíθa rótat]
gearbox	kutia e marsheve (f)	[kutía ɛ márʃɛvɛ]
automatic (adj)	automatik	[automatík]
mechanical (adj)	mekanik	[mɛkaník]
gear shift	levë e marshit (f)	[lévə ɛ márʃit]
headlight	dritë e përparme (f)	[drítə ɛ pərpármɛ]
headlights	dritat e përparme (pl)	[drítat ɛ pərpármɛ]
low beam	dritat e shkurtra (pl)	[drítat ɛ ʃkúrtra]
high beam	dritat e gjata (pl)	[drítat ɛ ɟáta]
brake light	dritat e frenave (pl)	[drítat ɛ frénavɛ]
parking lights	dritat për parkim (pl)	[drítat pər parkím]
hazard lights	sinjal për urgjencë (m)	[siɲál pər uɾɟéntsə]
fog lights	drita mjegulle (pl)	[dríta mjégułɛ]
turn signal	sinjali i kthesës (m)	[siɲáli i kθésəs]
back-up light	dritat e prapme (pl)	[drítat ɛ prápmɛ]

176. Cars. Passenger compartment

car inside (interior)	interier (m)	[intɛriér]
leather (as adj)	prej lëkure	[prɛj lǝkúrɛ]
velour (as adj)	kadife	[kadífɛ]
upholstery	veshje (f)	[véʃjɛ]

instrument (gage)	instrument (m)	[instrumént]
dashboard	panel instrumentesh (m)	[panél instruméntɛʃ]
speedometer	matës i shpejtësisë (m)	[mátǝs i ʃpɛjtǝsísǝ]
needle (pointer)	shigjetë (f)	[ʃijétǝ]

odometer	kilometrazh (m)	[kilomɛtráʒ]
indicator (sensor)	indikator (m)	[indikatór]
level	nivel (m)	[nivél]
warning light	dritë paralajmëruese (f)	[drítǝ paralajmǝrúɛsɛ]

steering wheel	timon (m)	[timón]
horn	bori (f)	[borí]
button	buton (m)	[butón]
switch	çelës drite (m)	[tʃélǝs drítɛ]

seat	karrige (f)	[karígɛ]
backrest	shpinore (f)	[ʃpinórɛ]
headrest	mbështetësja e kokës (m)	[mbǝʃtétǝsja ɛ kókǝs]
seat belt	rrip i sigurimit (m)	[rip i sigurímit]
to fasten the belt	lidh rripin e sigurimit	[lið rípin ɛ sigurímit]
adjustment (of seats)	rregulloj (m)	[rɛguɫój]

airbag	jastëk ajri (m)	[jastǝk ájri]
air-conditioner	kondicioner (m)	[konditsionér]

radio	radio (f)	[rádio]
CD player	disk CD (m)	[dísk tsɛdé]
to turn on	ndez	[ndɛz]
antenna	antenë (f)	[anténǝ]
glove box	kroskot (m)	[kroskót]
ashtray	taketuke (f)	[takɛtúkɛ]

177. Cars. Engine

engine, motor	motor (m)	[motór]
diesel (as adj)	me naftë	[mɛ náftǝ]
gasoline (as adj)	me benzinë	[mɛ bɛnzínǝ]

engine volume	vëllim i motorit (m)	[vǝɫím i motórit]
power	fuqi (f)	[fucí]
horsepower	kuaj-fuqi (f)	[kúaj-fucí]
piston	piston (m)	[pistón]

| cylinder | cilindër (m) | [tsilíndər] |
| valve | valvulë (f) | [valvúlə] |

injector	injektor (m)	[iɲɛktór]
generator (alternator)	gjenerator (m)	[ɟɛnɛratór]
carburetor	karburator (m)	[karburatór]
motor oil	vaj i motorit (m)	[vaj i motórit]

radiator	radiator (m)	[radiatór]
coolant	antifriz (m)	[antifríz]
cooling fan	ventilator (m)	[vɛntilatór]

battery (accumulator)	bateri (f)	[batɛrí]
starter	motorino (f)	[motoríno]
ignition	kuadër ndezës (m)	[kuádər ndézəs]
spark plug	kandelë (f)	[kandélə]

terminal (of battery)	morseta e baterisë (f)	[morséta ɛ batɛrísə]
positive terminal	kahu pozitiv (m)	[káhu pózitiv]
negative terminal	kahu negativ (m)	[káhu négativ]
fuse	siguresë (f)	[sigurésə]

air filter	filtri i ajrit (m)	[fíltri i ájrit]
oil filter	filtri i vajit (m)	[fíltri i vájit]
fuel filter	filtri i karburantit (m)	[fíltri i karburántit]

178. Cars. Crash. Repair

car crash	aksident (m)	[aksidént]
traffic accident	aksident rrugor (m)	[aksidént rúgor]
to crash (into the wall, etc.)	përplasem në mur	[pərplásɛm nə mur]

to get smashed up	aksident i rëndë	[aksidént i rəndə]
damage	dëm (m)	[dəm]
intact (unscathed)	pa dëmtime	[pa dəmtímɛ]

breakdown	avari (f)	[avarí]
to break down (vi)	prishet	[príʃɛt]
towrope	kabllo rimorkimi (f)	[kábɫo rimorkími]

puncture	shpim (m)	[ʃpim]
to be flat	shpohet	[ʃpóhɛt]
to pump up	fryj	[fryj]
pressure	presion (m)	[prɛsión]
to check (to examine)	kontrolloj	[kontroɫój]

repair	riparim (m)	[riparím]
auto repair shop	auto servis (m)	[áuto sɛrvís]
spare part	pjesë këmbimi (f)	[pjésə kəmbími]
part	pjesë (f)	[pjésə]

bolt (with nut)	**bulona** (f)	[bulóna]
screw (fastener)	**vida** (f)	[vída]
nut	**dado** (f)	[dádo]
washer	**rondelë** (f)	[rondélə]
bearing (e.g., ball ~)	**kushineta** (f)	[kuʃinéta]
tube	**tub** (m)	[tub]
gasket (head ~)	**rondelë** (f)	[rondélə]
cable, wire	**kabllo** (f)	[kábɫo]
jack	**krik** (m)	[krik]
wrench	**çelës** (m)	[tʃéləs]
hammer	**çekiç** (m)	[tʃɛkítʃ]
pump	**pompë** (f)	[pómpə]
screwdriver	**kaçavidë** (f)	[katʃavídə]
fire extinguisher	**bombolë kundër zjarrit** (f)	[bombólə kúndər zjárit]
warning triangle	**trekëndësh paralajmërues** (m)	[trékəndəʃ paralajmərúɛs]
to stall (vi)	**fiket**	[fíkɛt]
stall (n)	**fikje** (f)	[fíkjɛ]
to be broken	**prishet**	[príʃɛt]
to overheat (vi)	**nxehet**	[ndzéhɛt]
to be clogged up	**bllokohet**	[bɫokóhɛt]
to freeze up (pipes, etc.)	**ngrihet**	[ŋríhɛt]
to burst (vi, ab. tube)	**plas tubi**	[plas túbi]
pressure	**presion** (m)	[prɛsión]
level	**nivel** (m)	[nivél]
slack (~ belt)	**i lirshëm**	[i lírʃəm]
dent	**shtypje** (f)	[ʃtýpjɛ]
knocking noise (engine)	**zhurmë motori** (f)	[ʒúmə motóri]
crack	**çarje** (f)	[tʃárjɛ]
scratch	**gërvishtje** (f)	[gərvíʃtjɛ]

179. Cars. Road

road	**rrugë** (f)	[rúgə]
highway	**autostradë** (f)	[autostrádə]
freeway	**autostradë** (f)	[autostrádə]
direction (way)	**drejtim** (m)	[drɛjtím]
distance	**largësi** (f)	[largəsí]
bridge	**urë** (f)	[úrə]
parking lot	**parking** (m)	[parkíŋ]
square	**shesh** (m)	[ʃɛʃ]
interchange	**kryqëzim rrugësh** (m)	[krycəzím rúgəʃ]

tunnel	tunel (m)	[tunél]
gas station	pikë karburanti (f)	[píkə karburánti]
parking lot	parking (m)	[parkíŋ]
gas pump (fuel dispenser)	pompë karburanti (f)	[pómpə karburánti]
auto repair shop	auto servis (m)	[áuto sɛrvís]
to get gas (to fill up)	furnizohem me gaz	[furnizóhɛm mɛ gáz]
fuel	karburant (m)	[karburánt]
jerrycan	bidon (m)	[bidón]
asphalt	asfalt (m)	[asfált]
road markings	vijëzime të rrugës (pl)	[vijəzímɛ tə rúgəs]
curb	bordurë (f)	[bordúrə]
guardrail	parmakë të sigurisë (pl)	[parmákə tə sigurísə]
ditch	kanal (m)	[kanál]
roadside (shoulder)	shpatull rrugore (f)	[ʃpátuɬ rugórɛ]
lamppost	shtyllë dritash (f)	[ʃtýɬə drítaʃ]
to drive (a car)	ngas	[ŋas]
to turn (e.g., ~ left)	kthej	[kθɛj]
to make a U-turn	marr kthesë U	[mar kθésə u]
reverse (~ gear)	marsh prapa (m)	[marʃ prápa]
to honk (vi)	i bie borisë	[i bíɛ borísə]
honk (sound)	tyt (m)	[tyt]
to get stuck (in the mud, etc.)	ngec në baltë	[ŋɛts nə báltə]
to spin the wheels	xhiroj gomat	[dʒirój gómat]
to cut, to turn off (vt)	fik	[fik]
speed	shpejtësi (f)	[ʃpɛjtəsí]
to exceed the speed limit	kaloj minimumin e shpejtësisë	[kalój minimúmin ɛ ʃpɛjtəsísə]
to give a ticket	vë gjobë	[və ɟóbə]
traffic lights	semafor (m)	[sɛmafór]
driver's license	patentë shoferi (f)	[paténtə ʃoféri]
grade crossing	kalim hekurudhor (m)	[kalím hɛkuruðór]
intersection	kryqëzim (m)	[krycəzím]
crosswalk	kalim për këmbësorë (m)	[kalím pər kəmbəsórə]
bend, curve	kthesë (f)	[kθésə]
pedestrian zone	zonë këmbësorësh (f)	[zónə kəmbəsórəʃ]

180. Traffic signs

rules of the road	rregullat e trafikut rrugor (pl)	[réguɬat ɛ trafíkut rugór]
road sign (traffic sign)	shenjë trafiku (f)	[ʃéɲə trafíku]
passing (overtaking)	tejkalim	[tɛjkalím]
curve	kthesë	[kθésə]
U-turn	kthesë U	[kθésə u]

traffic circle	rrethrrotullim	[rɛθrotuɫím]
No entry	Ndalohet hyrja	[ndalóhɛt hýrja]
No vehicles allowed	Ndalohen automjetet	[ndalóhɛn automjétɛt]
No passing	Ndalohet tejkalimi	[ndalóhɛt tɛjkalími]
No parking	Ndalohet parkimi	[ndalóhɛt parkími]
No stopping	Ndalohet qëndrimi	[ndalóhɛt cəndrími]

dangerous bend	kthesë e rrezikshme	[kθésə ɛ rɛzíkʃmɛ]
steep descent	pjerrësi e fortë	[pjɛrəsí ɛ fórtə]
one-way traffic	rrugë me një drejtim	[rúgə mɛ ɲə drɛjtím]
crosswalk	kalim për këmbësorë (m)	[kalím pər kəmbəsórə]
slippery road	rrugë e rrëshqitshme	[rúgə ɛ rəʃcítʃmɛ]
YIELD	HAP UDHËN	[hap úðən]

PEOPLE. LIFE EVENTS

Life events

181. Holidays. Event

celebration, holiday	festë (f)	[féstə]
national day	festë kombëtare (f)	[féstə kombətárɛ]
public holiday	festë publike (f)	[féstə publíkɛ]
to commemorate (vt)	festoj	[fɛstój]
event (happening)	ceremoni (f)	[tsɛrɛmoní]
event (organized activity)	eveniment (m)	[ɛvɛnimént]
banquet (party)	banket (m)	[bankét]
reception (formal party)	pritje (f)	[prítjɛ]
feast	aheng (m)	[ahéŋ]
anniversary	përvjetor (m)	[pərvjɛtór]
jubilee	jubile (m)	[jubilé]
to celebrate (vt)	festoj	[fɛstój]
New Year	Viti i Ri (m)	[víti i rí]
Happy New Year!	Gëzuar Vitin e Ri!	[gəzúar vítin ɛ rí!]
Santa Claus	Santa Klaus (m)	[sánta kláus]
Christmas	Krishtlindje (f)	[kriʃtlíndjɛ]
Merry Christmas!	Gëzuar Krishtlindjen!	[gəzúar kriʃtlíndjɛn!]
Christmas tree	péma e Krishtlindjes (f)	[péma ɛ kriʃtlíndjɛs]
fireworks (fireworks show)	fishekzjarrë (m)	[fiʃɛkzjárə]
wedding	dasmë (f)	[dásmə]
groom	dhëndër (m)	[ðéndər]
bride	nuse (f)	[núsɛ]
to invite (vt)	ftoj	[ftoj]
invitation card	ftesë (f)	[ftésə]
guest	mysafir (m)	[mysafír]
to visit	vizitoj	[vizitój]
(~ your parents, etc.)		
to meet the guests	takoj të ftuarit	[takój tə ftúarit]
gift, present	dhuratë (f)	[ðurátə]
to give (sth as present)	dhuroj	[ðurój]
to receive gifts	marr dhurata	[mar ðuráta]

bouquet (of flowers)	buqetë (f)	[bucétə]
congratulations	urime (f)	[urímɛ]
to congratulate (vt)	përgëzoj	[pərgəzój]

greeting card	kartolinë (f)	[kartolínə]
to send a postcard	dërgoj kartolinë	[dərgój kartolínə]
to get a postcard	marr kartolinë	[mar kartolínə]

toast	dolli (f)	[dotí]
to offer (a drink, etc.)	qeras	[cɛrás]
champagne	shampanjë (f)	[ʃampáɲə]

to enjoy oneself	kënaqem	[kənácɛm]
merriment (gaiety)	gëzim (m)	[gəzím]
joy (emotion)	gëzim (m)	[gəzím]

| dance | vallëzim (m) | [vaɫəzím] |
| to dance (vi, vt) | vallëzoj | [vaɫəzój] |

| waltz | vals (m) | [vals] |
| tango | tango (f) | [táŋo] |

182. Funerals. Burial

cemetery	varreza (f)	[varéza]
grave, tomb	varr (m)	[var]
cross	kryq (m)	[kryc]
gravestone	gur varri (m)	[gur vári]
fence	gardh (m)	[garð]
chapel	kishëz (m)	[kíʃəz]

death	vdekje (f)	[vdékjɛ]
to die (vi)	vdes	[vdɛs]
the deceased	i vdekuri (m)	[i vdékuri]
mourning	zi (f)	[zi]
to bury (vt)	varros	[varós]
funeral home	agjenci funeralesh (f)	[aɟɛntsí funɛráleʃ]
funeral	funeral (m)	[funɛrál]

wreath	kurorë (f)	[kurórə]
casket, coffin	arkivol (m)	[arkivól]
hearse	makinë funebre (f)	[makínə funébrɛ]
shroud	qefin (m)	[cɛfín]

funeral procession	kortezh (m)	[kortéʒ]
funerary urn	urnë (f)	[úrnə]
crematory	kremator (m)	[krɛmatór]
obituary	përkujtim (m)	[pərkujtím]
to cry (weep)	qaj	[caj]
to sob (vi)	qaj me dënesë	[caj mɛ dənésə]

183. War. Soldiers

platoon	togë (f)	[tógə]
company	kompani (f)	[kompaní]
regiment	regjiment (m)	[rɛɟimént]
army	ushtri (f)	[uʃtrí]
division	divizion (m)	[divizión]
section, squad	skuadër (f)	[skuádər]
host (army)	armatë (f)	[armátə]
soldier	ushtar (m)	[uʃtár]
officer	oficer (m)	[ofitsér]
private	ushtar (m)	[uʃtár]
sergeant	rreshter (m)	[rɛʃtér]
lieutenant	toger (m)	[togér]
captain	kapiten (m)	[kapitén]
major	major (m)	[majór]
colonel	kolonel (m)	[kolonél]
general	gjeneral (m)	[ɟɛnɛrál]
sailor	marinar (m)	[marinár]
captain	kapiten (m)	[kapitén]
boatswain	kryemarinar (m)	[kryɛmarinár]
artilleryman	artiljer (m)	[artiljér]
paratrooper	parashutist (m)	[paraʃutíst]
pilot	pilot (m)	[pilót]
navigator	naviguers (m)	[navigúɛs]
mechanic	mekanik (m)	[mɛkaník]
pioneer (sapper)	xhenier (m)	[dʒɛniér]
parachutist	parashutist (m)	[paraʃutíst]
reconnaissance scout	agjent zbulimi (m)	[aɟént zbulími]
sniper	snajper (m)	[snajpér]
patrol (group)	patrullë (f)	[patrúłə]
to patrol (vt)	patrulloj	[patrułój]
sentry, guard	rojë (f)	[rójə]
warrior	luftëtar (m)	[luftətár]
patriot	patriot (m)	[patriót]
hero	hero (m)	[hɛró]
heroine	heroinë (f)	[hɛroínə]
traitor	tradhtar (m)	[traðtár]
to betray (vt)	tradhtoj	[traðtój]
deserter	dezertues (m)	[dɛzɛrtúɛs]
to desert (vi)	dezertoj	[dɛzɛrtój]

mercenary	mercenar (m)	[mɛrtsɛnár]
recruit	rekrut (m)	[rɛkrút]
volunteer	vullnetar (m)	[vułnɛtár]

dead (n)	vdekur (m)	[vdékuɾ]
wounded (n)	i plagosur (m)	[i plagósur]
prisoner of war	rob lufte (m)	[rob lúftɛ]

184. War. Military actions. Part 1

war	luftë (f)	[lúftə]
to be at war	në luftë	[nə lúftə]
civil war	luftë civile (f)	[lúftə tsivílɛ]

treacherously (adv)	pabesisht	[pabɛsíʃt]
declaration of war	shpallje lufte (f)	[ʃpátjɛ lúftɛ]
to declare (~ war)	shpall	[ʃpał]
aggression	agresion (m)	[agrɛsión]
to attack (invade)	sulmoj	[sulmój]

to invade (vt)	pushtoj	[puʃtój]
invader	pushtues (m)	[puʃtúɛs]
conqueror	pushtues (m)	[puʃtúɛs]

defense	mbrojtje (f)	[mbrójtjɛ]
to defend (a country, etc.)	mbroj	[mbrój]
to defend (against ...)	mbrohem	[mbróhɛm]

enemy	armik (m)	[armík]
foe, adversary	kundërshtar (m)	[kundərʃtár]
enemy (as adj)	armike	[armíkɛ]

| strategy | strategji (f) | [stratɛɟí] |
| tactics | taktikë (f) | [taktíkə] |

order	urdhër (m)	[úrðər]
command (order)	komandë (f)	[komándə]
to order (vt)	urdhëroj	[urðərój]
mission	mision (m)	[misión]
secret (adj)	sekret	[sɛkrét]

| battle, combat | betejë (f) | [bɛtéjə] |
| combat | luftim (m) | [luftím] |

attack	sulm (m)	[sulm]
charge (assault)	sulm (m)	[sulm]
to storm (vt)	sulmoj	[sulmój]
siege (to be under ~)	nën rrethim (m)	[nən rɛθím]
offensive (n)	sulm (m)	[sulm]
to go on the offensive	kaloj në sulm	[kalój nə súlm]

| retreat | tërheqje (f) | [tərhécjɛ] |
| to retreat (vi) | tërhiqem | [tərhícɛm] |

| encirclement | rrethim (m) | [rɛθím] |
| to encircle (vt) | rrethoj | [rɛθój] |

bombing (by aircraft)	bombardim (m)	[bombardím]
to drop a bomb	hedh bombë	[hɛð bómbə]
to bomb (vt)	bombardoj	[bombardój]
explosion	shpërthim (m)	[ʃpərθím]

shot	e shtënë (f)	[ɛ ʃtə́nə]
to fire (~ a shot)	qëlloj	[cəɫój]
firing (burst of ~)	të shtëna (pl)	[tə ʃtə́na]

to aim (to point a weapon)	vë në shënjestër	[və nə ʃəɲéstər]
to point (a gun)	drejtoj armën	[drɛjtój ármən]
to hit (the target)	qëlloj	[cəɫój]

to sink (~ a ship)	fundos	[fundós]
hole (in a ship)	vrimë (f)	[vrímə]
to founder, to sink (vi)	fundoset	[fundósɛt]

front (war ~)	front (m)	[front]
evacuation	evakuim (m)	[ɛvakuím]
to evacuate (vt)	evakuoj	[ɛvakuój]

trench	llogore (f)	[ɫogórɛ]
barbwire	tel me gjemba (m)	[tɛl mɛ ɟémba]
barrier (anti tank ~)	pengesë (f)	[pɛŋésə]
watchtower	kullë vrojtuese (f)	[kúɫə vrojtúɛsɛ]

military hospital	spital ushtarak (m)	[spitál uʃtarák]
to wound (vt)	plagos	[plagós]
wound	plagë (f)	[plágə]
wounded (n)	i plagosur (m)	[i plagósur]
to be wounded	jam i plagosur	[jam i plagósur]
serious (wound)	rëndë	[rə́ndə]

185. War. Military actions. Part 2

captivity	burgosje (f)	[burgósjɛ]
to take captive	zë rob	[zə rob]
to be held captive	mbahem rob	[mbáhɛm rób]
to be taken captive	zihem rob	[zíhɛm rob]

concentration camp	kamp përqendrimi (m)	[kamp pərcɛndrími]
prisoner of war	rob lufte (m)	[rob lúftɛ]
to escape (vi)	arratisem	[aratísɛm]
to betray (vt)	tradhtoj	[traðtój]

betrayer	**tradhtar** (m)	[traðtár]
betrayal	**tradhti** (f)	[traðtí]
to execute (by firing squad)	**ekzekutoj**	[ɛkzɛkutój]
execution (by firing squad)	**ekzekutim** (m)	[ɛkzɛkutím]
equipment (military gear)	**armatim** (m)	[armatím]
shoulder board	**spaletë** (f)	[spalétə]
gas mask	**maskë antigaz** (f)	[máskə antigáz]
field radio	**radiomarrëse** (f)	[radiomárəsɛ]
cipher, code	**kod sekret** (m)	[kód sɛkrét]
secrecy	**komplot** (m)	[komplót]
password	**fjalëkalim** (m)	[fjaləkalím]
land mine	**minë tokësore** (f)	[mínə tokəsórɛ]
to mine (road, etc.)	**minoj**	[minój]
minefield	**fushë e minuar** (f)	[fúʃə ɛ minúar]
air-raid warning	**alarm sulmi ajror** (m)	[alárm súlmi ajrór]
alarm (alert signal)	**alarm** (m)	[alárm]
signal	**sinjal** (m)	[siɲál]
signal flare	**sinjalizues** (m)	[siɲalizúɛs]
headquarters	**selia qendrore** (f)	[sɛlía cɛndrórɛ]
reconnaissance	**zbulim** (m)	[zbulím]
situation	**gjendje** (f)	[ɟéndjɛ]
report	**raport** (m)	[rapórt]
ambush	**pritë** (f)	[prítə]
reinforcement (of army)	**përforcim** (m)	[pərfortsím]
target	**shënjestër** (f)	[ʃəɲéstər]
proving ground	**poligon** (m)	[poligón]
military exercise	**manovra ushtarake** (f)	[manóvra uʃtarákɛ]
panic	**panik** (m)	[paník]
devastation	**shkatërrim** (m)	[ʃkatərím]
destruction, ruins	**gërmadha** (pl)	[gərmáða]
to destroy (vt)	**shkatërroj**	[ʃkatərój]
to survive (vi, vt)	**mbijetoj**	[mbijɛtój]
to disarm (vt)	**çarmatos**	[tʃarmatós]
to handle (~ a gun)	**manovroj**	[manovrój]
Attention!	**Gatitu!**	[gatitú!]
At ease!	**Qetësohu!**	[cɛtəsóhu!]
feat, act of courage	**akt heroik** (m)	[ákt hɛroík]
oath (vow)	**betim** (m)	[bɛtím]
to swear (an oath)	**betohem**	[bɛtóhɛm]
decoration (medal, etc.)	**dekoratë** (f)	[dɛkorátə]

to award (give medal to)	**dekoroj**	[dɛkorój]
medal	**medalje** (f)	[mɛdáljɛ]
order (e.g., ~ of Merit)	**urdhër medalje** (m)	[úrðər mɛdáljɛ]

victory	**fitore** (f)	[fitórɛ]
defeat	**humbje** (f)	[húmbjɛ]
armistice	**armëpushim** (m)	[arməpuʃím]

standard (battle flag)	**flamur beteje** (m)	[flamúr bɛtéjɛ]
glory (honor, fame)	**famë** (f)	[fámə]
parade	**paradë** (f)	[parádə]
to march (on parade)	**marshoj**	[marʃój]

186. Weapons

weapons	**armë** (f)	[ármə]
firearms	**armë zjarri** (f)	[ármə zjári]
cold weapons (knives, etc.)	**armë të ftohta** (pl)	[ármə tə ftóhta]

chemical weapons	**armë kimike** (f)	[ármə kimíkɛ]
nuclear (adj)	**nukleare**	[nuklɛárɛ]
nuclear weapons	**armë nukleare** (f)	[ármə nuklɛárɛ]

bomb	**bombë** (f)	[bómbə]
atomic bomb	**bombë atomike** (f)	[bómbə atomíkɛ]

pistol (gun)	**pistoletë** (f)	[pistolétə]
rifle	**pushkë** (f)	[púʃkə]
submachine gun	**mitraloz** (m)	[mitralóz]
machine gun	**mitraloz** (m)	[mitralóz]

muzzle	**grykë** (f)	[grýkə]
barrel	**tytë pushke** (f)	[týtə púʃkɛ]
caliber	**kalibër** (m)	[kalíbər]

trigger	**këmbëz** (f)	[kémbəz]
sight (aiming device)	**shënjestër** (f)	[ʃəɲéstər]
magazine	**karikator** (m)	[karikatór]
butt (shoulder stock)	**qytë** (f)	[cýtə]

hand grenade	**bombë dore** (f)	[bómbə dórɛ]
explosive	**eksploziv** (m)	[ɛksplozív]

bullet	**plumb** (m)	[plúmb]
cartridge	**fishek** (m)	[fiʃék]
charge	**karikim** (m)	[karikím]
ammunition	**municion** (m)	[munitsión]
bomber (aircraft)	**avion bombardues** (m)	[avión bombardúɛs]
fighter	**avion luftarak** (m)	[avión luftarák]

helicopter	helikopter (m)	[hɛlikoptér]
anti-aircraft gun	armë anti-ajrore (f)	[ármə ánti-ajrórɛ]
tank	tank (m)	[tank]
tank gun	top tanku (m)	[top tánku]

artillery	artileri (f)	[artilɛrí]
gun (cannon, howitzer)	top (m)	[top]
to lay (a gun)	vë në shënjestër	[və nə ʃəɲéstər]

shell (projectile)	mortajë (f)	[mortájə]
mortar bomb	bombë mortaje (f)	[bómbə mortájɛ]
mortar	mortajë (f)	[mortájə]
splinter (shell fragment)	copëz mortaje (f)	[tsópəz mortájɛ]

submarine	nëndetëse (f)	[nəndétəsɛ]
torpedo	silurë (f)	[silúrə]
missile	raketë (f)	[rakétə]

to load (gun)	mbush	[mbúʃ]
to shoot (vi)	qëlloj	[cəɫój]
to point at (the cannon)	drejtoj	[drɛjtój]
bayonet	bajonetë (f)	[bajonétə]

rapier	shpatë (f)	[ʃpátə]
saber (e.g., cavalry ~)	shpatë (f)	[ʃpátə]
spear (weapon)	shtizë (f)	[ʃtízə]
bow	hark (m)	[hárk]
arrow	shigjetë (f)	[ʃiɟétə]
musket	musketë (f)	[muskétə]
crossbow	pushkë-shigjetë (f)	[púʃkə-ʃiɟétə]

187. Ancient people

primitive (prehistoric)	prehistorik	[prɛhistorík]
prehistoric (adj)	prehistorike	[prɛhistoríkɛ]
ancient (~ civilization)	i lashtë	[i láʃtə]

Stone Age	Epoka e Gurit (f)	[ɛpóka ɛ gúrit]
Bronze Age	Epoka e Bronzit (f)	[ɛpóka ɛ brónzit]
Ice Age	Epoka e akullit (f)	[ɛpóka ɛ ákuɫit]

tribe	klan (m)	[klan]
cannibal	kanibal (m)	[kanibál]
hunter	gjahtar (m)	[ɟahtár]
to hunt (vi, vt)	dal për gjah	[dál pər ɟáh]
mammoth	mamut (m)	[mamút]

cave	shpellë (f)	[ʃpéɫə]
fire	zjarr (m)	[zjar]
campfire	zjarr kampingu (m)	[zjar kampíŋu]

cave painting	vizatim në shpella (m)	[vizatím nə ʃpéła]
tool (e.g., stone ax)	vegël (f)	[végəl]
spear	shtizë (f)	[ʃtízə]
stone ax	sëpatë guri (f)	[səpátə gúri]
to be at war	në luftë	[nə lúftə]
to domesticate (vt)	zbus	[zbus]

idol	idhull (m)	[íðuł]
to worship (vt)	adhuroj	[aðurój]
superstition	besëtytni (f)	[bɛsətytní]
rite	rit (m)	[rit]

evolution	evolucion (m)	[ɛvolutsión]
development	zhvillim (m)	[ʒviłím]
disappearance (extinction)	zhdukje (f)	[ʒdúkjɛ]
to adapt oneself	përshtatem	[pərʃtátɛm]

archeology	arkeologji (f)	[arkɛoloɟí]
archeologist	arkeolog (m)	[arkɛológ]
archeological (adj)	arkeologjike	[arkɛoloɟíkɛ]

excavation site	vendi i gërmimeve (m)	[véndi i gərmímɛvɛ]
excavations	gërmime (pl)	[gərmímɛ]
find (object)	zbulim (m)	[zbulím]
fragment	fragment (m)	[fragmént]

188. Middle Ages

people (ethnic group)	popull (f)	[pópuł]
peoples	popuj (pl)	[pópuj]
tribe	klan (m)	[klan]
tribes	klane (pl)	[klánɛ]

barbarians	barbarë (pl)	[barbárə]
Gauls	Galët (pl)	[gálət]
Goths	Gotët (pl)	[gótət]
Slavs	Sllavët (pl)	[słávət]
Vikings	Vikingët (pl)	[vikíŋət]

| Romans | Romakët (pl) | [romákət] |
| Roman (adj) | romak | [romák] |

Byzantines	Bizantinët (pl)	[bizantínət]
Byzantium	Bizanti (m)	[bizánti]
Byzantine (adj)	bizantine	[bizantínɛ]

emperor	perandor (m)	[pɛrandór]
leader, chief (tribal ~)	prijës (m)	[príjəs]
powerful (~ king)	i fuqishëm	[i fucíʃəm]
king	mbret (m)	[mbrét]

ruler (sovereign)	sundimtar (m)	[sundimtár]
knight	kalorës (m)	[kalórəs]
feudal lord	lord feudal (m)	[lórd fɛudál]
feudal (adj)	feudal	[fɛudál]
vassal	vasal (m)	[vasál]

duke	dukë (f)	[dúkə]
earl	kont (m)	[kont]
baron	baron (m)	[barón]
bishop	peshkop (m)	[pɛʃkóp]

armor	parzmore (f)	[parzmórɛ]
shield	mburojë (f)	[mburójə]
sword	shpatë (f)	[ʃpátə]
visor	ballnik (m)	[bałník]
chainmail	thurak (m)	[θurák]

| Crusade | Kryqëzata (f) | [krycəzáta] |
| crusader | kryqtar (m) | [kryctár] |

territory	territor (m)	[tɛritór]
to attack (invade)	sulmoj	[sulmój]
to conquer (vt)	mposht	[mpóʃt]
to occupy (invade)	pushtoj	[puʃtój]

siege (to be under ~)	nën rrethim (m)	[nən rɛθím]
besieged (adj)	i rrethuar	[i rɛθúar]
to besiege (vt)	rrethoj	[rɛθój]

inquisition	inkuizicion (m)	[inkuizitsión]
inquisitor	inkuizitor (m)	[inkuizitór]
torture	torturë (f)	[tortúrə]
cruel (adj)	mizor	[mizór]
heretic	heretik (m)	[hɛrɛtík]
heresy	herezi (f)	[hɛrɛzí]

seafaring	lundrim (m)	[lundrím]
pirate	pirat (m)	[pirát]
piracy	pirateri (f)	[piratɛrí]
boarding (attack)	sulm me anije (m)	[sulm mɛ aníjɛ]

| loot, booty | plaçkë (f) | [plátʃkə] |
| treasures | thesare (pl) | [θɛsárɛ] |

discovery	zbulim (m)	[zbulím]
to discover (new land, etc.)	zbuloj	[zbulój]
expedition	ekspeditë (f)	[ɛkspɛdítə]

musketeer	musketar (m)	[muskɛtár]
cardinal	kardinal (m)	[kardinál]
heraldry	heraldikë (f)	[hɛraldíkə]
heraldic (adj)	heraldik	[hɛraldík]

189. Leader. Chief. Authorities

king	**mbret** (m)	[mbrét]
queen	**mbretëreshë** (f)	[mbrɛtəréʃə]
royal (adj)	**mbretërore**	[mbrɛtərórɛ]
kingdom	**mbretëri** (f)	[mbrɛtərí]
prince	**princ** (m)	[prints]
princess	**princeshë** (f)	[printséʃə]
president	**president** (m)	[prɛsidént]
vice-president	**zëvendës president** (m)	[zəvéndəs prɛsidént]
senator	**senator** (m)	[sɛnatór]
monarch	**monark** (m)	[monárk]
ruler (sovereign)	**sundimtar** (m)	[sundimtár]
dictator	**diktator** (m)	[diktatór]
tyrant	**tiran** (m)	[tirán]
magnate	**manjat** (m)	[maɲát]
director	**drejtor** (m)	[drɛjtór]
chief	**udhëheqës** (m)	[uðəhécəs]
manager (director)	**drejtor** (m)	[drɛjtór]
boss	**bos** (m)	[bos]
owner	**pronar** (m)	[pronár]
leader	**lider** (m)	[lidér]
head (~ of delegation)	**kryetar** (m)	[kryɛtár]
authorities	**autoritetet** (pl)	[autoritétɛt]
superiors	**eprorët** (pl)	[ɛprórət]
governor	**guvernator** (m)	[guvɛrnatór]
consul	**konsull** (m)	[kónsuɫ]
diplomat	**diplomat** (m)	[diplomát]
mayor	**kryetar komune** (m)	[kryɛtár komúnɛ]
sheriff	**sherif** (m)	[ʃɛríf]
emperor	**perandor** (m)	[pɛrandór]
tsar, czar	**car** (m)	[tsár]
pharaoh	**faraon** (m)	[faraón]
khan	**khan** (m)	[khán]

190. Road. Way. Directions

road	**rrugë** (f)	[rúgə]
way (direction)	**drejtim** (m)	[drɛjtím]
freeway	**autostradë** (f)	[autostrádə]
highway	**autostradë** (f)	[autostrádə]

interstate	**rrugë nacionale** (f)	[rúgə natsionálɛ]
main road	**rrugë kryesore** (f)	[rúgə kryɛsórɛ]
dirt road	**rrugë fushe** (f)	[rúgə fúʃɛ]
pathway	**shteg** (m)	[ʃtɛg]
footpath (troddenpath)	**shteg** (m)	[ʃtɛg]
Where?	**Ku?**	[ku?]
Where (to)?	**Për ku?**	[pər ku?]
From where?	**Nga ku?**	[ŋa ku?]
direction (way)	**drejtim** (m)	[drɛjtím]
to point (~ the way)	**tregoj**	[trɛgój]
to the left	**në të majtë**	[nə tə májtə]
to the right	**në të djathtë**	[nə tə djáθtə]
straight ahead (adv)	**drejt**	[dréjt]
back (e.g., to turn ~)	**pas**	[pas]
bend, curve	**kthesë** (f)	[kθésə]
to turn (e.g., ~ left)	**kthej**	[kθɛj]
to make a U-turn	**marr kthesë U**	[mar kθésə u]
to be visible (mountains, castle, etc.)	**të dukshme**	[tə dúkʃmɛ]
to appear (come into view)	**shfaq**	[ʃfac]
stop, halt (e.g., during a trip)	**ndalesë** (f)	[ndalésə]
to rest, to pause (vi)	**pushoj**	[puʃój]
rest (pause)	**pushim** (m)	[puʃím]
to lose one's way	**humb rrugën**	[húmb rúgən]
to lead to ... (ab. road)	**të çon**	[tə tʃon]
to come out (e.g., on the highway)	**dal**	[dal]
stretch (of road)	**copëz** (m)	[tsópəz]
asphalt	**asfalt** (m)	[asfált]
curb	**bordurë** (f)	[bordúrə]
ditch	**kanal** (m)	[kanál]
manhole	**pusetë** (f)	[pusétə]
roadside (shoulder)	**shpatull rrugore** (f)	[ʃpátuɫ rugórɛ]
pit, pothole	**gropë** (f)	[grópə]
to go (on foot)	**ec në këmbë**	[ɛts nə kémbə]
to pass (overtake)	**tejkaloj**	[tɛjkalój]
step (footstep)	**hap** (m)	[hap]
on foot (adv)	**në këmbë**	[nə kémbə]
to block (road)	**bllokoj**	[bɫokój]
boom gate	**postbllok** (m)	[postbɫók]
dead end	**rrugë pa krye** (f)	[rúgə pa krýɛ]

191. Breaking the law. Criminals. Part 1

bandit	bandit (m)	[bandít]
crime	krim (m)	[krim]
criminal (person)	kriminel (m)	[kriminél]

thief	hajdut (m)	[hajdút]
to steal (vi, vt)	vjedh	[vjɛð]
stealing, theft	vjedhje (f)	[vjéðjɛ]

to kidnap (vt)	rrëmbej	[rəmbéj]
kidnapping	rrëmbim (m)	[rəmbím]
kidnapper	rrëmbyes (m)	[rəmbýɛs]

| ransom | shpërblesë (f) | [ʃpərblésə] |
| to demand ransom | kërkoj shpërblesë | [kərkój ʃpərblésə] |

to rob (vt)	grabis	[grabís]
robbery	grabitje (f)	[grabítjɛ]
robber	grabitës (m)	[grabítəs]

to extort (vt)	zhvat	[ʒvat]
extortionist	zhvatës (m)	[ʒvátəs]
extortion	zhvatje (f)	[ʒvátjɛ]

to murder, to kill	vras	[vras]
murder	vrasje (f)	[vrásjɛ]
murderer	vrasës (m)	[vrásəs]

gunshot	e shtënë (f)	[ɛ ʃténə]
to fire (~ a shot)	qëlloj	[cəɫój]
to shoot to death	qëlloj për vdekje	[cəɫój pər vdékjɛ]
to shoot (vi)	qëlloj	[cəɫój]
shooting	të shtëna (pl)	[tə ʃténa]

incident (fight, etc.)	incident (m)	[intsidént]
fight, brawl	përleshje (f)	[pərléʃɛ]
Help!	Ndihmë!	[ndíhmə!]
victim	viktimë (f)	[viktímə]

to damage (vt)	dëmtoj	[dəmtój]
damage	dëm (m)	[dəm]
dead body, corpse	kufomë (f)	[kufómə]
grave (~ crime)	i rëndë	[i réndə]

to attack (vt)	sulmoj	[sulmój]
to beat (to hit)	rrah	[rah]
to beat up	sakatoj	[sakatój]
to take (rob of sth)	rrëmbej	[rəmbéj]
to stab to death	ther për vdekje	[θɛr pər vdékjɛ]
to maim (vt)	gjymtoj	[ɟymtój]

to wound (vt)	plagos	[plagós]
blackmail	shantazh (m)	[ʃantáʒ]
to blackmail (vt)	bëj shantazh	[bəj ʃantáʒ]
blackmailer	shantazhist (m)	[ʃantaʒíst]

protection racket	rrjet mashtrimi (m)	[rjét maʃtrími]
racketeer	mashtrues (m)	[maʃtrúɛs]
gangster	gangster (m)	[gaŋstér]
mafia, Mob	mafia (f)	[máfia]

pickpocket	vjedhës xhepash (m)	[vjéðəs dʒépaʃ]
burglar	hajdut (m)	[hajdút]
smuggling	trafikim (m)	[trafikím]
smuggler	trafikues (m)	[trafikúɛs]

forgery	falsifikim (m)	[falsifikím]
to forge (counterfeit)	falsifikoj	[falsifikój]
fake (forged)	fals	[fáls]

192. Breaking the law. Criminals. Part 2

rape	përdhunim (m)	[pərðuním]
to rape (vt)	përdhunoj	[pərðunój]
rapist	përdhunues (m)	[pərðunúɛs]
maniac	maniak (m)	[maniák]

prostitute (fem.)	prostitutë (f)	[prostitútə]
prostitution	prostitucion (m)	[prostitutsión]
pimp	tutor (m)	[tutór]

| drug addict | narkoman (m) | [narkomán] |
| drug dealer | trafikant droge (m) | [trafikánt drógɛ] |

to blow up (bomb)	shpërthej	[ʃpərθéj]
explosion	shpërthim (m)	[ʃpərθím]
to set fire	vë flakën	[və flákən]
arsonist	zjarrvënës (m)	[zjarvénəs]

terrorism	terrorizëm (m)	[tɛrorízəm]
terrorist	terrorist (m)	[tɛroríst]
hostage	peng (m)	[pɛŋ]

to swindle (deceive)	mashtroj	[maʃtrój]
swindle, deception	mashtrim (m)	[maʃtrím]
swindler	mashtrues (m)	[maʃtrúɛs]

to bribe (vt)	jap ryshfet	[jap ryʃfét]
bribery	ryshfet (m)	[ryʃfét]
bribe	ryshfet (m)	[ryʃfét]
poison	helm (m)	[hɛlm]

| to poison (vt) | helmoj | [hɛlmój] |
| to poison oneself | helmohem | [hɛlmóhɛm] |

| suicide (act) | vetëvrasje (f) | [vɛtəvrásjɛ] |
| suicide (person) | vetëvrasës (m) | [vɛtəvrásəs] |

to threaten (vt)	kërcënoj	[kərtsənój]
threat	kërcënim (m)	[kərtsəním]
to make an attempt	tentoj	[tɛntój]
attempt (attack)	atentat (m)	[atɛntát]

| to steal (a car) | vjedh | [vjɛð] |
| to hijack (a plane) | rrëmbej | [rəmbéj] |

| revenge | hakmarrje (f) | [hakmárjɛ] |
| to avenge (get revenge) | hakmerrem | [hakmérɛm] |

to torture (vt)	torturoj	[torturój]
torture	torturë (f)	[tortúrə]
to torment (vt)	torturoj	[torturój]

pirate	pirat (m)	[pirát]
hooligan	huligan (m)	[huligán]
armed (adj)	i armatosur	[i armatósur]
violence	dhunë (f)	[ðúnə]
illegal (unlawful)	ilegal	[ilɛgál]

| spying (espionage) | spiunazh (m) | [spiunáʒ] |
| to spy (vi) | spiunoj | [spiunój] |

193. Police. Law. Part 1

| justice | drejtësi (f) | [drɛjtəsí] |
| court (see you in ~) | gjykatë (f) | [ɟykátə] |

judge	gjykatës (m)	[ɟykátəs]
jurors	anëtar jurie (m)	[anətár juríɛ]
jury trial	gjyq me juri (m)	[ɟýc mɛ jurí]
to judge, to try (vt)	gjykoj	[ɟykój]

lawyer, attorney	avokat (m)	[avokát]
defendant	pandehur (m)	[pandéhur]
dock	bankë e të pandehurit (f)	[bánkə ɛ tə pandéhurit]

| charge | akuzë (f) | [akúzə] |
| accused | i akuzuar (m) | [i akuzúar] |

sentence	vendim (m)	[vɛndím]
to sentence (vt)	dënoj	[dənój]
guilty (culprit)	fajtor (m)	[fajtór]

| to punish (vt) | ndëshkoj | [ndəʃkój] |
| punishment | ndëshkim (m) | [ndəʃkím] |

fine (penalty)	gjobë (f)	[ɟóbə]
life imprisonment	burgim i përjetshëm (m)	[burgím i pərjétʃəm]
death penalty	dënim me vdekje (m)	[dəním mɛ vdékjɛ]
electric chair	karrige elektrike (f)	[karígɛ ɛlɛktríkɛ]
gallows	varje (f)	[várjɛ]

| to execute (vt) | ekzekutoj | [ɛkzɛkutój] |
| execution | ekzekutim (m) | [ɛkzɛkutím] |

| prison, jail | burg (m) | [búrg] |
| cell | qeli (f) | [cɛlí] |

escort (convoy)	eskortë (f)	[ɛskórtə]
prison guard	gardian burgu (m)	[gardián búrgu]
prisoner	i burgosur (m)	[i burgósur]

| handcuffs | pranga (f) | [práŋa] |
| to handcuff (vt) | vë prangat | [və práŋat] |

prison break	arratisje nga burgu (f)	[aratísjɛ ŋa búrgu]
to break out (vi)	arratisem	[aratísɛm]
to disappear (vi)	zhduk	[ʒduk]
to release (from prison)	dal nga burgu	[dál ŋa búrgu]
amnesty	amnisti (f)	[amnistí]

police	polici (f)	[politsí]
police officer	polic (m)	[políts]
police station	komisariat (m)	[komisariát]
billy club	shkop gome (m)	[ʃkop gómɛ]
bullhorn	altoparlant (m)	[altoparlánt]

patrol car	makinë patrullimi (f)	[makínə patruɫími]
siren	alarm (m)	[alárm]
to turn on the siren	ndez sirenën	[ndɛz sirénən]
siren call	zhurmë alarmi (f)	[ʒúrmə alármi]

crime scene	skenë krimi (f)	[skénə krími]
witness	dëshmitar (m)	[dəʃmitár]
freedom	liri (f)	[lirí]
accomplice	bashkëpunëtor (m)	[baʃkəpunətór]
to flee (vi)	zhdukem	[ʒdúkɛm]
trace (to leave a ~)	gjurmë (f)	[ɟúrmə]

194. Police. Law. Part 2

| search (investigation) | kërkim (m) | [kərkím] |
| to look for ... | kërkoj ... | [kərkój ...] |

suspicion	dyshim (m)	[dyʃím]
suspicious (e.g., ~ vehicle)	i dyshuar	[i dyʃúar]
to stop (cause to halt)	ndaloj	[ndalój]
to detain (keep in custody)	mbaj të ndaluar	[mbáj tə ndalúar]

case (lawsuit)	padi (f)	[padí]
investigation	hetim (m)	[hɛtím]
detective	detektiv (m)	[dɛtɛktív]
investigator	hetues (m)	[hɛtúɛs]
hypothesis	hipotezë (f)	[hipotézə]

motive	motiv (m)	[motív]
interrogation	marrje në pyetje (f)	[márjɛ nə pýɛtjɛ]
to interrogate (vt)	marr në pyetje	[mar nə pýɛtjɛ]
to question	pyes	[pýɛs]
(~ neighbors, etc.)		
check (identity ~)	verifikim (m)	[vɛrifikím]

round-up (raid)	kontroll në grup (m)	[kontróɫ nə grúp]
search (~ warrant)	bastisje (f)	[bastísjɛ]
chase (pursuit)	ndjekje (f)	[ndjékjɛ]
to pursue, to chase	ndjek	[ndjék]
to track (a criminal)	ndjek	[ndjék]

arrest	arrestim (m)	[arɛstím]
to arrest (sb)	arrestoj	[arɛstój]
to catch (thief, etc.)	kap	[kap]
capture	kapje (f)	[kápjɛ]

document	dokument (m)	[dokumént]
proof (evidence)	provë (f)	[próvə]
to prove (vt)	dëshmoj	[dəʃmój]
footprint	gjurmë (f)	[ɟúrmə]
fingerprints	shenja gishtash (pl)	[ʃéɲa gíʃtaʃ]
piece of evidence	provë (f)	[próvə]

alibi	alibi (f)	[alibí]
innocent (not guilty)	i pafajshëm	[i pafájʃəm]
injustice	padrejtësi (f)	[padrɛjtəsí]
unjust, unfair (adj)	i padrejtë	[i padréjtə]

criminal (adj)	kriminale	[kriminálɛ]
to confiscate (vt)	konfiskoj	[konfiskój]
drug (illegal substance)	drogë (f)	[drógə]
weapon, gun	armë (f)	[ármə]
to disarm (vt)	çarmatos	[tʃarmatós]
to order (command)	urdhëroj	[urðərój]
to disappear (vi)	zhduk	[ʒduk]

law	ligj (m)	[liɟ]
legal, lawful (adj)	ligjor	[liɟór]
illegal, illicit (adj)	i paligjshëm	[i palíɟʃəm]

responsibility (blame)	**përgjegjësi** (f)	[pəɲɛɟəsí]
responsible (adj)	**përgjegjës**	[pəɲéɟəs]

NATURE

The Earth. Part 1

195. Outer space

space	hapësirë (f)	[hapəsírə]
space (as adj)	hapësinor	[hapəsinór]
outer space	kozmos (m)	[kozmós]
world	botë (f)	[bótə]
universe	univers	[univérs]
galaxy	galaksi (f)	[galaksí]
star	yll (m)	[ył]
constellation	yllësi (f)	[yłəsí]
planet	planet (m)	[planét]
satellite	satelit (m)	[satɛlít]
meteorite	meteor (m)	[mɛtɛór]
comet	kometë (f)	[kométə]
asteroid	asteroid (m)	[astɛroíd]
orbit	orbitë (f)	[orbítə]
to revolve (~ around the Earth)	rrotullohet	[rotułóhɛt]
atmosphere	atmosferë (f)	[atmosférə]
the Sun	Dielli (m)	[diéłi]
solar system	sistemi diellor (m)	[sistémi diɛłór]
solar eclipse	eklips diellor (m)	[ɛklíps diɛłór]
the Earth	Toka (f)	[tóka]
the Moon	Hëna (f)	[hóna]
Mars	Marsi (m)	[mársi]
Venus	Venera (f)	[vɛnéra]
Jupiter	Jupiteri (m)	[jupitéri]
Saturn	Saturni (m)	[satúrni]
Mercury	Merkuri (m)	[mɛrkúri]
Uranus	Urani (m)	[uráni]
Neptune	Neptuni (m)	[nɛptúni]
Pluto	Pluto (f)	[plúto]
Milky Way	Rruga e Qumështit (f)	[rúga ɛ cúməʃtit]

| Great Bear (Ursa Major) | Arusha e Madhe (f) | [arúʃa ɛ máðɛ] |
| North Star | ylli i Veriut (m) | [ýłi i vériut] |

Martian	Marsian (m)	[marsián]
extraterrestrial (n)	jashtëtokësor (m)	[jaʃtətokəsór]
alien	alien (m)	[alién]
flying saucer	disk fluturues (m)	[dísk fluturúɛs]

spaceship	anije kozmike (f)	[aníjɛ kozmíkɛ]
space station	stacion kozmik (m)	[statsión kozmík]
blast-off	ngritje (f)	[ŋrítjɛ]

engine	motor (m)	[motór]
nozzle	dizë (f)	[dízə]
fuel	karburant (m)	[karburánt]

cockpit, flight deck	kabinë pilotimi (f)	[kabínə pilotími]
antenna	antenë (f)	[anténə]
porthole	dritare anësore (f)	[dritárɛ anəsórɛ]
solar panel	panel solar (m)	[panél solár]
spacesuit	veshje astronauti (f)	[véʃjɛ astronáuti]

| weightlessness | mungesë graviteti (f) | [muŋésə gravitéti] |
| oxygen | oksigjen (m) | [oksiɟén] |

| docking (in space) | ndërlidhje në hapësirë (f) | [ndərlíðjɛ nə hapəsírə] |
| to dock (vi, vt) | stacionohem | [statsionóhɛm] |

observatory	observator (m)	[obsɛrvatór]
telescope	teleskop (m)	[tɛlɛskóp]
to observe (vt)	vëzhgoj	[vəʒgój]
to explore (vt)	eksploroj	[ɛksplorój]

196. The Earth

the Earth	Toka (f)	[tóka]
the globe (the Earth)	globi (f)	[glóbi]
planet	planet (m)	[planét]

atmosphere	atmosferë (f)	[atmosférə]
geography	gjeografi (f)	[ɟɛografí]
nature	natyrë (f)	[natýrə]

globe (table ~)	glob (m)	[glob]
map	hartë (f)	[hártə]
atlas	atlas (m)	[atlás]

Europe	Evropa (f)	[ɛvrópa]
Asia	Azia (f)	[azía]
Africa	Afrika (f)	[afríka]

Australia	**Australia** (f)	[australía]
America	**Amerika** (f)	[amɛríka]
North America	**Amerika Veriore** (f)	[amɛríka vɛriórɛ]
South America	**Amerika Jugore** (f)	[amɛríka jugórɛ]
Antarctica	**Antarktika** (f)	[antarktíka]
the Arctic	**Arktiku** (m)	[arktíku]

197. Cardinal directions

north	**veri** (m)	[vɛrí]
to the north	**drejt veriut**	[dréjt vériut]
in the north	**në veri**	[nə vɛrí]
northern (adj)	**verior**	[vɛriór]
south	**jug** (m)	[jug]
to the south	**drejt jugut**	[dréjt júgut]
in the south	**në jug**	[nə jug]
southern (adj)	**jugor**	[jugór]
west	**perëndim** (m)	[pɛrəndím]
to the west	**drejt perëndimit**	[dréjt pɛrəndímit]
in the west	**në perëndim**	[nə pɛrəndím]
western (adj)	**perëndimor**	[pɛrəndimór]
east	**lindje** (f)	[líndjɛ]
to the east	**drejt lindjes**	[dréjt líndjɛs]
in the east	**në lindje**	[nə líndjɛ]
eastern (adj)	**lindor**	[lindór]

198. Sea. Ocean

sea	**det** (m)	[dét]
ocean	**oqean** (m)	[ocɛán]
gulf (bay)	**gji** (m)	[ɟi]
straits	**ngushticë** (f)	[ŋuʃtítsə]
land (solid ground)	**tokë** (f)	[tókə]
continent (mainland)	**kontinent** (m)	[kontinént]
island	**ishull** (m)	[íʃuɫ]
peninsula	**gadishull** (m)	[gadíʃuɫ]
archipelago	**arkipelag** (m)	[arkipɛlág]
bay, cove	**gji** (m)	[ɟi]
harbor	**port** (m)	[port]
lagoon	**lagunë** (f)	[lagúnə]
cape	**kep** (m)	[kɛp]

atoll	atol (m)	[atól]
reef	shkëmb nënujor (m)	[ʃkəmb nənujór]
coral	koral (m)	[korál]
coral reef	korale nënujorë (f)	[korálɛ nənujórə]

deep (adj)	i thellë	[i θétə]
depth (deep water)	thellësi (f)	[θɛɫəsí]
abyss	humnerë (f)	[humnérə]
trench (e.g., Mariana ~)	hendek (m)	[hɛndék]
current (Ocean ~)	rrymë (f)	[rýmə]
to surround (bathe)	rrethohet	[rɛθóhɛt]

shore	breg (m)	[brɛg]
coast	bregdet (m)	[brɛgdét]

flow (flood tide)	batica (f)	[batítsa]
ebb (ebb tide)	zbaticë (f)	[zbatítsə]
shoal	cekëtinë (f)	[tsɛkətínə]
bottom (~ of the sea)	fund i detit (m)	[fúnd i détit]

wave	dallgë (f)	[dáɫgə]
crest (~ of a wave)	kreshtë (f)	[kréʃtə]
spume (sea foam)	shkumë (f)	[ʃkúmə]
storm (sea storm)	stuhi (f)	[stuhí]
hurricane	uragan (m)	[uragán]
tsunami	cunam (m)	[tsunám]
calm (dead ~)	qetësi (f)	[cɛtəsí]
quiet, calm (adj)	i qetë	[i cétə]

pole	pol (m)	[pol]
polar (adj)	polar	[polár]

latitude	gjerësi (f)	[ɟɛrəsí]
longitude	gjatësi (f)	[ɟatəsí]
parallel	paralele (f)	[paralélɛ]
equator	ekuator (m)	[ɛkuatór]

sky	qiell (m)	[cíɛɫ]
horizon	horizont (m)	[horizónt]
air	ajër (m)	[ájər]

lighthouse	fanar (m)	[fanár]
to dive (vi)	zhytem	[ʒýtɛm]
to sink (ab. boat)	fundosje	[fundósjɛ]
treasures	thesare (pl)	[θɛsárɛ]

199. Seas' and Oceans' names

Atlantic Ocean	Oqeani Atlantik (m)	[ocɛáni atlantík]
Indian Ocean	Oqeani Indian (m)	[ocɛáni indián]

| Pacific Ocean | Oqeani Paqësor (m) | [ocɛáni pacəsór] |
| Arctic Ocean | Oqeani Arktik (m) | [ocɛáni arktík] |

Black Sea	Deti i Zi (m)	[déti i zí]
Red Sea	Deti i Kuq (m)	[déti i kúc]
Yellow Sea	Deti i Verdhë (m)	[déti i vérðə]
White Sea	Deti i Bardhë (m)	[déti i bárðə]

Caspian Sea	Deti Kaspik (m)	[déti kaspík]
Dead Sea	Deti i Vdekur (m)	[déti i vdékur]
Mediterranean Sea	Deti Mesdhe (m)	[déti mɛsðé]

| Aegean Sea | Deti Egje (m) | [déti ɛɟé] |
| Adriatic Sea | Deti Adriatik (m) | [déti adriatík] |

Arabian Sea	Deti Arab (m)	[déti aráb]
Sea of Japan	Deti i Japonisë (m)	[déti i japonísə]
Bering Sea	Deti Bering (m)	[déti bériŋ]
South China Sea	Deti i Kinës Jugore (m)	[déti i kínəs jugórɛ]

Coral Sea	Deti Koral (m)	[déti korál]
Tasman Sea	Deti Tasman (m)	[déti tasmán]
Caribbean Sea	Deti i Karaibeve (m)	[déti i karaíbɛvɛ]

| Barents Sea | Deti Barents (m) | [déti barénts] |
| Kara Sea | Deti Kara (m) | [déti kára] |

North Sea	Deti i Veriut (m)	[déti i vériut]
Baltic Sea	Deti Baltik (m)	[déti baltík]
Norwegian Sea	Deti Norvegjez (m)	[déti norvɛɟéz]

200. Mountains

mountain	mal (m)	[mal]
mountain range	vargmal (m)	[vargmál]
mountain ridge	kresht malor (m)	[kréʃt malór]

summit, top	majë (f)	[májə]
peak	maja më e lartë (f)	[mája mə ɛ lártə]
foot (~ of the mountain)	rrëza e malit (f)	[rəza ɛ málit]
slope (mountainside)	shpat (m)	[ʃpat]

volcano	vullkan (m)	[vuɬkán]
active volcano	vullkan aktiv (m)	[vuɬkán aktív]
dormant volcano	vullkan i fjetur (m)	[vuɬkán i fjétur]

eruption	shpërthim (m)	[ʃpərθím]
crater	krater (m)	[kratér]
magma	magmë (f)	[mágmə]
lava	llavë (f)	[ɬávə]

molten (~ lava)	**i shkrirë**	[i ʃkrírə]
canyon	**kanion** (m)	[kanión]
gorge	**grykë** (f)	[grýkə]
crevice	**çarje** (f)	[tʃárjɛ]
abyss (chasm)	**humnerë** (f)	[humnérə]
pass, col	**kalim** (m)	[kalím]
plateau	**pllajë** (f)	[pɬájə]
cliff	**shkëmb** (m)	[ʃkəmb]
hill	**kodër** (f)	[kódər]
glacier	**akullnajë** (f)	[akuɬnájə]
waterfall	**ujëvarë** (f)	[ujəvárə]
geyser	**gejzer** (m)	[gɛjzér]
lake	**liqen** (m)	[licén]
plain	**fushë** (f)	[fúʃə]
landscape	**peizazh** (m)	[pɛizáʒ]
echo	**jehonë** (f)	[jɛhónə]
alpinist	**alpinist** (m)	[alpiníst]
rock climber	**alpinist shkëmbßinjsh** (m)	[alpiníst ʃkəmbiɲʃ]
to conquer (in climbing)	**pushtoj majën**	[puʃtój májən]
climb (an easy ~)	**ngjitje** (f)	[nɟítjɛ]

201. Mountains names

The Alps	**Alpet** (pl)	[alpét]
Mont Blanc	**Montblanc** (m)	[montblánk]
The Pyrenees	**Pirenejet** (pl)	[pirɛnéjɛt]
The Carpathians	**Karpatet** (m)	[karpátɛt]
The Ural Mountains	**Malet Urale** (pl)	[málɛt urálɛ]
The Caucasus Mountains	**Malet Kaukaze** (pl)	[málɛt kaukázɛ]
Mount Elbrus	**Mali Elbrus** (m)	[máli ɛlbrús]
The Altai Mountains	**Malet Altai** (pl)	[málɛt altái]
The Tian Shan	**Tian Shani** (m)	[tían ʃáni]
The Pamir Mountains	**Malet e Pamirit** (m)	[málɛt ɛ pamírit]
The Himalayas	**Himalajet** (pl)	[himalájɛt]
Mount Everest	**Mali Everest** (m)	[máli ɛvɛrést]
The Andes	**andet** (pl)	[ándɛt]
Mount Kilimanjaro	**Mali Kilimanxharo** (m)	[máli kilimandʒáro]

202. Rivers

river	**lum** (m)	[lum]
spring (natural source)	**burim** (m)	[burím]

riverbed (river channel)	**shtrat lumi** (m)	[ʃtrat lúmi]
basin (river valley)	**basen** (m)	[basén]
to flow into …	**rrjedh …**	[rjéð …]
tributary	**derdhje** (f)	[dérðjɛ]
bank (of river)	**breg** (m)	[brɛg]
current (stream)	**rrymë** (f)	[rýmə]
downstream (adv)	**rrjedhje e poshtme**	[rjéðjɛ ɛ póʃtmɛ]
upstream (adv)	**rrjedhje e sipërme**	[rjéðjɛ ɛ sípərmɛ]
inundation	**vërshim** (m)	[vərʃím]
flooding	**përmbytje** (f)	[pərmbýtjɛ]
to overflow (vi)	**vërshon**	[vərʃón]
to flood (vt)	**përmbytet**	[pərmbýtɛt]
shallow (shoal)	**cekëtinë** (f)	[tsɛkətínə]
rapids	**rrjedhë** (f)	[rjéðə]
dam	**digë** (f)	[dígə]
canal	**kanal** (m)	[kanál]
reservoir (artificial lake)	**rezervuar** (m)	[rɛzɛrvuár]
sluice, lock	**pendë ujore** (f)	[péndə ujórɛ]
water body (pond, etc.)	**plan hidrik** (m)	[plan hidrík]
swamp (marshland)	**kënetë** (f)	[kənétə]
bog, marsh	**moçal** (m)	[motʃ ál]
whirlpool	**vorbull** (f)	[vórbuɫ]
stream (brook)	**përrua** (f)	[pərúa]
drinking (ab. water)	**i pijshëm**	[i píjʃəm]
fresh (~ water)	**i freskët**	[i fréskət]
ice	**akull** (m)	[ákuɫ]
to freeze over (ab. river, etc.)	**ngrihet**	[ŋríhɛt]

203. Rivers' names

Seine	**Sena** (f)	[séna]
Loire	**Loire** (f)	[luar]
Thames	**Temza** (f)	[témza]
Rhine	**Rajnë** (m)	[rájnə]
Danube	**Danubi** (m)	[danúbi]
Volga	**Volga** (f)	[vólga]
Don	**Doni** (m)	[dóni]
Lena	**Lena** (f)	[léna]
Yellow River	**Lumi i Verdhë** (m)	[lúmi i vérðə]

Yangtze	Jangce (f)	[jaɲtsé]
Mekong	Mekong (m)	[mɛkóŋ]
Ganges	Gang (m)	[gaŋ]

Nile River	Lumi Nil (m)	[lúmi nil]
Congo River	Lumi Kongo (m)	[lúmi kóŋo]
Okavango River	Lumi Okavango (m)	[lúmi okaváŋo]
Zambezi River	Lumi Zambezi (m)	[lúmi zambézi]
Limpopo River	Lumi Limpopo (m)	[lúmi limpópo]
Mississippi River	Lumi Misisipi (m)	[lúmi misisípi]

204. Forest

| forest, wood | pyll (m) | [pyɫ] |
| forest (as adj) | pyjor | [pyjór] |

thick forest	pyll i ngjeshur (m)	[pyɫ i ɲjéʃur]
grove	zabel (m)	[zabél]
forest clearing	lëndinë (f)	[ləndínə]

| thicket | pyllëz (m) | [pýɫəz] |
| scrubland | shkurre (f) | [ʃkúrɛ] |

| footpath (troddenpath) | shteg (m) | [ʃtɛg] |
| gully | hon (m) | [hon] |

tree	pemë (f)	[pémə]
leaf	gjeth (m)	[ɟɛθ]
leaves (foliage)	gjethe (pl)	[ɟéθɛ]

fall of leaves	rënie e gjetheve (f)	[rəníɛ ɛ ɟéθɛvɛ]
to fall (ab. leaves)	bien	[bíɛn]
top (of the tree)	maje (f)	[májɛ]

branch	degë (f)	[dégə]
bough	degë (f)	[dégə]
bud (on shrub, tree)	syth (m)	[syθ]
needle (of pine tree)	shtiza pishe (f)	[ʃtíza píʃɛ]
pine cone	lule pishe (f)	[lúlɛ píʃɛ]

tree hollow	zgavër (f)	[zgávər]
nest	fole (f)	[folé]
burrow (animal hole)	strofull (f)	[strófuɫ]

trunk	trung (m)	[truŋ]
root	rrënjë (f)	[réɲə]
bark	lëvore (f)	[ləvórɛ]
moss	myshk (m)	[myʃk]
to uproot (remove trees or tree stumps)	shkul	[ʃkul]

to chop down	pres	[prɛs]
to deforest (vt)	shpyllëzoj	[ʃpyɫəzój]
tree stump	cung (m)	[tsúŋ]

campfire	zjarr kampingu (m)	[zjar kampíŋu]
forest fire	zjarr në pyll (m)	[zjar nə pyɫ]
to extinguish (vt)	shuaj	[ʃúaj]

forest ranger	roje pyjore (f)	[rójɛ pyjórɛ]
protection	mbrojtje (f)	[mbrójtjɛ]
to protect (~ nature)	mbroj	[mbrój]
poacher	gjahtar i jashtëligjshëm (m)	[ɟahtár i jaʃtəlíʃʃəm]
steel trap	grackë (f)	[grátskə]

| to gather, to pick (vt) | mbledh | [mbléð] |
| to lose one's way | humb rrugën | [húmb rúgən] |

205. Natural resources

natural resources	burime natyrore (pl)	[burímɛ natyrórɛ]
minerals	minerale (pl)	[minɛrálɛ]
deposits	depozita (pl)	[dɛpozíta]
field (e.g., oilfield)	fushë (f)	[fúʃə]

to mine (extract)	nxjerr	[ndzjér]
mining (extraction)	nxjerrje mineralesh (f)	[ndzjérjɛ minɛrálɛʃ]
ore	xehe (f)	[dzéhɛ]
mine (e.g., for coal)	minierë (f)	[miniérə]
shaft (mine ~)	nivel (m)	[nivél]
miner	minator (m)	[minatór]

| gas (natural ~) | gaz (m) | [gaz] |
| gas pipeline | gazsjellës (m) | [gazsjéɫəs] |

oil (petroleum)	naftë (f)	[náftə]
oil pipeline	naftësjellës (f)	[naftəsjéɫəs]
oil well	pus nafte (m)	[pus náftɛ]
derrick (tower)	burim nafte (m)	[burím náftɛ]
tanker	anije-cisternë (f)	[aníjɛ-tsistérnə]

sand	rërë (f)	[rərə]
limestone	gur gëlqeror (m)	[gur gəlcɛrór]
gravel	zhavorr (m)	[ʒavór]
peat	torfë (f)	[tórfə]
clay	argjilë (f)	[aɲílə]
coal	qymyr (m)	[cymýr]

| iron (ore) | hekur (m) | [hékur] |
| gold | ar (m) | [ár] |

silver	**argjend** (m)	[arɲénd]
nickel	**nikel** (m)	[nikél]
copper	**bakër** (m)	[bákər]

zinc	**zink** (m)	[zink]
manganese	**mangan** (m)	[maɲán]
mercury	**merkur** (m)	[mɛrkúɾ]
lead	**plumb** (m)	[plúmb]

mineral	**mineral** (m)	[minɛrál]
crystal	**kristal** (m)	[kristál]
marble	**mermer** (m)	[mɛrmér]
uranium	**uranium** (m)	[uraniúm]

The Earth. Part 2

206. Weather

weather	**moti** (m)	[móti]
weather forecast	**parashikimi i motit** (m)	[paraʃikími i mótit]
temperature	**temperaturë** (f)	[tɛmpɛratúrə]
thermometer	**termometër** (m)	[tɛrmométər]
barometer	**barometër** (m)	[barométər]
humid (adj)	**i lagësht**	[i lágəʃt]
humidity	**lagështi** (f)	[lagəʃtí]
heat (extreme ~)	**vapë** (f)	[vápə]
hot (torrid)	**shumë nxehtë**	[ʃúmə ndzéhtə]
it's hot	**është nxehtë**	[əʃtə ndzéhtə]
it's warm	**është ngrohtë**	[əʃtə ŋróhtə]
warm (moderately hot)	**ngrohtë**	[ŋróhtə]
it's cold	**bën ftohtë**	[bən ftóhtə]
cold (adj)	**i ftohtë**	[i ftóhtə]
sun	**diell** (m)	[díɛɫ]
to shine (vi)	**ndriçon**	[ndritʃón]
sunny (day)	**me diell**	[mɛ díɛɫ]
to come up (vi)	**agon**	[agón]
to set (vi)	**perëndon**	[pɛrəndón]
cloud	**re** (f)	[rɛ]
cloudy (adj)	**vranët**	[vránət]
rain cloud	**re shiu** (f)	[rɛ ʃiu]
somber (gloomy)	**vranët**	[vránət]
rain	**shi** (m)	[ʃi]
it's raining	**bie shi**	[bíɛ ʃi]
rainy (~ day, weather)	**me shi**	[mɛ ʃi]
to drizzle (vi)	**shi i imët**	[ʃi i ímət]
pouring rain	**shi litar** (m)	[ʃi litár]
downpour	**stuhi shiu** (f)	[stuhí ʃiu]
heavy (e.g., ~ rain)	**i fortë**	[i fórtə]
puddle	**brakë** (f)	[brákə]
to get wet (in rain)	**lagem**	[lágɛm]
fog (mist)	**mjegull** (f)	[mjéguɫ]
foggy	**e mjegullt**	[ɛ mjéguɫt]

| snow | borë (f) | [bórə] |
| it's snowing | bie borë | [bíɛ bórə] |

207. Severe weather. Natural disasters

thunderstorm	stuhi (f)	[stuhí]
lightning (~ strike)	vetëtimë (f)	[vɛtətímə]
to flash (vi)	vetëton	[vɛtətón]

thunder	bubullimë (f)	[bubuɫímə]
to thunder (vi)	bubullon	[bubuɫón]
it's thundering	bubullon	[bubuɫón]

| hail | breshër (m) | [bréʃər] |
| it's hailing | po bie breshër | [po biɛ bréʃər] |

| to flood (vt) | përmbytet | [pərmbýtɛt] |
| flood, inundation | përmbytje (f) | [pərmbýtjɛ] |

earthquake	tërmet (m)	[tərmét]
tremor, shoke	lëkundje (f)	[ləkúndjɛ]
epicenter	epiqendër (f)	[ɛpicéndər]
eruption	shpërthim (m)	[ʃpərθím]
lava	llavë (f)	[ɫávə]

twister	vorbull (f)	[vórbuɫ]
tornado	tornado (f)	[tornádo]
typhoon	tajfun (m)	[tajfún]

hurricane	uragan (m)	[uragán]
storm	stuhi (f)	[stuhí]
tsunami	cunam (m)	[tsunám]

cyclone	ciklon (m)	[tsiklón]
bad weather	mot i keq (m)	[mot i kɛc]
fire (accident)	zjarr (m)	[zjar]
disaster	fatkeqësi (f)	[fatkɛcəsí]
meteorite	meteor (m)	[mɛtɛór]

avalanche	ortek (m)	[orték]
snowslide	rrëshqitje bore (f)	[rəʃcítjɛ bórɛ]
blizzard	stuhi bore (f)	[stuhí bórɛ]
snowstorm	stuhi bore (f)	[stuhí bórɛ]

208. Noises. Sounds

| silence (quiet) | qetësi (f) | [cɛtəsí] |
| sound | tingull (m) | [tíŋuɫ] |

noise	zhurmë (f)	[ʒúrmə]
to make noise	bëj zhurmë	[bəj ʒúrmə]
noisy (adj)	i zhurmshëm	[i ʒúrmʃəm]

loudly (to speak, etc.)	me zë të lartë	[mɛ zə tə lártə]
loud (voice, etc.)	i lartë	[i lártə]
constant (e.g., ~ noise)	e përhershme	[ɛ pərhérʃmɛ]

cry, shout (n)	britmë (f)	[brítmə]
to cry, to shout (vi)	bërtas	[bərtás]
whisper	pëshpërimë (f)	[pəʃpərímə]
to whisper (vi, vt)	pëshpëris	[pəʃpərís]

barking (dog's ~)	lehje (f)	[léhjɛ]
to bark (vi)	leh	[lɛh]

groan (of pain, etc.)	rënkim (m)	[rənkím]
to groan (vi)	rënkoj	[rənkój]
cough	kollë (f)	[kóɫə]
to cough (vi)	kollitem	[koɫítɛm]

whistle	fishkëllimë (f)	[fiʃkəɫímə]
to whistle (vi)	fishkëlloj	[fiʃkəɫój]
knock (at the door)	trokitje (f)	[trokítjɛ]
to knock (on the door)	trokas	[trokás]

to crack (vi)	çahet	[tʃáhɛt]
crack (cracking sound)	krisje (f)	[krísjɛ]

siren	alarm (m)	[alárm]
whistle (factory ~, etc.)	fishkëllimë (f)	[fiʃkəɫímə]
to whistle (ab. train)	fishkëllen	[fiʃkəɫén]
honk (car horn sound)	bori (f)	[borí]
to honk (vi)	i bie borisë	[i bíɛ borísə]

209. Winter

winter (n)	dimër (m)	[dímər]
winter (as adj)	dimëror	[dimərór]
in winter	në dimër	[nə dímər]

snow	borë (f)	[bórə]
it's snowing	bie borë	[bíɛ bórə]
snowfall	reshje bore (f)	[réʃjɛ bórɛ]
snowdrift	mal dëbore (m)	[mal dəbórɛ]

snowflake	flok bore (m)	[flók bórɛ]
snowball	top bore (m)	[top bórɛ]
snowman	dordolec (m)	[dordoléts]
icicle	akull (m)	[ákuɫ]

December	Dhjetor (m)	[ðjɛtór]
January	Janar (m)	[janár]
February	Shkurt (m)	[ʃkurt]

| frost (severe ~, freezing cold) | ngricë (f) | [ŋrítsə] |
| frosty (weather, air) | me ngrica | [mɛ ŋrítsa] |

below zero (adv)	nën zero	[nən zéro]
first frost	ngrica e parë (f)	[ŋrítsa ɛ párə]
hoarfrost	brymë (f)	[brýmə]

| cold (cold weather) | ftohtë (f) | [ftóhtə] |
| it's cold | bën ftohtë | [bən ftóhtə] |

| fur coat | gëzof (m) | [gəzóf] |
| mittens | doreza (f) | [doréza] |

to get sick	sëmurem	[səmúrɛm]
cold (illness)	ftohje (f)	[ftóhjɛ]
to catch a cold	ftohem	[ftóhɛm]

ice	akull (m)	[ákuɫ]
black ice	akull transparent (m)	[ákuɫ transparént]
to freeze over (ab. river, etc.)	ngrihet	[ŋríhɛt]
ice floe	bllok akulli (m)	[bɫók ákuɫi]

skis	ski (pl)	[ski]
skier	skiator (m)	[skiatór]
to ski (vi)	bëj ski	[bəj skí]
to skate (vi)	bëj patinazh	[bəj patináʒ]

Fauna

210. Mammals. Predators

predator	**grabitqar** (m)	[grabitcár]
tiger	**tigër** (m)	[tígər]
lion	**luan** (m)	[luán]
wolf	**ujk** (m)	[ujk]
fox	**dhelpër** (f)	[ðélpər]
jaguar	**jaguar** (m)	[jaguár]
leopard	**leopard** (m)	[lɛopárd]
cheetah	**gepard** (m)	[gɛpárd]
black panther	**panterë e zezë** (f)	[pantérə ɛ zézə]
puma	**puma** (f)	[púma]
snow leopard	**leopard i borës** (m)	[lɛopárd i bórəs]
lynx	**rrëqebull** (m)	[rəcébuł]
coyote	**kojotë** (f)	[kojótə]
jackal	**çakall** (m)	[tʃakáł]
hyena	**hienë** (f)	[hiénə]

211. Wild animals

animal	**kafshë** (f)	[káfʃə]
beast (animal)	**bishë** (f)	[bíʃə]
squirrel	**ketër** (m)	[kétər]
hedgehog	**iriq** (m)	[iríc]
hare	**lepur i egër** (m)	[lépur i égər]
rabbit	**lepur** (m)	[lépur]
badger	**vjedull** (f)	[vjéduł]
raccoon	**rakun** (m)	[rakún]
hamster	**hamster** (m)	[hamstér]
marmot	**marmot** (m)	[marmót]
mole	**urith** (m)	[uríθ]
mouse	**mi** (m)	[mi]
rat	**mi** (m)	[mi]
bat	**lakuriq** (m)	[lakuríc]
ermine	**herminë** (f)	[hɛrmínə]
sable	**kunadhe** (f)	[kunáðɛ]

marten	shqarth (m)	[ʃcarθ]
weasel	nuselalë (f)	[nusɛlálə]
mink	vizon (m)	[vizón]

| beaver | kastor (m) | [kastór] |
| otter | vidër (f) | [vídər] |

horse	kali (m)	[káli]
moose	dre brilopatë (m)	[drɛ brilopátə]
deer	dre (f)	[drɛ]
camel	deve (f)	[dévɛ]

bison	bizon (m)	[bizón]
wisent	bizon evropian (m)	[bizón ɛvropián]
buffalo	buall (m)	[búaɫ]

zebra	zebër (f)	[zébər]
antelope	antilopë (f)	[antilópə]
roe deer	dre (f)	[drɛ]
fallow deer	dre ugar (m)	[drɛ ugár]
chamois	kamosh (m)	[kamóʃ]
wild boar	derr i egër (m)	[dér i égər]

whale	balenë (f)	[balénə]
seal	fokë (f)	[fókə]
walrus	lopë deti (f)	[lópə déti]
fur seal	fokë (f)	[fókə]
dolphin	delfin (m)	[dɛlfín]

bear	ari (m)	[arí]
polar bear	ari polar (m)	[arí polár]
panda	panda (f)	[pánda]

monkey	majmun (m)	[majmún]
chimpanzee	shimpanze (f)	[ʃimpánzɛ]
orangutan	orangutan (m)	[oraŋután]
gorilla	gorillë (f)	[goríɫə]
macaque	majmun makao (m)	[majmún makáo]
gibbon	gibon (m)	[gibón]

elephant	elefant (m)	[ɛlɛfánt]
rhinoceros	rinoqeront (m)	[rinocɛrónt]
giraffe	gjirafë (f)	[ɟiráfə]
hippopotamus	hipopotam (m)	[hipopotám]

| kangaroo | kangur (m) | [kaŋúr] |
| koala (bear) | koala (f) | [koála] |

mongoose	mangustë (f)	[maŋústə]
chinchilla	çinçila (f)	[tʃintʃíla]
skunk	qelbës (m)	[célbəs]
porcupine	ferrëgjatë (m)	[fɛrəɟátə]

212. Domestic animals

cat	**mace** (f)	[mátsɛ]
tomcat	**maçok** (m)	[matʃók]
dog	**qen** (m)	[cɛn]
horse	**kali** (m)	[káli]
stallion (male horse)	**hamshor** (m)	[hamʃór]
mare	**pelë** (f)	[pélə]
cow	**lopë** (f)	[lópə]
bull	**dem** (m)	[dém]
ox	**ka** (m)	[ka]
sheep (ewe)	**dele** (f)	[délɛ]
ram	**dash** (m)	[daʃ]
goat	**dhi** (f)	[ði]
billy goat, he-goat	**cjap** (m)	[tsjáp]
donkey	**gomar** (m)	[gomár]
mule	**mushkë** (f)	[múʃkə]
pig, hog	**derr** (m)	[dɛr]
piglet	**derrkuc** (m)	[dɛrkúts]
rabbit	**lepur** (m)	[lépur]
hen (chicken)	**pulë** (f)	[púlə]
rooster	**gjel** (m)	[ɟél]
duck	**rosë** (f)	[rósə]
drake	**rosak** (m)	[rosák]
goose	**patë** (f)	[pátə]
tom turkey, gobbler	**gjel deti i egër** (m)	[ɟél déti i égər]
turkey (hen)	**gjel deti** (m)	[ɟél déti]
domestic animals	**kafshë shtëpiake** (f)	[káfʃə ʃtəpiákɛ]
tame (e.g., ~ hamster)	**i zbutur**	[i zbútur]
to tame (vt)	**zbus**	[zbus]
to breed (vt)	**rrit**	[rit]
farm	**fermë** (f)	[férmə]
poultry	**pulari** (f)	[pularí]
cattle	**bagëti** (f)	[bagətí]
herd (cattle)	**kope** (f)	[kopé]
stable	**stallë** (f)	[stáłə]
pigpen	**stallë e derrave** (f)	[stáłə ɛ déravɛ]
cowshed	**stallë e lopëve** (f)	[stáłə ɛ lópəvɛ]
rabbit hutch	**kolibe lepujsh** (f)	[kolíbɛ lépujʃ]
hen house	**kotec** (m)	[kotéts]

213. Dogs. Dog breeds

dog	qen (m)	[cɛn]
sheepdog	qen dhensh (m)	[cɛn ðɛnʃ]
German shepherd	pastor gjerman (m)	[pastór ɟɛrmán]
poodle	pudël (f)	[púdəl]
dachshund	dakshund (m)	[dákshund]
bulldog	bulldog (m)	[buɫdóg]
boxer	bokser (m)	[boksér]
mastiff	mastif (m)	[mastíf]
Rottweiler	rotvailer (m)	[rotvailér]
Doberman	doberman (m)	[dobɛrmán]
basset	baset (m)	[basét]
bobtail	bishtshkurtër (m)	[biʃtʃkúrtər]
Dalmatian	dalmat (m)	[dalmát]
cocker spaniel	koker spaniel (m)	[kokér spaniél]
Newfoundland	terranova (f)	[tɛranóva]
Saint Bernard	Seint-Bernard (m)	[séint-bɛrnárd]
husky	haski (m)	[háski]
Chow Chow	çau çau (m)	[tʃáu tʃáu]
spitz	dhelpërush (m)	[ðɛlpərúʃ]
pug	karlino (m)	[karlíno]

214. Sounds made by animals

barking (n)	lehje (f)	[léhjɛ]
to bark (vi)	leh	[lɛh]
to meow (vi)	mjaullin	[mjauɫín]
to purr (vi)	gërhimë	[gərhímə]
to moo (vi)	bën mu	[bən mú]
to bellow (bull)	pëllet	[pəɫét]
to growl (vi)	hungërin	[huŋərín]
howl (n)	hungërimë (f)	[huŋərímə]
to howl (vi)	hungëroj	[huŋərój]
to whine (vi)	angullin	[aŋuɫín]
to bleat (sheep)	blegërin	[blɛgərín]
to oink, to grunt (pig)	hungërin	[huŋərín]
to squeal (vi)	klith	[kliθ]
to croak (vi)	bën kuak	[bən kuák]
to buzz (insect)	zukat	[zukát]
to chirp (crickets, grasshopper)	gumëzhin	[guməʒín]

215. Young animals

cub	këlysh (m)	[kəlýʃ]
kitten	kotele (f)	[kotélɛ]
baby mouse	miush (m)	[miúʃ]
puppy	këlysh qeni (m)	[kəlýʃ céni]
leveret	lepurush (m)	[lɛpurúʃ]
baby rabbit	lepurush i butë (m)	[lɛpurúʃ i bútə]
wolf cub	këlysh ujku (m)	[kəlýʃ újku]
fox cub	këlysh dhelpre (m)	[kəlýʃ ðélprɛ]
bear cub	këlysh ariu (m)	[kəlýʃ aríu]
lion cub	këlysh luani (m)	[kəlýʃ luáni]
tiger cub	këlysh tigri (m)	[kəlýʃ tígri]
elephant calf	këlysh elefanti (m)	[kəlýʃ ɛlɛfánti]
piglet	derrkuc (m)	[dɛrkúts]
calf (young cow, bull)	viç (m)	[vitʃ]
kid (young goat)	kec (m)	[kéts]
lamb	qengj (m)	[cɛɲɟ]
fawn (young deer)	kaproll (m)	[kaprót]
young camel	këlysh deveje (m)	[kəlýʃ dɛvéjɛ]
snakelet (baby snake)	gjarpër i vogël (m)	[ɟárpər i vógəl]
froglet (baby frog)	këlysh bretkose (m)	[kəlýʃ brɛtkósɛ]
baby bird	zog i vogël (m)	[zog i vógəl]
chick (of chicken)	zog pule (m)	[zog púlɛ]
duckling	zog rose (m)	[zog rósɛ]

216. Birds

bird	zog (m)	[zog]
pigeon	pëllumb (m)	[pəɫúmb]
sparrow	harabel (m)	[harabél]
tit (great tit)	xhixhimës (m)	[dʒidʒimés]
magpie	laraskë (f)	[laráskə]
raven	korb (m)	[korb]
crow	sorrë (f)	[sórə]
jackdaw	galë (f)	[gálə]
rook	sorrë (f)	[sórə]
duck	rosë (f)	[rósə]
goose	patë (f)	[pátə]
pheasant	fazan (m)	[fazán]
eagle	shqiponjë (f)	[ʃcipóɲə]
hawk	gjeraqinë (f)	[ɟɛracínə]

falcon	**fajkua** (f)	[fajkúa]
vulture	**hutë** (f)	[hútə]
condor (Andean ~)	**kondor** (m)	[kondór]

swan	**mjellmë** (f)	[mjéłmə]
crane	**lejlek** (m)	[lɛjlék]
stork	**lejlek** (m)	[lɛjlék]

parrot	**papagall** (m)	[papagáł]
hummingbird	**kolibri** (m)	[kolíbri]
peacock	**pallua** (m)	[pałúa]

ostrich	**struc** (m)	[struts]
heron	**çafkë** (f)	[tʃáfkə]
flamingo	**flamingo** (m)	[flamíŋo]
pelican	**pelikan** (m)	[pɛlikán]

| nightingale | **bilbil** (m) | [bilbíl] |
| swallow | **dallëndyshe** (f) | [dałəndýʃɛ] |

thrush	**mëllenjë** (f)	[məłéɲə]
song thrush	**grifsha** (f)	[grífʃa]
blackbird	**mëllenjë** (f)	[məłéɲə]

swift	**dallëndyshe** (f)	[dałəndýʃɛ]
lark	**thëllëzë** (f)	[θəłə́zə]
quail	**trumcak** (m)	[trumtsák]

woodpecker	**qukapik** (m)	[cukapík]
cuckoo	**kukuvajkë** (f)	[kukuvájkə]
owl	**buf** (m)	[buf]
eagle owl	**buf mbretëror** (m)	[buf mbrɛtərór]
wood grouse	**fazan i pyllit** (m)	[fazán i pýłit]
black grouse	**fazan i zi** (m)	[fazán i zí]
partridge	**thëllëzë** (f)	[θəłə́zə]

starling	**gargull** (m)	[gárguł]
canary	**kanarinë** (f)	[kanarínə]
hazel grouse	**fazan mali** (m)	[fazán máli]
chaffinch	**trishtil** (m)	[triʃtíl]
bullfinch	**trishtil dimri** (m)	[triʃtíl dímri]

seagull	**pulëbardhë** (f)	[puləbárðə]
albatross	**albatros** (m)	[albatrós]
penguin	**penguin** (m)	[pɛɲuín]

217. Birds. Singing and sounds

| to sing (vi) | **këndoj** | [kəndój] |
| to call (animal, bird) | **thërras** | [θərás] |

| to crow (rooster) | kakaris | [kakarís] |
| cock-a-doodle-doo | kikiriku | [kikiríku] |

to cluck (hen)	kakaris	[kakarís]
to caw (crow call)	krokas	[krokás]
to quack (duck call)	bën kuak kuak	[bən kuák kuák]
to cheep (vi)	pisket	[piskét]
to chirp, to twitter	cicëroj	[tsitsərój]

218. Fish. Marine animals

bream	krapuliq (m)	[krapulíc]
carp	krap (m)	[krap]
perch	perç (m)	[pɛrtʃ]
catfish	mustak (m)	[musták]
pike	mlysh (m)	[mlýʃ]

| salmon | salmon (m) | [salmón] |
| sturgeon | bli (m) | [blí] |

herring	harengë (f)	[haréŋə]
Atlantic salmon	salmon Atlantiku (m)	[salmón atlantíku]
mackerel	skumbri (m)	[skúmbri]
flatfish	shojzë (f)	[ʃójzə]

zander, pike perch	troftë (f)	[tróftə]
cod	merluc (m)	[mɛrlúts]
tuna	tunë (f)	[túnə]
trout	troftë (f)	[tróftə]
eel	ngjalë (f)	[ɲálə]
electric ray	peshk elektrik (m)	[pɛʃk ɛlɛktrík]
moray eel	ngjalë morel (f)	[ɲálə morél]
piranha	piranja (f)	[piráɲa]

shark	peshkaqen (m)	[pɛʃkacén]
dolphin	delfin (m)	[dɛlfín]
whale	balenë (f)	[balénə]

crab	gaforre (f)	[gafórɛ]
jellyfish	kandil deti (m)	[kandíl déti]
octopus	oktapod (m)	[oktapód]

starfish	yll deti (m)	[yɫ déti]
sea urchin	iriq deti (m)	[iríc déti]
seahorse	kalë deti (m)	[kálə déti]

oyster	midhje (f)	[míðjɛ]
shrimp	karkalec (m)	[karkaléts]
lobster	karavidhe (f)	[karavíðɛ]
spiny lobster	karavidhe (f)	[karavíðɛ]

219. Amphibians. Reptiles

snake	gjarpër (m)	[ɲárpər]
venomous (snake)	helmues	[hɛlmúɛs]
viper	nepërka (f)	[nɛpərka]
cobra	kobra (f)	[kóbra]
python	piton (m)	[pitón]
boa	boa (f)	[bóa]
grass snake	kular (m)	[kulár]
rattle snake	gjarpër me zile (m)	[ɲárpər mɛ zílɛ]
anaconda	anakonda (f)	[anakónda]
lizard	hardhucë (f)	[harðútsə]
iguana	iguana (f)	[iguána]
monitor lizard	varan (m)	[varán]
salamander	salamandër (f)	[salamándər]
chameleon	kameleon (m)	[kamɛlɛón]
scorpion	akrep (m)	[akrép]
turtle	breshkë (f)	[bréʃkə]
frog	bretkosë (f)	[brɛtkósə]
toad	zhabë (f)	[ʒábə]
crocodile	krokodil (m)	[krokodíl]

220. Insects

insect, bug	insekt (m)	[insékt]
butterfly	flutur (f)	[flútur]
ant	milingonë (f)	[miliŋónə]
fly	mizë (f)	[mízə]
mosquito	mushkonjë (f)	[muʃkóɲə]
beetle	brumbull (m)	[brúmbuɫ]
wasp	grerëz (f)	[grérəz]
bee	bletë (f)	[blétə]
bumblebee	greth (m)	[grɛθ]
gadfly (botfly)	zekth (m)	[zɛkθ]
spider	merimangë (f)	[mɛrimáɲə]
spiderweb	rrjetë merimange (f)	[rjétə mɛrimáɲɛ]
dragonfly	pilivesë (f)	[pilivésə]
grasshopper	karkalec (m)	[karkaléts]
moth (night butterfly)	molë (f)	[mólə]
cockroach	kacabu (f)	[katsabú]
tick	rriqër (m)	[rícər]

| flea | plesht (m) | [plɛʃt] |
| midge | mushicë (f) | [muʃítsə] |

locust	gjinkallë (f)	[ɟinkálə]
snail	kërmill (m)	[kərmíɫ]
cricket	bulkth (m)	[búlkθ]

lightning bug	xixëllonjë (f)	[dzidzəɫóɲə]
ladybug	mollëkuqe (f)	[moɫəkúcɛ]
cockchafer	vizhë (f)	[víʒə]

leech	shushunjë (f)	[ʃuʃúɲə]
caterpillar	vemje (f)	[vémjɛ]
earthworm	krimb toke (m)	[krímb tókɛ]
larva	larvë (f)	[lárvə]

221. Animals. Body parts

beak	sqep (m)	[scɛp]
wings	flatra (pl)	[flátra]
foot (of bird)	këmbë (f)	[kə́mbə]
feathers (plumage)	pupla (pl)	[púpla]

| feather | pupël (f) | [púpəl] |
| crest | kreshtë (f) | [kréʃtə] |

gills	velëz (f)	[véləz]
spawn	vezë peshku (f)	[vézə péʃku]
larva	larvë (f)	[lárvə]

| fin | krah (m) | [krah] |
| scales (of fish, reptile) | luspë (f) | [lúspə] |

fang (canine)	dhëmb prerës (m)	[ðəmb prérəs]
paw (e.g., cat's ~)	shputë (f)	[ʃpútə]
muzzle (snout)	turi (m)	[turí]
maw (mouth)	gojë (f)	[gójə]

| tail | bisht (m) | [biʃt] |
| whiskers | mustaqe (f) | [mustácɛ] |

| hoof | thundër (f) | [θúndər] |
| horn | bri (m) | [brí] |

carapace	karapaks (m)	[karapáks]
shell (of mollusk)	guaskë (f)	[guáskə]
eggshell	lëvozhgë veze (f)	[ləvóʒgə vézɛ]

| animal's hair (pelage) | qime (f) | [címɛ] |
| pelt (hide) | lëkurë kafshe (f) | [ləkúrə káfʃɛ] |

222. Actions of animals

to fly (vi)	fluturoj	[fluturój]
to fly in circles	fluturoj përreth	[fluturój pəréθ]
to fly away	fluturoj tutje	[fluturój tútjɛ]
to flap (~ the wings)	rrah	[rah]

to peck (vi)	qukas	[cukás]
to sit on eggs	ngroh vezët	[ŋróh vézət]
to hatch out (vi)	çelin vezët	[tʃélin vézət]
to build a nest	ngre fole	[ŋré folé]

to slither, to crawl	gjarpëroj	[ɟarpərój]
to sting, to bite (insect)	pickoj	[pitskój]
to bite (ab. animal)	kafshoj	[kafʃój]

to sniff (vt)	nuhas	[nuhás]
to bark (vi)	leh	[lɛh]
to hiss (snake)	fërshëllej	[fərʃəɫéj]
to scare (vt)	tremb	[trɛmb]
to attack (vt)	sulmoj	[sulmój]

to gnaw (bone, etc.)	brej	[brɛj]
to scratch (with claws)	gërvisht	[gərvíʃt]
to hide (vi)	fsheh	[fʃéh]

to play (kittens, etc.)	luaj	[lúaj]
to hunt (vi, vt)	dal për gjah	[dál pər ɟáh]
to hibernate (vi)	fle gjumë letargjik	[flɛ ɟúmə lɛtaɾɟík]
to go extinct	zhdukem	[ʒdúkɛm]

223. Animals. Habitats

| habitat | banesë (f) | [banésə] |
| migration | migrim (m) | [migrím] |

mountain	mal (m)	[mal]
reef	shkëmb nënujor (m)	[ʃkəmb nənujór]
cliff	shkëmb (m)	[ʃkəmb]

forest	pyll (m)	[pyɫ]
jungle	xhungël (f)	[dʒúŋəl]
savanna	savana (f)	[savána]
tundra	tundra (f)	[túndra]

steppe	stepa (f)	[stépa]
desert	shkretëtirë (f)	[ʃkrɛtətírə]
oasis	oazë (f)	[oázə]
sea	det (m)	[dét]

| lake | liqen (m) | [licén] |
| ocean | oqean (m) | [ocεán] |

swamp (marshland)	kënetë (f)	[kənétə]
freshwater (adj)	ujëra të ëmbla	[újəra tə əmbla]
pond	pellg (m)	[pεłg]
river	lum (m)	[lum]

den (bear's ~)	strofull (f)	[strófuł]
nest	fole (f)	[folé]
tree hollow	zgavër (f)	[zgávər]
burrow (animal hole)	strofull (f)	[strófuł]
anthill	mal milingonash (m)	[mal miliŋónaʃ]

224. Animal care

| zoo | kopsht zoologjik (m) | [kópʃt zooloɉík] |
| nature preserve | rezervat natyror (m) | [rεzεrvát natyrór] |

breeder (cattery, kennel, etc.)	mbarështues (m)	[mbarəʃtúεs]
open-air cage	kafaz i hapur (m)	[kafáz i hápur]
cage	kafaz (m)	[kafáz]
doghouse (kennel)	kolibe qeni (f)	[kolíbε céni]

dovecot	kafaz pëllumbash (m)	[kafáz pəłúmbaʃ]
aquarium (fish tank)	akuarium (m)	[akuariúm]
dolphinarium	akuarium për delfinë (m)	[akuariúm pər dεlfínə]

to breed (animals)	mbarështoj	[mbarəʃtój]
brood, litter	këlysh (m)	[kəlýʃ]
to tame (vt)	zbus	[zbus]
to train (animals)	stërvit	[stərvít]
feed (fodder, etc.)	ushqim (m)	[uʃcím]
to feed (vt)	ushqej	[uʃcéj]

pet store	dyqan kafshësh (m)	[dycán káfʃəʃ]
muzzle (for dog)	maskë turiri (f)	[máskə turíri]
collar (e.g., dog ~)	kollare (f)	[kołárε]
name (of animal)	emri (m)	[émri]
pedigree (of dog)	raca (f)	[rátsa]

225. Animals. Miscellaneous

pack (wolves)	tufë (f)	[túfə]
flock (birds)	tufë (f)	[túfə]
shoal, school (fish)	grup (m)	[grup]
herd (horses)	tufë (f)	[túfə]

| male (n) | mashkull (m) | [máʃkuɫ] |
| female (n) | femër (f) | [fémər] |

hungry (adj)	i uritur	[i urítur]
wild (adj)	i egër	[i égər]
dangerous (adj)	i rrezikshëm	[i rɛzíkʃəm]

226. Horses

| horse | kali (m) | [káli] |
| breed (race) | raca (f) | [rátsa] |

| foal | mëzi (m) | [mézi] |
| mare | pelë (f) | [pélə] |

mustang	kalë mustang (m)	[kálə mustáŋ]
pony	poni (m)	[póni]
draft horse	kalë pune (f)	[kálə púnɛ]

| mane | kreshtë (f) | [kréʃtə] |
| tail | bisht (m) | [biʃt] |

hoof	thundër (f)	[θúndər]
horseshoe	patkua (f)	[patkúa]
to shoe (vt)	mbath	[mbáθ]
blacksmith	farkëtar (m)	[farkətár]

saddle	shalë (f)	[ʃálə]
stirrup	yzengji (f)	[yzɛnɟí]
bridle	gojëz (f)	[gójəz]
reins	frenat (pl)	[frénat]
whip (for riding)	kamxhik (m)	[kamdʒík]

rider	kalorës (m)	[kalórəs]
to saddle up (vt)	shaloj	[ʃalój]
to mount a horse	hip në kalë	[hip nə kálə]

gallop	galop (m)	[galóp]
to gallop (vi)	ec me galop	[ɛts mɛ galóp]
trot (n)	trok (m)	[trok]
at a trot (adv)	me trok	[mɛ trók]
to go at a trot	ec me trok	[ɛts mɛ trók]

| racehorse | kalë garash (m) | [kálə gáraʃ] |
| horse racing | garë kuajsh (f) | [gárə kúajʃ] |

stable	stallë (f)	[stáɫə]
to feed (vt)	ushqej	[uʃcéj]
hay	kashtë (f)	[káʃtə]
to water (animals)	i jap ujë	[i jap újə]

to wash (horse)	laj	[laj]
horse-drawn cart	karrocë me kalë (f)	[karótsə mɛ kálə]
to graze (vi)	kullos	[kuɫós]
to neigh (vi)	hingëlloj	[hiŋəɫój]
to kick (to buck)	gjuaj me shkelma	[ɟúaj mɛ ʃkélma]

Flora

227. Trees

tree	pemë (f)	[pémə]
deciduous (adj)	gjethor	[ɟɛθór]
coniferous (adj)	halor	[halór]
evergreen (adj)	përherë të gjelbra	[pərhérə tə ɟélbra]
apple tree	pemë molle (f)	[pémə mółɛ]
pear tree	pemë dardhe (f)	[pémə dárðɛ]
sweet cherry tree	pemë qershie (f)	[pémə cɛrʃíɛ]
sour cherry tree	pemë qershi vishnje (f)	[pémə cɛrʃí víʃnɛ]
plum tree	pemë kumbulle (f)	[pémə kúmbułɛ]
birch	mështekna (f)	[məʃtékna]
oak	lis (m)	[lis]
linden tree	bli (m)	[blí]
aspen	plep i egër (m)	[plɛp i égər]
maple	panjë (f)	[páɲə]
spruce	bredh (m)	[brɛð]
pine	pishë (f)	[píʃə]
larch	larsh (m)	[lárʃ]
fir tree	bredh i bardhë (m)	[brɛð i bárðə]
cedar	kedër (m)	[kédər]
poplar	plep (m)	[plɛp]
rowan	vadhë (f)	[váðə]
willow	shelg (m)	[ʃɛlg]
alder	verr (m)	[vɛr]
beech	ah (m)	[ah]
elm	elm (m)	[élm]
ash (tree)	shelg (m)	[ʃɛlg]
chestnut	gështenjë (f)	[gəʃtéɲə]
magnolia	manjolia (f)	[maɲólia]
palm tree	palma (f)	[pálma]
cypress	qiparis (m)	[ciparís]
mangrove	rizoforë (f)	[rizofórə]
baobab	baobab (m)	[baobáb]
eucalyptus	eukalipt (m)	[ɛukalípt]
sequoia	sekuojë (f)	[sɛkuójə]

228. Shrubs

bush	**shkurre** (f)	[ʃkúrɛ]
shrub	**kaçube** (f)	[katʃúbɛ]
grapevine	**hardhi** (f)	[harðí]
vineyard	**vreshtë** (f)	[vréʃtə]
raspberry bush	**mjedër** (f)	[mjédər]
blackcurrant bush	**kaliboba e zezë** (f)	[kalibóba ɛ zézə]
redcurrant bush	**kaliboba e kuqe** (f)	[kalibóba ɛ kúcɛ]
gooseberry bush	**shkurre kulumbrie** (f)	[ʃkúrɛ kulumbríɛ]
acacia	**akacie** (f)	[akátsiɛ]
barberry	**krespinë** (f)	[krɛspínə]
jasmine	**jasemin** (m)	[jasɛmín]
juniper	**dëllinjë** (f)	[dəlíɲə]
rosebush	**trëndafil** (m)	[trəndafíl]
dog rose	**trëndafil i egër** (m)	[trəndafíl i égər]

229. Mushrooms

mushroom	**kërpudhë** (f)	[kərpúðə]
edible mushroom	**kërpudhë ushqyese** (f)	[kərpúðə uʃcýɛsɛ]
poisonous mushroom	**kërpudhë helmuese** (f)	[kərpúðə hɛlmúɛsɛ]
cap (of mushroom)	**koka e kërpudhës** (f)	[kóka ɛ kərpúðəs]
stipe (of mushroom)	**bishti i kërpudhës** (m)	[bíʃti i kərpúðəs]
cep (Boletus edulis)	**porcini** (m)	[portsíni]
orange-cap boletus	**kërpudhë kapuç-verdhë** (f)	[kərpúðə kapútʃ-vérðə]
birch bolete	**porcinela** (f)	[portsinéla]
chanterelle	**shanterele** (f)	[ʃantɛrélɛ]
russula	**rusula** (f)	[rúsula]
morel	**morele** (f)	[morélɛ]
fly agaric	**kësulkuqe** (f)	[kəsulkúcɛ]
death cap	**kërpudha e vdekjes** (f)	[kərpúðə ɛ vdékjɛs]

230. Fruits. Berries

fruit	**frut** (m)	[frut]
fruits	**fruta** (pl)	[frúta]
apple	**mollë** (f)	[móɬə]
pear	**dardhë** (f)	[dárðə]

plum	kumbull (f)	[kúmbuɫ]
strawberry (garden ~)	luleshtrydhe (f)	[luleʃtrýðɛ]
sour cherry	qershi vishnje (f)	[cɛrʃi víʃɲɛ]
sweet cherry	qershi (f)	[cɛrʃi]
grape	rrush (m)	[ruʃ]

raspberry	mjedër (f)	[mjédər]
blackcurrant	kaliboba e zezë (f)	[kalibóba ɛ zézə]
redcurrant	kaliboba e kuqe (f)	[kalibóba ɛ kúcɛ]
gooseberry	kulumbri (f)	[kulumbrí]
cranberry	boronica (f)	[boronítsa]

orange	portokall (m)	[portokáɫ]
mandarin	mandarinë (f)	[mandarínə]
pineapple	ananas (m)	[ananás]
banana	banane (f)	[banánɛ]
date	hurmë (f)	[húrmə]

lemon	limon (m)	[limón]
apricot	kajsi (f)	[kajsí]
peach	pjeshkë (f)	[pjéʃkə]
kiwi	kivi (m)	[kívi]
grapefruit	grejpfrut (m)	[grɛjpfrút]

berry	manë (f)	[mánə]
berries	mana (f)	[mána]
cowberry	boronicë mirtile (f)	[boronítsə mirtílɛ]
wild strawberry	luleshtrydhe e egër (f)	[luleʃtrýðɛ ɛ égər]
bilberry	boronicë (f)	[boronítsə]

231. Flowers. Plants

flower	lule (f)	[lúlɛ]
bouquet (of flowers)	buqetë (f)	[bucétə]

rose (flower)	trëndafil (m)	[trəndafíl]
tulip	tulipan (m)	[tulipán]
carnation	karafil (m)	[karafíl]
gladiolus	gladiolë (f)	[gladiólə]

cornflower	lule misri (f)	[lúlɛ mísri]
harebell	lule këmborë (f)	[lúlɛ kəmbórə]
dandelion	luleradhiqe (f)	[lulɛraðícɛ]
camomile	kamomil (m)	[kamomíl]

aloe	aloe (f)	[alóɛ]
cactus	kaktus (m)	[kaktús]
rubber plant, ficus	fikus (m)	[fíkus]
lily	zambak (m)	[zambák]
geranium	barbarozë (f)	[barbarózə]

hyacinth	zymbyl (m)	[zymbýl]
mimosa	mimoza (f)	[mimóza]
narcissus	narcis (m)	[nartsís]
nasturtium	lule këmbore (f)	[lúlɛ kəmbórɛ]

orchid	orkide (f)	[orkidé]
peony	bozhure (f)	[boʒúrɛ]
violet	vjollcë (f)	[vjółtsə]
pansy	lule vjollca (f)	[lúlɛ vjółtsa]
forget-me-not	mosmëharro (f)	[mosməharó]
daisy	margaritë (f)	[margarítə]

poppy	lulëkuqe (f)	[luləkúcɛ]
hemp	kërp (m)	[kérp]
mint	mendër (f)	[méndər]

lily of the valley	zambak i fushës (m)	[zambák i fúʃəs]
snowdrop	luleborë (f)	[lulɛbórə]

nettle	hithra (f)	[híθra]
sorrel	lëpjeta (f)	[ləpjéta]
water lily	zambak uji (m)	[zambák új̈i]
fern	fier (m)	[fíɛr]
lichen	likene (f)	[likénɛ]
conservatory (greenhouse)	serrë (f)	[sérə]
lawn	lëndinë (f)	[ləndínə]
flowerbed	kënd lulishteje (m)	[kənd lulíʃtɛjɛ]

plant	bimë (f)	[bímə]
grass	bar (m)	[bar]
blade of grass	fije bari (f)	[fíjɛ bári]

leaf	gjeth (m)	[ɟɛθ]
petal	petale (f)	[pɛtálɛ]
stem	bisht (m)	[biʃt]
tuber	zhardhok (m)	[ʒarðók]

young plant (shoot)	filiz (m)	[filíz]
thorn	gjemb (m)	[ɟémb]

to blossom (vi)	lulëzoj	[luləzój]
to fade, to wither	vyshket	[výʃkɛt]
smell (odor)	aromë (f)	[arómə]
to cut (flowers)	pres lulet	[prɛs lúlɛt]
to pick (a flower)	mbledh lule	[mbléð lúlɛ]

232. Cereals, grains

grain	drithë (m)	[dríθə]
cereal crops	drithëra (pl)	[dríθəra]

ear (of barley, etc.)	kaush (m)	[kaúʃ]
wheat	grurë (f)	[grúrə]
rye	thekër (f)	[θékər]
oats	tërshërë (f)	[tərʃérə]
millet	mel (m)	[mɛl]
barley	elb (m)	[ɛlb]

corn	misër (m)	[mísər]
rice	oriz (m)	[oríz]
buckwheat	hikërr (m)	[híkər]

pea plant	bizele (f)	[bizélɛ]
kidney bean	groshë (f)	[gróʃə]
soy	sojë (f)	[sójə]
lentil	thjerrëz (f)	[θjérəz]
beans (pulse crops)	fasule (f)	[fasúlɛ]

233. Vegetables. Greens

| vegetables | perime (pl) | [pɛrímɛ] |
| greens | zarzavate (pl) | [zarzavátɛ] |

tomato	domate (f)	[domátɛ]
cucumber	kastravec (m)	[kastravéts]
carrot	karotë (f)	[karótə]
potato	patate (f)	[patátɛ]
onion	qepë (f)	[cépə]
garlic	hudhër (f)	[húðər]

cabbage	lakër (f)	[lákər]
cauliflower	lulelakër (f)	[lulɛlákər]
Brussels sprouts	lakër Brukseli (f)	[lákər brukséli]
broccoli	brokoli (m)	[brókoli]

beet	panxhar (m)	[pandʒár]
eggplant	patëllxhan (m)	[patəłdʒán]
zucchini	kungulleshë (m)	[kuŋułéʃə]
pumpkin	kungull (m)	[kúŋuł]
turnip	rrepë (f)	[répə]

parsley	majdanoz (m)	[majdanóz]
dill	kopër (f)	[kópər]
lettuce	sallatë jeshile (f)	[sałátə jɛʃílɛ]
celery	selino (f)	[sɛlíno]
asparagus	asparagus (m)	[asparágus]
spinach	spinaq (m)	[spináć]

pea	bizele (f)	[bizélɛ]
beans	fasule (f)	[fasúlɛ]
corn (maize)	misër (m)	[mísər]

kidney bean	**groshë** (f)	[gróʃə]
pepper	**spec** (m)	[spɛts]
radish	**rrepkë** (f)	[répkə]
artichoke	**angjinare** (f)	[anɟinárɛ]

REGIONAL GEOGRAPHY

Countries. Nationalities

234. Western Europe

Europe	**Evropa** (f)	[ɛvrópa]
European Union	**Bashkimi Evropian** (m)	[baʃkími ɛvropián]
European (n)	**Evropian** (m)	[ɛvropián]
European (adj)	**evropian**	[ɛvropián]
Austria	**Austri** (f)	[austrí]
Austrian (masc.)	**Austriak** (m)	[austriák]
Austrian (fem.)	**Austriake** (f)	[austriákɛ]
Austrian (adj)	**austriak**	[austriák]
Great Britain	**Britani e Madhe** (f)	[brítani ɛ máðɛ]
England	**Angli** (f)	[aŋlí]
British (masc.)	**Britanik** (m)	[britaník]
British (fem.)	**Britanike** (f)	[britaníkɛ]
English, British (adj)	**anglez**	[aŋléz]
Belgium	**Belgjikë** (f)	[bɛʎíkə]
Belgian (masc.)	**Belg** (m)	[bɛlg]
Belgian (fem.)	**Belge** (f)	[bélgɛ]
Belgian (adj)	**belg**	[bɛlg]
Germany	**Gjermani** (f)	[ʝɛrmaní]
German (masc.)	**Gjerman** (m)	[ʝɛrmán]
German (fem.)	**Gjermane** (f)	[ʝɛrmánɛ]
German (adj)	**gjerman**	[ʝɛrmán]
Netherlands	**Holandë** (f)	[holándə]
Holland	**Holandë** (f)	[holándə]
Dutch (masc.)	**Holandez** (m)	[holandéz]
Dutch (fem.)	**Holandeze** (f)	[holandézɛ]
Dutch (adj)	**holandez**	[holandéz]
Greece	**Greqi** (f)	[grɛcí]
Greek (masc.)	**Grek** (m)	[grɛk]
Greek (fem.)	**Greke** (f)	[grékɛ]
Greek (adj)	**grek**	[grɛk]
Denmark	**Danimarkë** (f)	[danimárkə]
Dane (masc.)	**Danez** (m)	[danéz]

| Dane (fem.) | Daneze (f) | [danézɛ] |
| Danish (adj) | danez | [danéz] |

Ireland	Irlandë (f)	[irlándə]
Irish (masc.)	Irlandez (m)	[irlandéz]
Irish (fem.)	Irlandeze (f)	[irlandézɛ]
Irish (adj)	irlandez	[irlandéz]

Iceland	Islandë (f)	[islándə]
Icelander (masc.)	Islandez (m)	[islandéz]
Icelander (fem.)	Islandeze (f)	[islandézɛ]
Icelandic (adj)	islandez	[islandéz]

Spain	Spanjë (f)	[spáɲə]
Spaniard (masc.)	Spanjoll (m)	[spaɲóɫ]
Spaniard (fem.)	Spanjolle (f)	[spaɲóɫɛ]
Spanish (adj)	spanjoll	[spaɲóɫ]

Italy	Itali (f)	[italí]
Italian (masc.)	Italian (m)	[italián]
Italian (fem.)	Italiane (f)	[italiánɛ]
Italian (adj)	italian	[italián]

Cyprus	Qipro (f)	[cípro]
Cypriot (masc.)	Qipriot (m)	[cipriót]
Cypriot (fem.)	Qipriote (f)	[cipriótɛ]
Cypriot (adj)	qipriot	[cipriót]

Malta	Maltë (f)	[máltə]
Maltese (masc.)	Maltez (m)	[maltéz]
Maltese (fem.)	Malteze (f)	[maltézɛ]
Maltese (adj)	maltez	[maltéz]

Norway	Norvegji (f)	[norvɛɟí]
Norwegian (masc.)	Norvegjez (m)	[norvɛɟéz]
Norwegian (fem.)	Norvegjeze (f)	[norvɛɟézɛ]
Norwegian (adj)	norvegjez	[norvɛɟéz]

Portugal	Portugali (f)	[portugalí]
Portuguese (masc.)	Portugez (m)	[portugéz]
Portuguese (fem.)	Portugeze (f)	[portugézɛ]
Portuguese (adj)	portugez	[portugéz]

Finland	Finlandë (f)	[finlándə]
Finn (masc.)	Finlandez (m)	[finlandéz]
Finn (fem.)	Finlandeze (f)	[finlandézɛ]
Finnish (adj)	finlandez	[finlandéz]

France	Francë (f)	[frántsə]
French (masc.)	Francez (m)	[frantséz]
French (fem.)	Franceze (f)	[frantsézɛ]
French (adj)	francez	[frantséz]

Sweden	Suedi (f)	[suɛdí]
Swede (masc.)	Suedez (m)	[suɛdéz]
Swede (fem.)	Suedeze (f)	[suɛdézɛ]
Swedish (adj)	suedez	[suɛdéz]

Switzerland	Zvicër (f)	[zvítsər]
Swiss (masc.)	Zviceran (m)	[zvitsɛrán]
Swiss (fem.)	Zvicerane (f)	[zvitsɛránɛ]
Swiss (adj)	zviceran	[zvitsɛrán]

Scotland	Skoci (f)	[skotsí]
Scottish (masc.)	Skocez (m)	[skotséz]
Scottish (fem.)	Skoceze (f)	[skotsézɛ]
Scottish (adj)	skocez	[skotséz]

Vatican	Vatikan (m)	[vatikán]
Liechtenstein	Lichtenstein (m)	[litshtɛnstéin]
Luxembourg	Luksemburg (m)	[luksɛmbúrg]
Monaco	Monako (f)	[monáko]

235. Central and Eastern Europe

Albania	Shqipëri (f)	[ʃcipərí]
Albanian (masc.)	Shqiptar (m)	[ʃciptár]
Albanian (fem.)	Shqiptare (f)	[ʃciptárɛ]
Albanian (adj)	shqiptar	[ʃciptár]

Bulgaria	Bullgari (f)	[buɫgarí]
Bulgarian (masc.)	Bullgar (m)	[buɫgár]
Bulgarian (fem.)	Bullgare (f)	[buɫgárɛ]
Bulgarian (adj)	bullgar	[buɫgár]

Hungary	Hungari (f)	[huɲarí]
Hungarian (masc.)	Hungarez (m)	[huɲaréz]
Hungarian (fem.)	Hungareze (f)	[huɲarézɛ]
Hungarian (adj)	hungarez	[huɲaréz]

Latvia	Letoni (f)	[lɛtoní]
Latvian (masc.)	Letonez (m)	[lɛtonéz]
Latvian (fem.)	Letoneze (f)	[lɛtonézɛ]
Latvian (adj)	letonez	[lɛtonéz]

Lithuania	Lituani (f)	[lituaní]
Lithuanian (masc.)	Lituanez (m)	[lituanéz]
Lithuanian (fem.)	Lituaneze (f)	[lituanézɛ]
Lithuanian (adj)	lituanez	[lituanéz]

Poland	Poloni (f)	[poloní]
Pole (masc.)	Polak (m)	[polák]
Pole (fem.)	Polake (f)	[polákɛ]

Polish (adj)	polak	[polák]
Romania	Rumani (f)	[rumaní]
Romanian (masc.)	Rumun (m)	[rumún]
Romanian (fem.)	Rumune (f)	[rumúnɛ]
Romanian (adj)	rumun	[rumún]

Serbia	Serbi (f)	[sɛrbí]
Serbian (masc.)	Serb (m)	[sɛrb]
Serbian (fem.)	Serbe (f)	[sérbɛ]
Serbian (adj)	serb	[sɛrb]

Slovakia	Sllovaki (f)	[słovakí]
Slovak (masc.)	Sllovak (m)	[słovák]
Slovak (fem.)	Sllovake (f)	[słovákɛ]
Slovak (adj)	sllovak	[słovák]

Croatia	Kroaci (f)	[kroatsí]
Croatian (masc.)	Kroat (m)	[kroát]
Croatian (fem.)	Kroate (f)	[kroátɛ]
Croatian (adj)	kroat	[kroát]

Czech Republic	Republika Çeke (f)	[rɛpublíka tʃékɛ]
Czech (masc.)	Çek (m)	[tʃɛk]
Czech (fem.)	Çeke (f)	[tʃékɛ]
Czech (adj)	çek	[tʃɛk]

Estonia	Estoni (f)	[ɛstoní]
Estonian (masc.)	Estonez (m)	[ɛstonéz]
Estonian (fem.)	Estoneze (f)	[ɛstonézɛ]
Estonian (adj)	estonez	[ɛstonéz]

Bosnia and Herzegovina	Bosnje Herzegovina (f)	[bósɲɛ hɛrzɛgovína]
Macedonia (Republic of ~)	Maqedonia (f)	[macɛdonía]
Slovenia	Sllovenia (f)	[słovɛnía]
Montenegro	Mali i Zi (m)	[máli i zí]

236. Former USSR countries

Azerbaijan	Azerbajxhan (m)	[azɛrbajdʒán]
Azerbaijani (masc.)	Azerbajxhanas (m)	[azɛrbajdʒánas]
Azerbaijani (fem.)	Azerbajxhanase (f)	[azɛrbajdʒánasɛ]
Azerbaijani, Azeri (adj)	azerbajxhanas	[azɛrbajdʒánas]

Armenia	Armeni (f)	[armɛní]
Armenian (masc.)	Armen (m)	[armén]
Armenian (fem.)	Armene (f)	[arménɛ]
Armenian (adj)	armen	[armén]

| Belarus | Bjellorusi (f) | [bjɛłorusí] |
| Belarusian (masc.) | Bjellorus (m) | [bjɛłorús] |

| Belarusian (fem.) | Bjelloruse (f) | [bjɛɫorúsɛ] |
| Belarusian (adj) | bjellorus | [bjɛɫorús] |

Georgia	Gjeorgji (f)	[ɟeorɟí]
Georgian (masc.)	Gjeorgjian (m)	[ɟeorɟián]
Georgian (fem.)	Gjeorgjiane (f)	[ɟeorɟiánɛ]
Georgian (adj)	gjeorgjian	[ɟeorɟián]
Kazakhstan	Kazakistan (m)	[kazakistán]
Kazakh (masc.)	Kazakistanez (m)	[kazakistanéz]
Kazakh (fem.)	Kazakistaneze (f)	[kazakistanézɛ]
Kazakh (adj)	kazakistanez	[kazakistanéz]

Kirghizia	Kirgistan (m)	[kirgistán]
Kirghiz (masc.)	Kirgistanez (m)	[kirgistanéz]
Kirghiz (fem.)	Kirgistaneze (f)	[kirgistanézɛ]
Kirghiz (adj)	kirgistanez	[kirgistanéz]

Moldova, Moldavia	Moldavi (f)	[moldaví]
Moldavian (masc.)	Moldav (m)	[moldáv]
Moldavian (fem.)	Moldave (f)	[moldávɛ]
Moldavian (adj)	moldav	[moldáv]
Russia	Rusi (f)	[rusí]
Russian (masc.)	Rus (m)	[rus]
Russian (fem.)	Ruse (f)	[rúsɛ]
Russian (adj)	rus	[rus]

Tajikistan	Taxhikistan (m)	[tadʒikistán]
Tajik (masc.)	Taxhikistanez (m)	[tadʒikistanéz]
Tajik (fem.)	Taxhikistaneze (f)	[tadʒikistanézɛ]
Tajik (adj)	taxhikistanez	[tadʒikistanéz]

Turkmenistan	Turkmenistan (m)	[turkmɛnistán]
Turkmen (masc.)	Turkmen (m)	[turkmén]
Turkmen (fem.)	Turkmene (f)	[turkménɛ]
Turkmenian (adj)	Turkmen	[turkmén]

Uzbekistan	Uzbekistan (m)	[uzbɛkistán]
Uzbek (masc.)	Uzbek (m)	[uzbék]
Uzbek (fem.)	Uzbeke (f)	[uzbékɛ]
Uzbek (adj)	uzbek	[uzbék]

Ukraine	Ukrainë (f)	[ukraínə]
Ukrainian (masc.)	Ukrainas (m)	[ukraínas]
Ukrainian (fem.)	Ukrainase (f)	[ukraínasɛ]
Ukrainian (adj)	ukrainas	[ukraínas]

237. Asia

| Asia | Azia (f) | [azía] |
| Asian (adj) | Aziatik | [aziatík] |

Vietnam	Vietnam (m)	[viɛtnám]
Vietnamese (masc.)	Vietnamez (m)	[viɛtnaméz]
Vietnamese (fem.)	Vietnameze (f)	[viɛtnamézɛ]
Vietnamese (adj)	vietnamez	[viɛtnaméz]

India	Indi (f)	[indí]
Indian (masc.)	Indian (m)	[indián]
Indian (fem.)	Indiane (f)	[indiánɛ]
Indian (adj)	indian	[indián]

Israel	Izrael (m)	[izraél]
Israeli (masc.)	Izaelit (m)	[izaɛlít]
Israeli (fem.)	Izraelite (f)	[izraɛlítɛ]
Israeli (adj)	izraelit	[izraɛlít]

Jew (n)	hebre (m)	[hɛbré]
Jewess (n)	hebre (f)	[hɛbré]
Jewish (adj)	hebraike	[hɛbraíkɛ]

China	Kinë (f)	[kínə]
Chinese (masc.)	Kinez (m)	[kinéz]
Chinese (fem.)	Kineze (f)	[kinézɛ]
Chinese (adj)	kinez	[kinéz]

Korean (masc.)	Korean (m)	[korɛán]
Korean (fem.)	Koreane (f)	[korɛánɛ]
Korean (adj)	korean	[korɛán]

Lebanon	Liban (m)	[libán]
Lebanese (masc.)	Libanez (m)	[libanéz]
Lebanese (fem.)	Libaneze (f)	[libanézɛ]
Lebanese (adj)	libanez	[libanéz]

Mongolia	Mongoli (f)	[moŋolí]
Mongolian (masc.)	Mongol (m)	[moŋól]
Mongolian (fem.)	Mongole (f)	[moŋólɛ]
Mongolian (adj)	mongol	[moŋól]

Malaysia	Malajzi (f)	[malajzí]
Malaysian (masc.)	Malajzian (m)	[malajzián]
Malaysian (fem.)	Malajziane (f)	[malajziánɛ]
Malaysian (adj)	malajzian	[malajzián]

Pakistan	Pakistan (m)	[pakistán]
Pakistani (masc.)	Pakistanez (m)	[pakistanéz]
Pakistani (fem.)	Pakistaneze (f)	[pakistanézɛ]
Pakistani (adj)	pakistanez	[pakistanéz]

Saudi Arabia	Arabia Saudite (f)	[arabía saudítɛ]
Arab (masc.)	Arab (m)	[aráb]
Arab (fem.)	Arabe (f)	[arábɛ]
Arab, Arabic (adj)	arabik	[arabík]

Thailand	**Tajlandë** (f)	[tajlándə]
Thai (masc.)	**Tajlandez** (m)	[tajlandéz]
Thai (fem.)	**Tajlandeze** (f)	[tajlandézɛ]
Thai (adj)	**tajlandez**	[tajlandéz]
Taiwan	**Tajvan** (m)	[tajván]
Taiwanese (masc.)	**Tajvanez** (m)	[tajvanéz]
Taiwanese (fem.)	**Tajvaneze** (f)	[tajvanézɛ]
Taiwanese (adj)	**tajvanez**	[tajvanéz]
Turkey	**Turqi** (f)	[turcí]
Turk (masc.)	**Turk** (m)	[turk]
Turk (fem.)	**Turke** (f)	[túrkɛ]
Turkish (adj)	**turk**	[turk]
Japan	**Japoni** (f)	[japoní]
Japanese (masc.)	**Japonez** (m)	[japonéz]
Japanese (fem.)	**Japoneze** (f)	[japonézɛ]
Japanese (adj)	**japonez**	[japonéz]
Afghanistan	**Afganistan** (m)	[afganistán]
Bangladesh	**Bangladesh** (m)	[baŋladéʃ]
Indonesia	**Indonezi** (f)	[indonɛzí]
Jordan	**Jordani** (f)	[jordaní]
Iraq	**Irak** (m)	[irak]
Iran	**Iran** (m)	[irán]
Cambodia	**Kamboxhia** (f)	[kambódʒia]
Kuwait	**Kuvajt** (m)	[kuvájt]
Laos	**Laos** (m)	[láos]
Myanmar	**Mianmar** (m)	[mianmár]
Nepal	**Nepal** (m)	[nɛpál]
United Arab Emirates	**Emiratet e Bashkuara Arabe** (pl)	[ɛmirátɛt ɛ baʃkúara arábɛ]
Syria	**Siri** (f)	[sirí]
Palestine	**Palestinë** (f)	[palɛstínə]
South Korea	**Korea e Jugut** (f)	[koréa ɛ júgut]
North Korea	**Korea e Veriut** (f)	[koréa ɛ vériut]

238. North America

United States of America	**Shtetet e Bashkuara të Amerikës**	[ʃtétɛt ɛ baʃkúara tə amɛríkəs]
American (masc.)	**Amerikan** (m)	[amɛrikán]
American (fem.)	**Amerikane** (f)	[amɛrikánɛ]
American (adj)	**amerikan**	[amɛrikán]
Canada	**Kanada** (f)	[kanadá]
Canadian (masc.)	**Kanadez** (m)	[kanadéz]

| Canadian (fem.) | Kanadeze (f) | [kanadézɛ] |
| Canadian (adj) | kanadez | [kanadéz] |

Mexico	Meksikë (f)	[mɛksíkə]
Mexican (masc.)	Meksikan (m)	[mɛksikán]
Mexican (fem.)	Meksikane (f)	[mɛksikánɛ]
Mexican (adj)	meksikan	[mɛksikán]

239. Central and South America

Argentina	Argjentinë (f)	[arɟɛntínə]
Argentinian (masc.)	Argjentinas (m)	[arɟɛntínas]
Argentinian (fem.)	Argjentinase (f)	[arɟɛntínasɛ]
Argentinian (adj)	argjentinas	[arɟɛntínas]

Brazil	Brazil (m)	[brazíl]
Brazilian (masc.)	Brazilian (m)	[brazilián]
Brazilian (fem.)	Braziliane (f)	[braziliánɛ]
Brazilian (adj)	brazilian	[brazilián]

Colombia	Kolumbi (f)	[kolumbí]
Colombian (masc.)	Kolumbian (m)	[kolumbián]
Colombian (fem.)	Kolumbiane (f)	[kolumbiánɛ]
Colombian (adj)	kolumbian	[kolumbián]

Cuba	Kuba (f)	[kúba]
Cuban (masc.)	Kuban (m)	[kubán]
Cuban (fem.)	Kubane (f)	[kubánɛ]
Cuban (adj)	kuban	[kubán]

Chile	Kili (m)	[kíli]
Chilean (masc.)	Kilian (m)	[kilián]
Chilean (fem.)	Kiliane (f)	[kiliánɛ]
Chilean (adj)	kilian	[kilián]

| Bolivia | Bolivi (f) | [boliví] |
| Venezuela | Venezuelë (f) | [vɛnɛzuélə] |

| Paraguay | Paraguai (m) | [paraguái] |
| Peru | Peru (f) | [pɛrú] |

Suriname	Surinam (m)	[surinám]
Uruguay	Uruguai (m)	[uruguái]
Ecuador	Ekuador (m)	[ɛkuadór]

The Bahamas	Bahamas (m)	[bahámas]
Haiti	Haiti (m)	[haíti]
Dominican Republic	Republika Dominikane (f)	[rɛpublíka dominikánɛ]
Panama	Panama (f)	[panamá]
Jamaica	Xhamajka (f)	[dʒamájka]

240. Africa

Egypt	Egjipt (m)	[ɛɟípt]
Egyptian (masc.)	Egjiptian (m)	[ɛɟiptián]
Egyptian (fem.)	Egjiptiane (f)	[ɛɟiptiánɛ]
Egyptian (adj)	egjiptian	[ɛɟiptián]
Morocco	Marok (m)	[marók]
Moroccan (masc.)	Maroken (m)	[marokén]
Moroccan (fem.)	Marokene (f)	[marokénɛ]
Moroccan (adj)	maroken	[marokén]
Tunisia	Tunizi (f)	[tunizí]
Tunisian (masc.)	Tunizian (m)	[tunizián]
Tunisian (fem.)	Tuniziane (f)	[tuniziánɛ]
Tunisian (adj)	tunizian	[tunizián]
Ghana	Gana (f)	[gána]
Zanzibar	Zanzibar (m)	[zanzibár]
Kenya	Kenia (f)	[kénia]
Libya	Libia (f)	[libía]
Madagascar	Madagaskar (m)	[madagaskár]
Namibia	Namibia (f)	[namíbia]
Senegal	Senegal (m)	[sɛnɛgál]
Tanzania	Tanzani (f)	[tanzaní]
South Africa	Afrika e Jugut (f)	[afríka ɛ júgut]
African (masc.)	Afrikan (m)	[afrikán]
African (fem.)	Afrikane (f)	[afrikánɛ]
African (adj)	Afrikan	[afrikán]

241. Australia. Oceania

Australia	Australia (f)	[australía]
Australian (masc.)	Australian (m)	[australián]
Australian (fem.)	Australiane (f)	[australiánɛ]
Australian (adj)	australian	[australián]
New Zealand	Zelandë e Re (f)	[zɛlándə ɛ ré]
New Zealander (masc.)	Zelandez (m)	[zɛlandéz]
New Zealander (fem.)	Zelandeze (f)	[zɛlandézɛ]
New Zealand (as adj)	zelandez	[zɛlandéz]
Tasmania	Tasmani (f)	[tasmaní]
French Polynesia	Polinezia Franceze (f)	[polinɛzía frantsézɛ]

242. Cities

Amsterdam	Amsterdam (m)	[amstɛrdám]
Ankara	Ankara (f)	[ankará]
Athens	Athinë (f)	[aθínə]
Baghdad	Bagdad (m)	[bagdád]
Bangkok	Bangkok (m)	[baŋkók]
Barcelona	Barcelonë (f)	[bartsɛlónə]
Beijing	Pekin (m)	[pɛkín]
Beirut	Bejrut (m)	[bɛjrút]
Berlin	Berlin (m)	[bɛrlín]
Mumbai (Bombay)	Mumbai (m)	[mumbái]
Bonn	Bon (m)	[bon]
Bordeaux	Bordo (f)	[bordó]
Bratislava	Bratislavë (f)	[bratislávə]
Brussels	Bruksel (m)	[bruksél]
Bucharest	Bukuresht (m)	[bukuréʃt]
Budapest	Budapest (m)	[budapést]
Cairo	Kajro (f)	[kájro]
Kolkata (Calcutta)	Kalkutë (f)	[kalkútə]
Chicago	Çikago (f)	[tʃikágo]
Copenhagen	Kopenhagen (m)	[kopɛnhágɛn]
Dar-es-Salaam	Dar es Salam (m)	[dar ɛs salám]
Delhi	Delhi (f)	[délhi]
Dubai	Dubai (m)	[dubái]
Dublin	Dublin (m)	[dúblin]
Düsseldorf	Dyseldorf (m)	[dysɛldórf]
Florence	Firence (f)	[firéntsɛ]
Frankfurt	Frankfurt (m)	[frankfúrt]
Geneva	Gjenevë (f)	[ɟɛnévə]
The Hague	Hagë (f)	[hágə]
Hamburg	Hamburg (m)	[hambúrg]
Hanoi	Hanoi (m)	[hanói]
Havana	Havana (f)	[havána]
Helsinki	Helsinki (m)	[hɛlsínki]
Hiroshima	Hiroshimë (f)	[hiroʃímə]
Hong Kong	Hong Kong (m)	[hoŋ kóŋ]
Istanbul	Stamboll (m)	[stambóɫ]
Jerusalem	Jerusalem (m)	[jɛrusalém]
Kyiv	Kiev (m)	[kíɛv]
Kuala Lumpur	Kuala Lumpur (m)	[kuála lumpúr]
Lisbon	Lisbonë (f)	[lisbónə]
London	Londër (f)	[lóndər]
Los Angeles	Los Anxhelos (m)	[lós andʒɛlós]

Lyons	Lion (m)	[lión]
Madrid	Madrid (m)	[madríd]
Marseille	Marsejë (f)	[marséjə]
Mexico City	Meksiko Siti (m)	[méksiko síti]
Miami	Majami (m)	[majámi]
Montreal	Montreal (m)	[montrɛál]
Moscow	Moskë (f)	[móskə]
Munich	Munih (m)	[muníh]

Nairobi	Najrobi (m)	[najróbi]
Naples	Napoli (m)	[nápoli]
New York	Nju Jork (m)	[ɲu jork]
Nice	Nisë (m)	[nísə]
Oslo	oslo (f)	[óslo]
Ottawa	Otava (f)	[otáva]

Paris	Paris (m)	[parís]
Prague	Pragë (f)	[prágə]
Rio de Janeiro	Rio de Zhaneiro (m)	[río dɛ ʒanéiro]
Rome	Romë (f)	[rómə]

Saint Petersburg	Shën Petersburg (m)	[ʃən pɛtɛrsbúrg]
Seoul	Seul (m)	[sɛúl]
Shanghai	Shangai (m)	[ʃaɲái]
Singapore	Singapor (m)	[siɲapór]
Stockholm	Stokholm (m)	[stokhólm]
Sydney	Sidney (m)	[sidnéy]

Taipei	Taipei (m)	[taipéi]
Tokyo	Tokio (f)	[tókio]
Toronto	Toronto (f)	[torónto]

Venice	Venecia (f)	[vɛnétsia]
Vienna	Vjenë (f)	[vjénə]
Warsaw	Varshavë (f)	[varʃávə]
Washington	Uashington (m)	[vaʃiɲtón]

243. Politics. Government. Part 1

politics	politikë (f)	[politíkə]
political (adj)	politike	[politíkɛ]
politician	politikan (m)	[politikán]

state (country)	shtet (m)	[ʃtɛt]
citizen	nënshtetas (m)	[nənʃtétas]
citizenship	nënshtetësi (f)	[nənʃtɛtəsí]

national emblem	simbol kombëtar (m)	[simból kombətár]
national anthem	himni kombëtar (m)	[hímni kombətár]
government	qeveri (f)	[cɛvɛrí]

head of state	kreu i shtetit (m)	[kréu i ʃtétit]
parliament	parlament (m)	[parlamént]
party	parti (f)	[partí]
capitalism	kapitalizëm (m)	[kapitalízəm]
capitalist (adj)	kapitalist	[kapitalíst]
socialism	socializëm (m)	[sotsialízəm]
socialist (adj)	socialist	[sotsialíst]
communism	komunizëm (m)	[komunízəm]
communist (adj)	komunist	[komuníst]
communist (n)	komunist (m)	[komuníst]
democracy	demokraci (f)	[dɛmokratsí]
democrat	demokrat (m)	[dɛmokrát]
democratic (adj)	demokratik	[dɛmokratík]
Democratic party	parti demokratike (f)	[partí dɛmokratíkɛ]
liberal (n)	liberal (m)	[libɛrál]
liberal (adj)	liberal	[libɛrál]
conservative (n)	konservativ (m)	[konsɛrvatív]
conservative (adj)	konservativ	[konsɛrvatív]
republic (n)	republikë (f)	[rɛpublíkə]
republican (n)	republikan (m)	[rɛpublikán]
Republican party	parti republikane (f)	[partí rɛpublikánɛ]
elections	zgjedhje (f)	[zɟéðjɛ]
to elect (vt)	zgjedh	[zɟɛð]
elector, voter	zgjedhës (m)	[zɟéðəs]
election campaign	fushatë zgjedhore (f)	[fuʃátə zɟɛðórɛ]
voting (n)	votim (m)	[votím]
to vote (vi)	votoj	[votój]
suffrage, right to vote	e drejta e votës (f)	[ɛ dréjta ɛ vótəs]
candidate	kandidat (m)	[kandidát]
to be a candidate	jam kandidat	[jam kandidát]
campaign	fushatë (f)	[fuʃátə]
opposition (as adj)	opozitar	[opozitár]
opposition (n)	opozitë (f)	[opozítə]
visit	vizitë (f)	[vizítə]
official visit	vizitë zyrtare (f)	[vizítə zyrtárɛ]
international (adj)	ndërkombëtar	[ndərkombətár]
negotiations	negociata (f)	[nɛgotsiáta]
to negotiate (vi)	negocioj	[nɛgotsiój]

244. Politics. Government. Part 2

society	**shoqëri** (f)	[ʃocərí]
constitution	**kushtetutë** (f)	[kuʃtɛtútə]
power (political control)	**pushtet** (m)	[puʃtét]
corruption	**korrupsion** (m)	[korupsión]
law (justice)	**ligj** (m)	[liɟ]
legal (legitimate)	**ligjor**	[liɟór]
justice (fairness)	**drejtësi** (f)	[drɛjtəsí]
just (fair)	**e drejtë**	[ɛ dréjtə]
committee	**komitet** (m)	[komitét]
bill (draft law)	**projektligj** (m)	[projɛktlíɟ]
budget	**buxhet** (m)	[budʒét]
policy	**politikë** (f)	[politíkə]
reform	**reformë** (f)	[rɛfórmə]
radical (adj)	**radikal**	[radikál]
power (strength, force)	**fuqi** (f)	[fucí]
powerful (adj)	**i fuqishëm**	[i fucíʃəm]
supporter	**mbështetës** (m)	[mbəʃtétəs]
influence	**ndikim** (m)	[ndikím]
regime (e.g., military ~)	**regjim** (m)	[rɛɟím]
conflict	**konflikt** (m)	[konflíkt]
conspiracy (plot)	**komplot** (m)	[komplót]
provocation	**provokim** (m)	[provokím]
to overthrow (regime, etc.)	**rrëzoj**	[rəzój]
overthrow (of government)	**rrëzim** (m)	[rəzím]
revolution	**revolucion** (m)	[rɛvolutsión]
coup d'état	**grusht shteti** (m)	[grúʃt ʃtéti]
military coup	**puç ushtarak** (m)	[putʃ uʃtarák]
crisis	**krizë** (f)	[krízə]
economic recession	**recesion ekonomik** (m)	[rɛtsɛsión ɛkonomík]
demonstrator (protester)	**protestues** (m)	[protɛstúɛs]
demonstration	**protestë** (f)	[protéstə]
martial law	**ligj ushtarak** (m)	[liɟ uʃtarák]
military base	**bazë ushtarake** (f)	[bázə uʃtarákɛ]
stability	**stabilitet** (m)	[stabilitét]
stable (adj)	**stabil**	[stabíl]
exploitation	**shfrytëzim** (m)	[ʃfrytəzím]
to exploit (workers)	**shfrytëzoj**	[ʃfrytəzój]
racism	**racizëm** (m)	[ratsízəm]
racist	**racist** (m)	[ratsíst]

fascism	**fashizëm** (m)	[faʃízəm]
fascist	**fashist** (m)	[faʃíst]

245. Countries. Miscellaneous

foreigner	**i huaj** (m)	[i húaj]
foreign (adj)	**huaj**	[húaj]
abroad (in a foreign country)	**jashtë shteti**	[jáʃtə ʃtéti]
emigrant	**emigrant** (m)	[ɛmigránt]
emigration	**emigracion** (m)	[ɛmigratsión]
to emigrate (vi)	**emigroj**	[ɛmigrój]
the West	**Perëndimi** (m)	[pɛrəndími]
the East	**Lindja** (f)	[líndja]
the Far East	**Lindja e Largët** (f)	[líndja ɛ lárgət]
civilization	**civilizim** (m)	[tsivilizím]
humanity (mankind)	**njerëzia** (f)	[ɲɛrəzía]
the world (earth)	**bota** (f)	[bóta]
peace	**paqe** (f)	[pácɛ]
worldwide (adj)	**botëror**	[botərór]
homeland	**atdhe** (f)	[atðé]
people (population)	**njerëz** (m)	[ɲérəz]
population	**popullsi** (f)	[popuɫsí]
people (a lot of ~)	**njerëz** (m)	[ɲérəz]
nation (people)	**komb** (m)	[komb]
generation	**brez** (m)	[brɛz]
territory (area)	**zonë** (f)	[zónə]
region	**rajon** (m)	[rajón]
state (part of a country)	**shtet** (m)	[ʃtɛt]
tradition	**traditë** (f)	[tradítə]
custom (tradition)	**zakon** (m)	[zakón]
ecology	**ekologjia** (f)	[ɛkoloɟía]
Indian (Native American)	**Indian të Amerikës** (m)	[indián tə amɛríkəs]
Gypsy (masc.)	**jevg** (m)	[jɛvg]
Gypsy (fem.)	**jevge** (f)	[jévgɛ]
Gypsy (adj)	**jevg**	[jɛvg]
empire	**perandori** (f)	[pɛrandorí]
colony	**koloni** (f)	[koloní]
slavery	**skllevëri** (m)	[skɫɛvərí]
invasion	**pushtim** (m)	[puʃtím]
famine	**uria** (f)	[uría]

246. Major religious groups. Confessions

religion	religjion (m)	[rɛliɟión]
religious (adj)	religjioz	[rɛliɟióz]
faith, belief	fe, besim (m)	[fé], [bɛsím]
to believe (in God)	besoj	[bɛsój]
believer	besimtar (m)	[bɛsimtár]
atheism	ateizëm (m)	[atɛízəm]
atheist	ateist (m)	[atɛíst]
Christianity	Krishterimi (m)	[kriʃtɛrími]
Christian (n)	i krishterë (m)	[i kriʃtérə]
Christian (adj)	krishterë	[kriʃtérə]
Catholicism	Katolicizëm (m)	[katolitsízəm]
Catholic (n)	Katolik (m)	[katolík]
Catholic (adj)	katolik	[katolík]
Protestantism	Protestantizëm (m)	[protɛstantízəm]
Protestant Church	Kishë Protestante (f)	[kíʃə protɛstántɛ]
Protestant (n)	Protestant (m)	[protɛstánt]
Orthodoxy	Ortodoksia (f)	[ortodoksía]
Orthodox Church	Kishë Ortodokse (f)	[kíʃə ortodóksɛ]
Orthodox (n)	Ortodoks (m)	[ortodóks]
Presbyterianism	Presbiterian (m)	[prɛsbitɛrián]
Presbyterian Church	Kishë Presbiteriane (f)	[kíʃə prɛsbitɛriánɛ]
Presbyterian (n)	Presbiterian (m)	[prɛsbitɛrián]
Lutheranism	Luterianizëm (m)	[lutɛrianízəm]
Lutheran (n)	Luterian (m)	[lutɛrián]
Baptist Church	Kishë Baptiste (f)	[kíʃə baptístɛ]
Baptist (n)	Baptist (m)	[baptíst]
Anglican Church	Kishë Anglikane (f)	[kíʃə aŋlikánɛ]
Anglican (n)	Anglikan (m)	[aŋlikán]
Mormonism	Mormonizëm (m)	[mormonízəm]
Mormon (n)	Mormon (m)	[mormón]
Judaism	Judaizëm (m)	[judaízəm]
Jew (n)	çifut (m)	[tʃifút]
Buddhism	Budizëm (m)	[budízəm]
Buddhist (n)	Budist (m)	[budíst]
Hinduism	Hinduizëm (m)	[hinduízəm]
Hindu (n)	Hindu (m)	[híndu]

Islam	Islam (m)	[islám]
Muslim (n)	Mysliman (m)	[myslimán]
Muslim (adj)	Mysliman	[myslimán]

| Shiah Islam | Islami Shia (m) | [islámi ʃia] |
| Shiite (n) | Shiitë (f) | [ʃiitə] |

| Sunni Islam | Islami Suni (m) | [islámi súni] |
| Sunnite (n) | Sunit (m) | [sunít] |

247. Religions. Priests

| priest | prift (m) | [prift] |
| the Pope | Papa (f) | [pápa] |

monk, friar	murg, frat (m)	[murg], [frat]
nun	murgeshë (f)	[murgéʃə]
pastor	pastor (m)	[pastór]

abbot	abat (m)	[abát]
vicar (parish priest)	famullitar (m)	[famuɫitár]
bishop	peshkop (m)	[pɛʃkóp]
cardinal	kardinal (m)	[kardinál]

preacher	predikues (m)	[prɛdikúɛs]
preaching	predikim (m)	[prɛdikím]
parishioners	faullistë (f)	[fauɫístə]

| believer | besimtar (m) | [bɛsimtár] |
| atheist | ateist (m) | [atɛíst] |

248. Faith. Christianity. Islam

| Adam | Adam (m) | [adám] |
| Eve | eva (f) | [éva] |

God	Zot (m)	[zot]
the Lord	Zoti (m)	[zóti]
the Almighty	i Plotfuqishmi (m)	[i plotfucíʃmi]

sin	mëkat (m)	[məkát]
to sin (vi)	mëkatoj	[məkatój]
sinner (masc.)	mëkatar (m)	[məkatár]
sinner (fem.)	mëkatare (f)	[məkatárɛ]

hell	ferr (m)	[fɛr]
paradise	parajsë (f)	[parájsə]
Jesus	Jezus (m)	[jézus]

Jesus Christ	Jezu Krishti (m)	[jézu kríʃti]
the Holy Spirit	Shpirti i Shenjtë (m)	[ʃpírti i ʃéɲtə]
the Savior	Shpëtimtar (m)	[ʃpətimtár]
the Virgin Mary	e Virgjëra Meri (f)	[ε víɾɟəra méri]

the Devil	Djalli (m)	[djáɬi]
devil's (adj)	i djallit	[i djáɬit]
Satan	Satani (m)	[satáni]
satanic (adj)	satanik	[sataník]

angel	engjëll (m)	[éɲɟəɬ]
guardian angel	engjëlli mbrojtës (m)	[éɲɟəɬi mbrójtəs]
angelic (adj)	engjëllor	[εɲɟətór]

apostle	apostull (m)	[apóstuɬ]
archangel	kryeengjëll (m)	[kryεéɲɟəɬ]
the Antichrist	Antikrishti (m)	[antikríʃti]

Church	Kishë (f)	[kíʃə]
Bible	Bibla (f)	[bíbla]
biblical (adj)	biblik	[biblík]

Old Testament	Dhiata e Vjetër (f)	[ðiáta ε vjétər]
New Testament	Dhiata e Re (f)	[ðiáta ε ré]
Gospel	ungjill (m)	[uɲɟíɬ]
Holy Scripture	Libri i Shenjtë (m)	[líbri i ʃéɲtə]
Heaven	parajsa (f)	[parájsa]

Commandment	urdhëresë (f)	[urðərésə]
prophet	profet (m)	[profét]
prophecy	profeci (f)	[profεtsí]

Allah	Allah (m)	[aɬáh]
Mohammed	Muhamed (m)	[muhaméd]
the Koran	Kurani (m)	[kuráni]

mosque	xhami (f)	[dʒamí]
mullah	hoxhë (m)	[hódʒə]
prayer	lutje (f)	[lútjε]
to pray (vi, vt)	lutem	[lútεm]

pilgrimage	pelegrinazh (m)	[pεlεgrináʒ]
pilgrim	pelegrin (m)	[pεlεgrín]
Mecca	Mekë (f)	[mékə]

church	kishë (f)	[kíʃə]
temple	tempull (m)	[témpuɬ]
cathedral	katedrale (f)	[katεdrálε]
Gothic (adj)	Gotik	[gotík]
synagogue	sinagogë (f)	[sinagógə]
mosque	xhami (f)	[dʒamí]
chapel	kishëz (m)	[kíʃəz]

| abbey | abaci (f) | [ábatsi] |
| monastery | manastir (m) | [manastír] |

bell (church ~s)	kambanë (f)	[kambánə]
bell tower	kulla e kambanës (f)	[kúɫa ɛ kambánəs]
to ring (ab. bells)	bien	[bíɛn]

cross	kryq (m)	[kryc]
cupola (roof)	kupola (f)	[kupóla]
icon	ikona (f)	[ikóna]

soul	shpirt (m)	[ʃpirt]
fate (destiny)	fat (m)	[fat]
evil (n)	e keqe (f)	[ɛ kécɛ]
good (n)	e mirë (f)	[ɛ mírə]

vampire	vampir (m)	[vampír]
witch (evil ~)	shtrigë (f)	[ʃtrígə]
demon	djall (m)	[djáɫ]
spirit	shpirt (m)	[ʃpirt]

| redemption (giving us ~) | shëlbim (m) | [ʃəlbím] |
| to redeem (vt) | shëlbej | [ʃəlbéj] |

church service, mass	meshë (f)	[méʃə]
to say mass	lus meshë	[lús méʃə]
confession	rrëfim (m)	[rəfím]
to confess (vi)	rrëfej	[rəféj]

saint (n)	shenjt (m)	[ʃɛɲt]
sacred (holy)	i shenjtë	[i ʃéɲtə]
holy water	ujë i bekuar (m)	[újə i bɛkúar]

ritual (n)	ritual (m)	[rituál]
ritual (adj)	ritual	[rituál]
sacrifice	sakrificë (f)	[sakrifítsə]

superstition	besëtytni (f)	[bɛsətytní]
superstitious (adj)	supersticioz	[supɛrstitsióz]
afterlife	jeta e përtejme (f)	[jéta ɛ pərtéjmɛ]
eternal life	përjetësia (f)	[pərjɛtəsía]

MISCELLANEOUS

249. Various useful words

background (green ~)	sfond (m)	[sfónd]
balance (of situation)	ekuilibër (m)	[εkuilibər]
barrier (obstacle)	pengesë (f)	[pεŋésə]
base (basis)	bazë (f)	[bázə]
beginning	fillim (m)	[fiłím]
category	kategori (f)	[katεgorí]
cause (reason)	shkak (m)	[ʃkak]
choice	zgjedhje (f)	[zɟéðjε]
coincidence	rastësi (f)	[rastəsí]
comfortable (~ chair)	i rehatshëm	[i rεhátʃəm]
comparison	krahasim (m)	[krahasím]
compensation	shpërblim (m)	[ʃpərblím]
degree (extent, amount)	nivel (m)	[nivél]
development	zhvillim (m)	[ʒviłím]
difference	ndryshim (m)	[ndryʃím]
effect (e.g., of drugs)	efekt (m)	[εfékt]
effort (exertion)	përpjekje (f)	[pərpjékjε]
element	element (m)	[εlεmént]
end (finish)	fund (m)	[fund]
example (illustration)	shembull (m)	[ʃémbuł]
fact	fakt (m)	[fakt]
frequent (adj)	i shpeshtë	[i ʃpéʃtə]
growth (development)	rritje (f)	[rítjε]
help	ndihmë (f)	[ndíhmə]
ideal	ideal (m)	[idεál]
kind (sort, type)	lloj (m)	[łoj]
labyrinth	labirint (m)	[labirínt]
mistake, error	gabim (m)	[gabím]
moment	moment (m)	[momént]
object (thing)	objekt (m)	[objékt]
obstacle	pengesë (f)	[pεŋésə]
original (original copy)	origjinal (m)	[oriʝinál]
part (~ of sth)	pjesë (f)	[pjésə]
particle, small part	grimcë (f)	[grímtsə]
pause (break)	pushim (m)	[puʃím]

position	pozicion (m)	[pozitsión]
principle	parim (m)	[parím]
problem	problem (m)	[problém]

process	proces (m)	[protsés]
progress	ecje përpara (f)	[étsjɛ pərpára]
property (quality)	cilësi (f)	[tsiləsí]

reaction	reagim (m)	[rɛagím]
risk	rrezik (m)	[rɛzík]

secret	sekret (m)	[sɛkrét]
series	seri (f)	[sɛrí]
shape (outer form)	formë (f)	[fórmə]
situation	situatë (f)	[situátə]
solution	zgjidhje (f)	[zɟíðjɛ]

standard (adj)	standard	[standárd]
standard (level of quality)	standard (m)	[standárd]
stop (pause)	pauzë (f)	[paúzə]
style	stil (m)	[stil]

system	sistem (m)	[sistém]
table (chart)	tabelë (f)	[tabélə]
tempo, rate	ritëm (m)	[rítəm]
term (word, expression)	term (m)	[tɛrm]

thing (object, item)	gjë (f)	[ɟə]
truth (e.g., moment of ~)	e vërtetë (f)	[ɛ vərtétə]
turn (please wait your ~)	kthesë (f)	[kθésə]
type (sort, kind)	tip (m)	[tip]
urgent (adj)	urgjent	[urɲént]

urgently (adv)	urgjentisht	[urɲɛntíʃt]
utility (usefulness)	vegël (f)	[végəl]
variant (alternative)	variant (m)	[variánt]
way (means, method)	rrugëzgjidhje (f)	[rugəzɟíðjɛ]
zone	zonë (f)	[zónə]

250. Modifiers. Adjectives. Part 1

additional (adj)	shtesë	[ʃtésə]
ancient (~ civilization)	i lashtë	[i láʃtə]
artificial (adj)	artificial	[artifitsiál]
back, rear (adj)	i pasmë	[i pásmə]
bad (adj)	i keq	[i kéc]

beautiful (~ palace)	i bukur	[i búkuɾ]
beautiful (person)	i bukur	[i búkuɾ]
big (in size)	i madh	[i máð]

bitter (taste)	i hidhur	[i híður]
blind (sightless)	i verbër	[i vérbər]
calm, quiet (adj)	i qetë	[i cétə]
careless (negligent)	i pakujdesshëm	[i pakujdésʃəm]
caring (~ father)	i dashur	[i dáʃur]
central (adj)	qendror	[cɛndrór]
cheap (low-priced)	i lirë	[i lírə]
cheerful (adj)	i gëzuar	[i gəzúar]
children's (adj)	i fëmijëve	[i fəmíjəvɛ]
civil (~ law)	civil	[tsivíl]
clandestine (secret)	klandestin	[klandɛstín]
clean (free from dirt)	i pastër	[i pástər]
clear (explanation, etc.)	i qartë	[i cártə]
clever (smart)	i zgjuar	[i zɟúar]
close (near in space)	i afërt	[i áfərt]
closed (adj)	i mbyllur	[i mbýɬur]
cloudless (sky)	pa re	[pa rɛ]
cold (drink, weather)	i ftohtë	[i ftóhtə]
compatible (adj)	i përshtatshëm	[i pərʃtátʃəm]
contented (satisfied)	i kënaqur	[i kənácur]
continuous (uninterrupted)	i vazhdueshëm	[i vaʒdúɛʃəm]
cool (weather)	i ftohtë	[i ftóhtə]
dangerous (adj)	i rrezikshëm	[i rɛzíkʃəm]
dark (room)	i errët	[i érət]
dead (not alive)	i vdekur	[i vdékur]
dense (fog, smoke)	i dendur	[i déndur]
destitute (extremely poor)	i mjerë	[i mjérə]
different (not the same)	i ndryshëm	[i ndrýʃəm]
difficult (decision)	i vështirë	[i vəʃtírə]
difficult (problem, task)	i vështirë	[i vəʃtírə]
dim, faint (light)	i zbehtë	[i zbéhtə]
dirty (not clean)	i pistë	[i pístə]
distant (in space)	i largët	[i lárgət]
dry (clothes, etc.)	i thatë	[i θátə]
easy (not difficult)	i lehtë	[i léhtə]
empty (glass, room)	zbrazët	[zbrázət]
even (e.g., ~ surface)	i barabartë	[i barabártə]
exact (amount)	i saktë	[i sáktə]
excellent (adj)	i shkëlqyer	[i ʃkəlcýɛr]
excessive (adj)	i tepërt	[i tépərt]
expensive (adj)	i shtrenjtë	[i ʃtréɲtə]
exterior (adj)	i jashtëm	[i jáʃtəm]
far (the ~ East)	larg	[larg]

fast (quick)	i shpejtë	[i ʃpéjtə]
fatty (food)	i yndyrshëm	[i yndýrʃəm]
fertile (land, soil)	pjellore	[pjɛłórɛ]

flat (~ panel display)	i sheshtë	[i ʃéʃtə]
foreign (adj)	huaj	[húaj]
fragile (china, glass)	delikat	[dɛlikát]
free (at no cost)	falas	[fálas]
free (unrestricted)	i lirë	[i lírə]

fresh (~ water)	i freskët	[i fréskət]
fresh (e.g., ~ bread)	i freskët	[i fréskət]
frozen (food)	i ngrirë	[i ŋrírə]
full (completely filled)	i mbushur	[i mbúʃur]
gloomy (house, forecast)	i vrazhdë	[i vráʒdə]

good (book, etc.)	i mirë	[i mírə]
good, kind (kindhearted)	i mirë	[i mírə]
grateful (adj)	mirënjohës	[mirəɲóhəs]
happy (adj)	i lumtur	[i lúmtur]
hard (not soft)	i fortë	[i fórtə]

heavy (in weight)	i rëndë	[i rɛ́ndə]
hostile (adj)	armiqësor	[armicəsór]
hot (adj)	i nxehtë	[i ndzéhtə]
huge (adj)	i madh	[i máð]

humid (adj)	i lagësht	[i lágəʃt]
hungry (adj)	i uritur	[i urítur]
ill (sick, unwell)	i sëmurë	[i səmúrə]
immobile (adj)	i palëvizshëm	[i paləvízʃəm]

important (adj)	i rëndësishëm	[i rəndəsíʃəm]
impossible (adj)	i pamundur	[i pamúndur]
incomprehensible	i pakuptueshëm	[i pakuptúɛʃəm]
indispensable (adj)	i pazëvendësueshëm	[i pazɛvɛndəsúɛʃəm]

inexperienced (adj)	i papërvojë	[i papərvójə]
insignificant (adj)	i parëndësishëm	[i parəndəsíʃəm]
interior (adj)	i brendshëm	[i bréndʃəm]
joint (~ decision)	i përbashkët	[i pərbáʃkət]
last (e.g., ~ week)	i fundit	[i fúndit]

last (final)	i fundit	[i fúndit]
left (e.g., ~ side)	majtë	[májtə]
legal (legitimate)	ligjor	[liɟór]
light (in weight)	i lehtë	[i léhtə]
light (pale color)	i çelët	[i tʃélət]

limited (adj)	i kufizuar	[i kufizúar]
liquid (fluid)	i lëngët	[i lə́ŋət]
long (e.g., ~ hair)	i gjatë	[i ɟátə]

| loud (voice, etc.) | i lartë | [i lártə] |
| low (voice) | i ulët | [i úlət] |

251. Modifiers. Adjectives. Part 2

main (principal)	kryesor	[kryɛsór]
matt, matte	mat	[mat]
meticulous (job)	i hollësishëm	[i hoɫəsíʃəm]
mysterious (adj)	misterioz	[mistɛrióz]
narrow (street, etc.)	i ngushtë	[i ŋúʃtə]

native (~ country)	autokton	[autoktón]
nearby (adj)	pranë	[pránə]
nearsighted (adj)	miop	[mióp]
needed (necessary)	i nevojshëm	[i nɛvójʃəm]
negative (~ response)	negativ	[nɛgatív]

neighboring (adj)	fqinj	[fcíɲ]
nervous (adj)	nervoz	[nɛrvóz]
new (adj)	i ri	[i rí]
next (e.g., ~ week)	tjetër	[tjétər]

nice (agreeable)	i mirë	[i mírə]
pleasant (voice)	i bukur	[i búkur]
normal (adj)	normal	[noɾmál]
not big (adj)	jo i madh	[jo i máð]
not difficult (adj)	jo i vështirë	[jo i vəʃtírə]

obligatory (adj)	i detyrueshëm	[i dɛtyrúɛʃəm]
old (house)	i vjetër	[i vjétər]
open (adj)	i hapur	[i hápur]
opposite (adj)	i kundërt	[i kúndərt]

ordinary (usual)	i zakonshëm	[i zakónʃəm]
original (unusual)	origjinal	[oriɟinál]
past (recent)	kaluar	[kalúar]
permanent (adj)	i përhershëm	[i pərhérʃəm]
personal (adj)	personal	[pɛrsonál]

polite (adj)	i sjellshëm	[i sjéɫʃəm]
poor (not rich)	i varfër	[i várfər]
possible (adj)	i mundur	[i múndur]
present (current)	i pranishëm	[i praníʃəm]
previous (adj)	i mëparshëm	[i məpárʃəm]

principal (main)	kryesor	[kryɛsór]
private (~ jet)	privat	[prívat]
probable (adj)	i mundshëm	[i múndʃəm]
prolonged (e.g., ~ applause)	i zgjatur	[i zɟátur]

public (open to all)	publik	[publík]
punctual (person)	i përpiktë	[i pərpíktə]
quiet (tranquil)	i qetë	[i cétə]
rare (adj)	i rrallë	[i rátə]
raw (uncooked)	i gjallë	[i ɟátə]
right (not left)	djathtë	[djáθtə]

right, correct (adj)	i saktë	[i sáktə]
ripe (fruit)	i pjekur	[i pjékur]
risky (adj)	i rrezikshëm	[i rɛzíkʃəm]
sad (~ look)	i mërzitur	[i mərzítur]

sad (depressing)	i mërzitur	[i mərzítur]
safe (not dangerous)	i sigurt	[i sígurt]
salty (food)	kripur	[krípur]
satisfied (customer)	i kënaqur	[i kənácur]

second hand (adj)	i përdorur	[i pərdórur]
shallow (water)	i cekët	[i tsékət]
sharp (blade, etc.)	i mprehtë	[i mpréhtə]
short (in length)	i shkurtër	[i ʃkúrtər]

short, short-lived (adj)	jetëshkurtër	[jɛtəʃkúrtər]
significant (notable)	i rëndësishëm	[i rəndəsíʃəm]
similar (adj)	i ngjashëm	[i nɟáʃəm]
simple (easy)	i thjeshtë	[i θjéʃtə]
skinny	i hollë	[i hótə]

small (in size)	i vogël	[i vógəl]
smooth (surface)	i lëmuar	[i ləmúar]
soft (~ toys)	i butë	[i bútə]
solid (~ wall)	i ngjeshur	[i nɟéʃur]

sour (flavor, taste)	i hidhur	[i híður]
spacious (house, etc.)	i bollshëm	[i bótʃəm]
special (adj)	i veçantë	[i vɛtʃántə]
straight (line, road)	i drejtë	[i dréjtə]
strong (person)	i fortë	[i fórtə]

stupid (foolish)	budalla	[budałá]
suitable (e.g., ~ for drinking)	i përshtatshëm	[i pərʃtátʃəm]
sunny (day)	me diell	[mɛ díɛt]
superb, perfect (adj)	i përsosur	[i pərsósur]
swarthy (adj)	zeshkan	[zɛʃkán]

sweet (sugary)	i ëmbël	[i ə́mbəl]
tan (adj)	i nxirë	[i ndzírə]
tasty (delicious)	i shijshëm	[i ʃíjʃəm]
tender (affectionate)	i ndjeshëm	[i ndjéʃəm]
the highest (adj)	më i larti	[mə i lárti]
the most important	më i rëndësishmi	[mə i rəndəsíʃmi]

the nearest	më i afërti	[mə i áfərti]
the same, equal (adj)	i njëjtë	[i ɲéjtə]
thick (e.g., ~ fog)	i trashë	[i tráʃə]
thick (wall, slice)	i trashë	[i tráʃə]

thin (person)	i dobët	[i dóbət]
tight (~ shoes)	ngushtë	[ŋúʃtə]
tired (exhausted)	i lodhur	[i lóðuɾ]
tiring (adj)	i mundimshëm	[i mundímʃəm]

transparent (adj)	i tejdukshëm	[i tɛjdúkʃəm]
unclear (adj)	i paqartë	[i pacártə]
unique (exceptional)	unik	[uník]
various (adj)	i ndryshëm	[i ndrýʃəm]

warm (moderately hot)	ngrohtë	[ŋróhtə]
wet (e.g., ~ clothes)	i lagur	[i láguɾ]
whole (entire, complete)	i plotë	[i plótə]
wide (e.g., ~ road)	i gjerë	[i ɟérə]
young (adj)	i ri	[i rí]

MAIN 500 VERBS

252. Verbs A-C

to accompany (vt)	shoqëroj	[ʃoɡərój]
to accuse (vt)	akuzoj	[akuzój]
to acknowledge (admit)	pranoj	[pranój]
to act (take action)	veproj	[vɛprój]

to add (supplement)	shtoj	[ʃtoj]
to address (speak to)	i drejtohem	[i drɛjtóhɛm]
to admire (vi)	admiroj	[admirój]
to advertise (vt)	reklamoj	[rɛklamój]

to advise (vt)	këshilloj	[kəʃiłój]
to affirm (assert)	pohoj	[pohój]
to agree (say yes)	bie dakord	[bíɛ dakórd]
to aim (to point a weapon)	vë në shënjestër	[və nə ʃəɲéstər]

to allow (sb to do sth)	lejoj	[lɛjój]
to amputate (vt)	amputoj	[amputój]
to answer (vi, vt)	përgjigjem	[pərɟíɟɛm]
to apologize (vi)	kërkoj falje	[kərkój fáljɛ]

to appear (come into view)	shfaq	[ʃfac]
to applaud (vi, vt)	duartrokas	[duartrokás]
to appoint (assign)	caktoj	[tsaktój]
to approach (come closer)	afrohem	[afróhɛm]

to arrive (ab. train)	arrij	[aríj]
to ask (~ sb to do sth)	pyes	[pýɛs]
to aspire to ...	synoj ...	[synój ...]
to assist (help)	ndihmoj	[ndihmój]

to attack (mil.)	sulmoj	[sulmój]
to attain (objectives)	arrij	[aríj]
to avenge (get revenge)	hakmerrem	[hakmérɛm]
to avoid (danger, task)	shmang	[ʃmaŋ]

| to award (give medal to) | dekoroj | [dɛkorój] |
| to battle (vi) | luftoj | [luftój] |

to be (vi)	jam	[jam]
to be a cause of ...	shkaktoj ...	[ʃkaktój ...]
to be afraid	kam frikë	[kam fríkə]
to be angry (with ...)	revoltohem	[rɛvoltóhɛm]

to be at war	në luftë	[nə lúftə]
to be based (on ...)	bazuar	[bazúar]
to be bored	mërzitem	[mərzítɛm]
to be convinced	bindem	[bíndɛm]
to be enough	mjafton	[mjaftón]
to be envious	xhelozoj	[dʒɛlozój]
to be indignant	zemërohem	[zɛməróhɛm]
to be interested in ...	interesohem ...	[intɛrɛsóhɛm ...]
to be lost in thought	humbas në mendime	[humbás nə mɛndímɛ]
to be lying (~ on the table)	shtrihem	[ʃtríhɛm]
to be needed	nevojitet	[nɛvojítɛt]
to be perplexed (puzzled)	jam në mëdyshje	[jam nə mədýʃʃɛ]
to be preserved	ruhem	[rúhɛm]
to be required	kërkohet	[kərkóhɛt]
to be surprised	çuditem	[tʃudítɛm]
to be worried	shqetësohem	[ʃcɛtəsóhɛm]
to beat (to hit)	rrah	[rah]
to become (e.g., ~ old)	bëhem	[béhɛm]
to behave (vi)	sillem	[síɫɛm]
to believe (think)	besoj	[bɛsój]
to belong to ...	përkas ...	[pərkás ...]
to berth (moor)	ankoroj	[ankorój]
to blind (other drivers)	zë rrugën	[zə rúgən]
to blow (wind)	fryn	[fryn]
to blush (vi)	skuqem	[skúcɛm]
to boast (vi)	mburrem	[mbúrɛm]
to borrow (money)	marr borxh	[mar bórdʒ]
to break (branch, toy, etc.)	thyej	[θýɛj]
to breathe (vi)	marr frymë	[mar frýmə]
to bring (sth)	sjell	[sjɛɫ]
to burn (paper, logs)	djeg	[djég]
to buy (purchase)	blej	[blɛj]
to call (~ for help)	thërras	[θərás]
to call (yell for sb)	thërras	[θərás]
to calm down (vt)	qetësoj	[cɛtəsój]
can (v aux)	mund	[mund]
to cancel (call off)	anuloj	[anulój]
to cast off (of a boat or ship)	hedh poshtë	[hɛð póʃtə]
to catch (e.g., ~ a ball)	kap	[kap]
to change (~ one's opinion)	ndryshoj	[ndryʃój]
to change (exchange)	shkëmbej	[ʃkəmbéj]
to charm (vt)	tërheq	[tərhéc]
to choose (select)	zgjedh	[zɟɛð]

to chop off (with an ax)	këpus	[kəpús]
to clean (e.g., kettle from scale)	pastroj	[pastrój]
to clean (shoes, etc.)	pastroj	[pastrój]

to clean up (tidy)	rregulloj	[rɛgułój]
to close (vt)	mbyll	[mbyɫ]
to comb one's hair	kreh flokët	[kréh flókət]
to come down (the stairs)	zbres	[zbrɛs]

to come out (book)	del	[dɛl]
to compare (vt)	krahasoj	[krahasój]
to compensate (vt)	kompensoj	[kompɛnsój]
to compete (vi)	konkurroj	[konkurój]

to compile (~ a list)	përgatis	[pərgatís]
to complain (vi, vt)	ankohem	[ankóhɛm]
to complicate (vt)	komplikoj	[komplikój]
to compose (music, etc.)	kompozoj	[kompozój]

to compromise (reputation)	komprometoj	[kompromɛtój]
to concentrate (vi)	përqendrohem	[pərcɛndróhɛm]
to confess (criminal)	rrëfehem	[rəféhɛm]
to confuse (mix up)	ngatërroj	[ŋatərój]

to congratulate (vt)	përgëzoj	[pərgəzój]
to consult (doctor, expert)	konsultohem	[konsultóhɛm]
to continue (~ to do sth)	vazhdoj	[vaʒdój]
to control (vt)	kontrolloj	[kontroɫój]

to convince (vt)	bind	[bínd]
to cooperate (vi)	bashkëpunoj	[baʃkəpunój]
to coordinate (vt)	koordinoj	[koordinój]
to correct (an error)	korrigjoj	[koriɟój]

to cost (vt)	kushton	[kuʃtón]
to count (money, etc.)	numëroj	[numərój]
to count on ...	mbështetem ...	[mbəʃtétɛm ...]
to crack (ceiling, wall)	plasarit	[plasarít]

to create (vt)	krijoj	[krijój]
to crush, to squash (~ a bug)	shtyp	[ʃtyp]
to cry (weep)	qaj	[caj]
to cut off (with a knife)	pres	[prɛs]

253. Verbs D-G

to dare (~ to do sth)	guxoj	[gudzój]
to date from ...	daton ...	[datón ...]

to deceive (vi, vt)	mashtroj	[maʃtrój]
to decide (~ to do sth)	vendos	[vɛndós]
to decorate (tree, street)	zbukuroj	[zbukurój]
to dedicate (book, etc.)	dedikoj	[dɛdikój]
to defend (a country, etc.)	mbroj	[mbrój]
to defend oneself	mbrohem	[mbróhɛm]
to demand (request firmly)	kërkoj	[kərkój]
to denounce (vt)	denoncoj	[dɛnontsój]
to deny (vt)	mohoj	[mohój]
to depend on ...	varem nga ...	[várɛm ŋa ...]
to deprive (vt)	heq	[hɛc]
to deserve (vt)	meritoj	[mɛritój]
to design (machine, etc.)	projektoj	[projɛktój]
to desire (want, wish)	dëshiroj	[dəʃirój]
to despise (vt)	përbuz	[pərbúz]
to destroy (documents, etc.)	shkatërroj	[ʃkatərój]
to differ (from sth)	ndryshoj	[ndryʃój]
to dig (tunnel, etc.)	gërmoj	[gərmój]
to direct (point the way)	drejtoj	[drɛjtój]
to disappear (vi)	zhduk	[ʒduk]
to discover (new land, etc.)	zbuloj	[zbulój]
to discuss (vt)	diskutoj	[diskutój]
to distribute (leaflets, etc.)	shpërndaj	[ʃpərndáj]
to disturb (vt)	shqetësoj	[ʃcɛtəsój]
to dive (vi)	zhytem	[ʒýtɛm]
to divide (math)	pjesëtoj	[pjɛsətój]
to do (vt)	bëj	[bəj]
to do the laundry	laj rroba	[laj róba]
to double (increase)	dyfishoj	[dyfiʃój]
to doubt (have doubts)	dyshoj	[dyʃój]
to draw a conclusion	nxjerr konkluzion	[ndzjér konkluzión]
to dream (daydream)	ëndërroj	[əndərój]
to dream (in sleep)	ëndërroj	[əndərój]
to drink (vi, vt)	pi	[pi]
to drive a car	ngas makinën	[ŋas makínən]
to drive away (scare away)	largoj	[largój]
to drop (let fall)	lëshoj	[ləʃój]
to drown (ab. person)	mbytem	[mbýtɛm]
to dry (clothes, hair)	thaj	[θaj]
to eat (vi, vt)	ha	[ha]
to eavesdrop (vi)	dëgjoj fshehurazi	[dəɟój fʃéhurazi]

to emit (diffuse - odor, etc.)	emetoj	[ɛmɛtój]
to enjoy oneself	kënaqem	[kənácɛm]
to enter (on the list)	përfshij	[pərfʃíj]
to enter (room, house, etc.)	hyj	[hyj]
to entertain (amuse)	argëtoj	[argətój]
to equip (fit out)	pajis	[pajís]
to examine (proposal)	ekzaminoj	[ɛkzaminój]
to exchange (sth)	shkëmbej	[ʃkəmbéj]
to excuse (forgive)	fal	[fal]
to exist (vi)	ekzistoj	[ɛkzistój]
to expect (anticipate)	pres	[prɛs]
to expect (foresee)	parashikoj	[paraʃikój]
to expel (from school, etc.)	përjashtohem	[pərjaʃtóhɛm]
to explain (vt)	shpjegoj	[ʃpjɛgój]
to express (vt)	shpreh	[ʃprɛh]
to extinguish (a fire)	shuaj	[ʃúaj]
to fall in love (with ...)	bie në dashuri	[bíɛ nə daʃurí]
to feed (provide food)	ushqej	[uʃcéj]
to fight (against the enemy)	luftoj	[luftój]
to fight (vi)	luftoj	[luftój]
to fill (glass, bottle)	mbush	[mbúʃ]
to find (~ lost items)	gjej	[ɟéj]
to finish (vt)	përfundoj	[pərfundój]
to fish (angle)	peshkoj	[pɛʃkój]
to fit (ab. dress, etc.)	më rri mirë	[mə ri mírə]
to flatter (vt)	lajkatoj	[lajkatój]
to fly (bird, plane)	fluturoj	[fluturój]
to follow ... (come after)	ndjek ...	[ndjék ...]
to forbid (vt)	ndaloj	[ndalój]
to force (compel)	detyroj	[dɛtyrój]
to forget (vi, vt)	harroj	[harój]
to forgive (pardon)	fal	[fal]
to form (constitute)	formoj	[formój]
to get dirty (vi)	bëhem pis	[béhɛm pis]
to get infected (with ...)	infektohem ...	[infɛktóhɛm ...]
to get irritated	acarohem	[atsaróhɛm]
to get married	martohem	[martóhɛm]
to get rid of ...	heq qafe ...	[hɛc cáfɛ ...]
to get tired	lodhem	[lóðɛm]
to get up (arise from bed)	ngrihem	[ŋríhɛm]

| to give (vt) | jap | [jap] |
| to give a bath (to bath) | lahem | [láhɛm] |

to give a hug, to hug (vt)	përqafoj	[pǝrcafój]
to give in (yield to)	tërhiqem	[tǝrhícɛm]
to glimpse (vt)	hedh një sy	[hɛð ɲǝ sý]
to go (by car, etc.)	shkoj	[ʃkoj]

to go (on foot)	ec në këmbë	[ɛts nǝ kémbǝ]
to go for a swim	notoj	[notój]
to go out (for dinner, etc.)	dal	[dal]
to go to bed (go to sleep)	shtrihem	[ʃtríhɛm]

to greet (vt)	përshëndes	[pǝrʃǝndés]
to grow (plants)	rris	[ris]
to guarantee (vt)	garantoj	[garantój]
to guess (the answer)	hamendësoj	[hamɛndǝsój]

254. Verbs H-M

to hand out (distribute)	shpërndaj	[ʃpǝrndáj]
to hang (curtains, etc.)	var	[var]
to have (vt)	kam	[kam]
to have a try	përpiqem	[pǝrpícɛm]
to have breakfast	ha mëngjes	[ha mǝɲɟés]

to have dinner	ha darkë	[ha dárkǝ]
to have lunch	ha drekë	[ha drékǝ]
to head (group, etc.)	drejtoj	[drɛjtój]
to hear (vt)	dëgjoj	[dǝɟój]
to heat (vt)	ngroh	[ŋróh]

to help (vt)	ndihmoj	[ndihmój]
to hide (vt)	fsheh	[fʃéh]
to hire (e.g., ~ a boat)	marr me qira	[mar mɛ cirá]
to hire (staff)	punësoj	[punǝsój]
to hope (vi, vt)	shpresoj	[ʃprɛsój]

to hunt (for food, sport)	dal për gjah	[dál pǝr ɟáh]
to hurry (vi)	nxitoj	[ndzitój]
to imagine (to picture)	imagjinoj	[imaɟinój]
to imitate (vt)	imitoj	[imitój]
to implore (vt)	përgjërohem	[pǝrɟǝróhɛm]
to import (vt)	importoj	[importój]
to increase (vi)	shtoj	[ʃtoj]
to increase (vt)	rritem	[rítɛm]
to infect (vt)	ndot	[ndot]
to influence (vt)	ndikoj	[ndikój]
to inform (e.g., ~ the police about)	njoftoj	[ɲoftój]

to inform (vt)	informoj	[informój]
to inherit (vt)	trashëgoj	[traʃəgój]
to inquire (about ...)	pyes për	[pýɛs pər]

to insert (put in)	fus	[fus]
to insinuate (imply)	nënkuptoj	[nənkuptój]
to insist (vi, vt)	këmbëngul	[kəmbəŋúl]
to inspire (vt)	frymëzoj	[frymǝzój]
to instruct (teach)	udhëzoj	[uðǝzój]

to insult (offend)	fyej	[fýɛj]
to interest (vt)	interesohem	[intɛrɛsóhɛm]
to intervene (vi)	ndërhyj	[ndǝrhýj]
to introduce (sb to sb)	prezantoj	[prɛzantój]
to invent (machine, etc.)	shpik	[ʃpik]

to invite (vt)	ftoj	[ftoj]
to iron (clothes)	hekuros	[hɛkurós]
to irritate (annoy)	acaroj	[atsarój]
to isolate (vt)	izoloj	[izolój]
to join (political party, etc.)	i bashkohem	[i baʃkóhɛm]

to joke (be kidding)	bëj shaka	[bǝj ʃaká]
to keep (old letters, etc.)	mbaj	[mbáj]
to keep silent, to hush	hesht	[hɛʃt]
to kill (vt)	vras	[vras]
to knock (on the door)	trokas	[trokás]

to know (sb)	njoh	[ɲóh]
to know (sth)	di	[di]
to laugh (vi)	qesh	[cɛʃ]
to launch (start up)	nis	[nis]

to leave (~ for Mexico)	largohem	[largóhɛm]
to leave (forget sth)	harroj	[harój]
to leave (spouse)	lë	[lǝ]
to liberate (city, etc.)	çliroj	[tʃlirój]
to lie (~ on the floor)	shtrihem	[ʃtríhɛm]

to lie (tell untruth)	gënjej	[gǝɲéj]
to light (campfire, etc.)	ndez	[ndɛz]
to light up (illuminate)	ndriçoj	[ndritʃój]
to like (I like ...)	pëlqej	[pǝlcéj]
to limit (vt)	kufizoj	[kufizój]

to listen (vi)	dëgjoj	[dǝɟój]
to live (~ in France)	jetoj	[jɛtój]
to live (exist)	jetoj	[jɛtój]
to load (gun)	mbush	[mbúʃ]
to load (vehicle, etc.)	ngarkoj	[ŋarkój]
to look (I'm just ~ing)	shikoj	[ʃikój]
to look for ... (search)	kërkoj ...	[kǝrkój ...]

to look like (resemble)	ngjasoj	[ɲasój]
to lose (umbrella, etc.)	humb	[húmb]
to love (e.g., ~ dancing)	më pëlqen	[mə pəlcén]
to love (sb)	dashuroj	[daʃurój]
to lower (blind, head)	ul	[ul]
to make (~ dinner)	përgatis	[pərgatís]
to make a mistake	gaboj	[gabój]
to make angry	zemëroj	[zɛmərój]
to make easier	lehtësoj	[lɛhtəsój]
to make multiple copies	shumëfishoj	[ʃuməfiʃój]
to make the acquaintance	njihem me	[ɲíhɛm mɛ]
to make use (of ...)	përdor	[pərdór]
to manage, to run	drejtoj	[drɛjtój]
to mark (make a mark)	shënjoj	[ʃəɲój]
to mean (signify)	nënkuptoj	[nənkuptój]
to memorize (vt)	mbaj mend	[mbáj ménd]
to mention (talk about)	përmend	[pərménd]
to miss (school, etc.)	humbas	[humbás]
to mix (combine, blend)	përziej	[pərzíɛj]
to mock (make fun of)	tallem	[táɫɛm]
to move (to shift)	lëviz	[ləvíz]
to multiply (math)	shumëzoj	[ʃuməzój]
must (v aux)	duhet	[dúhɛt]

255. Verbs N-R

to name, to call (vt)	emërtoj	[ɛmərtój]
to negotiate (vi)	negocioj	[nɛgotsiój]
to note (write down)	shënoj	[ʃənój]
to notice (see)	vërej	[vəréj]
to obey (vi, vt)	bindem	[bíndɛm]
to object (vi, vt)	kundërshtoj	[kundərʃtój]
to observe (see)	vëzhgoj	[vəʒgój]
to offend (vt)	ofendoj	[ofɛndój]
to omit (word, phrase)	heq	[hɛc]
to open (vt)	hap	[hap]
to order (in restaurant)	porosis	[porosís]
to order (mil.)	urdhëroj	[urðərój]
to organize (concert, party)	organizoj	[organizój]
to overestimate (vt)	mbivlerësoj	[mbivlɛrəsój]
to own (possess)	zotëroj	[zotərój]
to participate (vi)	marr pjesë	[mar pjésə]
to pass through (by car, etc.)	kaloj	[kalój]

to pay (vi, vt)	paguaj	[pagúaj]
to peep, spy on	spiunoj	[spiunój]
to penetrate (vt)	depërtoj	[dɛpərtój]
to permit (vt)	lejoj	[lɛjój]
to pick (flowers)	këpus	[kəpús]

to place (put, set)	vendos	[vɛndós]
to plan (~ to do sth)	planifikoj	[planifikój]
to play (actor)	luaj	[lúaj]
to play (children)	luaj	[lúaj]
to point (~ the way)	tregoj	[trɛgój]

to pour (liquid)	derdh	[dérð]
to pray (vi, vt)	lutem	[lútɛm]
to prefer (vt)	preferoj	[prɛfɛrój]
to prepare (~ a plan)	përgatis	[pərgatís]
to present (sb to sb)	prezantoj	[prɛzantój]

to preserve (peace, life)	ruaj	[rúaj]
to prevail (vt)	mbizotëroj	[mbizotərój]
to progress (move forward)	ec përpara	[ɛts pərpára]
to promise (vt)	premtoj	[prɛmtój]

to pronounce (vt)	shqiptoj	[ʃciptój]
to propose (vt)	propozoj	[propozój]
to protect (e.g., ~ nature)	mbroj	[mbrój]
to protest (vi)	protestoj	[protɛstój]

to prove (vt)	dëshmoj	[dəʃmój]
to provoke (vt)	provokoj	[provokój]
to pull (~ the rope)	tërheq	[tərhéc]
to punish (vt)	ndëshkoj	[ndəʃkój]

to push (~ the door)	shtyj	[ʃtyj]
to put away (vt)	largoj	[largój]
to put in order	rregulloj	[rɛguɫój]
to put, to place	vendos	[vɛndós]

to quote (cite)	citoj	[tsitój]
to reach (arrive at)	arrij	[aríj]
to read (vi, vt)	lexoj	[lɛdzój]
to realize (a dream)	përmbush	[pərmbúʃ]
to recognize (identify sb)	njoh	[ɲóh]

to recommend (vt)	rekomandoj	[rɛkomandój]
to recover (~ from flu)	shërohem	[ʃəróhɛm]
to redo (do again)	ribëj	[ribéj]
to reduce (speed, etc.)	ul	[ul]

to refuse (~ sb)	refuzoj	[rɛfuzój]
to regret (be sorry)	pendohem	[pɛndóhɛm]

to reinforce (vt)	përforcoj	[pərfortsój]
to remember (Do you ~ me?)	kujtoj	[kujtój]
to remember (I can't ~ her name)	kujtohem	[kujtóhɛm]
to remind of ...	më kujton ...	[mə kujtón ...]
to remove (~ a stain)	heq	[hɛc]
to remove (~ an obstacle)	largoj	[largój]
to rent (sth from sb)	marr me qira	[mar mɛ cirá]
to repair (mend)	riparoj	[riparój]
to repeat (say again)	përsëris	[pərsərís]
to report (make a report)	raportoj	[raportój]
to reproach (vt)	qortoj	[cortój]
to reserve, to book	rezervoj	[rɛzɛrvój]
to restrain (hold back)	ruhem	[rúhɛm]
to return (come back)	kthehem	[kθéhɛm]
to risk, to take a risk	rrezikoj	[rɛzikój]
to rub out (erase)	fshij	[fʃíj]
to run (move fast)	vrapoj	[vrapój]
to rush (hurry sb)	nxitoj	[ndzitój]

256. Verbs S-W

to satisfy (please)	kënaq	[kənác]
to save (rescue)	shpëtoj	[ʃpətój]
to say (~ thank you)	them	[θɛm]
to scold (vt)	qortoj	[cortój]
to scratch (with claws)	gërvisht	[gərvíʃt]
to select (to pick)	zgjedh	[zɟɛð]
to sell (goods)	shes	[ʃɛs]
to send (a letter)	dërgoj	[dərgój]
to send back (vt)	kthej mbrapsht	[kθɛj mbrápʃt]
to sense (~ danger)	parandiej	[parandíɛj]
to sentence (vt)	dënoj	[dənój]
to serve (in restaurant)	shërbej	[ʃərbéj]
to settle (a conflict)	zgjidh	[zɟíð]
to shake (vt)	tund	[tund]
to shave (vi)	rruhem	[rúhɛm]
to shine (gleam)	shkëlqej	[ʃkəlcéj]
to shiver (with cold)	dridhem	[dríðɛm]
to shoot (vi)	qëlloj	[cətój]
to shout (vi)	bërtas	[bərtás]

to show (to display)	tregoj	[trɛgój]
to shudder (vi)	rrëqethem	[rəcéθɛm]
to sigh (vi)	psherëtij	[pʃɛrətíj]
to sign (document)	nënshkruaj	[nənʃkrúaj]
to signify (mean)	nënkuptoj	[nənkuptój]
to simplify (vt)	thjeshtoj	[θjɛʃtój]
to sin (vi)	mëkatoj	[məkatój]
to sit (be sitting)	ulem	[úlɛm]
to sit down (vi)	ulem	[úlɛm]
to smell (emit an odor)	mban erë	[mbán érə]
to smell (inhale the odor)	nuhas	[nuhás]
to smile (vi)	buzëqesh	[buzəcéʃ]
to snap (vi, ab. rope)	këpus	[kəpús]
to solve (problem)	zgjidh	[zɟið]
to sow (seed, crop)	mbjell	[mbjéɫ]
to spill (liquid)	derdh	[dérð]
to spill out, scatter (flour, etc.)	derdh	[dérð]
to spit (vi)	pështyj	[pəʃtýj]
to stand (toothache, cold)	duroj	[durój]
to start (begin)	filloj	[fiɫój]
to steal (money, etc.)	vjedh	[vjɛð]
to stop (for pause, etc.)	ndaloj	[ndalój]
to stop (please ~ calling me)	ndaloj	[ndalój]
to stop talking	ndaloj së foluri	[ndalój sə fóluri]
to stroke (caress)	përkëdhel	[pərkəðél]
to study (vt)	studioj	[studiój]
to suffer (feel pain)	vuaj	[vúaj]
to support (cause, idea)	mbështes	[mbəʃtés]
to suppose (assume)	supozoj	[supozój]
to surface (ab. submarine)	dal në sipërfaqe	[dál nə sipərfácɛ]
to surprise (amaze)	befasoj	[bɛfasój]
to suspect (vt)	dyshoj	[dyʃój]
to swim (vi)	notoj	[notój]
to take (get hold of)	marr	[mar]
to take a bath	lahem	[láhɛm]
to take a rest	pushoj	[puʃój]
to take away (e.g., about waiter)	heq	[hɛc]
to take off (airplane)	nisem	[nísɛm]
to take off (painting, curtains, etc.)	heq	[hɛc]

to take pictures	bëj foto	[bəj fóto]
to talk to ...	bisedoj ...	[bisɛdój ...]
to teach (give lessons)	mësoj	[məsój]

to tear off, to rip off (vt)	gris	[gris]
to tell (story, joke)	tregoj	[trɛgój]
to thank (vt)	falënderoj	[faləndɛrój]
to think (believe)	besoj	[bɛsój]

to think (vi, vt)	mendoj	[mɛndój]
to threaten (vt)	kërcënoj	[kərtsənój]
to throw (stone, etc.)	hedh	[hɛð]
to tie to ...	lidh ...	[lið ...]

to tie up (prisoner)	prangos	[praŋós]
to tire (make tired)	lodh	[loð]
to touch (one's arm, etc.)	prek	[prɛk]
to tower (over ...)	ngrihem mbi	[ŋríhɛm mbi]

to train (animals)	stërvit	[stərvít]
to train (sb)	stërvit	[stərvít]
to train (vi)	stërvitem	[stərvítɛm]
to transform (vt)	shndërrohem	[ʃndəróhɛm]

to translate (vt)	përkthej	[pərkθéj]
to treat (illness)	kuroj	[kurój]
to trust (vt)	besoj	[bɛsój]
to try (attempt)	përpiqem	[pərpícɛm]

to turn (e.g., ~ left)	kthej	[kθɛj]
to turn away (vi)	largohem	[largóhɛm]
to turn off (the light)	fik	[fik]
to turn on (computer, etc.)	ndez	[ndɛz]
to turn over (stone, etc.)	kthej	[kθɛj]

to underestimate (vt)	nënvlerësoj	[nənvlɛrəsój]
to underline (vt)	nënvijëzoj	[nənvijəzój]
to understand (vt)	kuptoj	[kuptój]
to undertake (vt)	ndërmarr	[ndərmár]

to unite (vt)	bashkoj	[baʃkój]
to untie (vt)	zgjidh	[zɟið]
to use (phrase, word)	përdor	[pərdór]
to vaccinate (vt)	vaksinoj	[vaksinój]

to vote (vi)	votoj	[votój]
to wait (vt)	pres	[prɛs]
to wake (sb)	zgjoj	[zɟoj]
to want (wish, desire)	dëshiroj	[dəʃirój]

| to warn (of the danger) | paralajmëroj | [paralajmərój] |
| to wash (clean) | laj | [laj] |

to water (plants)	**ujis**	[ujís]
to wave (the hand)	**bëj me dorë**	[bəj mɛ dórə]
to weigh (have weight)	**peshoj**	[pɛʃój]
to work (vi)	**punoj**	[punój]
to worry (make anxious)	**preokupoj**	[prɛokupój]
to worry (vi)	**shqetësohem**	[ʃcɛtəsóhɛm]
to wrap (parcel, etc.)	**mbështjell**	[mbəʃtjéɫ]
to wrestle (sport)	**ndeshem**	[ndéʃɛm]
to write (vt)	**shkruaj**	[ʃkrúaj]
to write down	**mbaj shënim**	[mbáj ʃəním]

Made in United States
Orlando, FL
03 November 2025

71903215R00154